RACEFANS™ REFERENCE

UNDERSTANDING WINSTON CUP RACING

BY

WILLIAM M. BURT

1ST EDITION

1ST PRINTING

ACKNOWLEDGMENTS

A special thanks to those who helped make this book possible.

BOBBY ALLISON MOTORSPORTS TEAM, INC.
COMPETITION CAMS
HUTCHERSON-PAGAN
KEMPS CONNECTING POINT

SCOOTER BROTHERS
MACK BURT
BETTY CARLAN
EDDIE DICKERSON
MIKE EAGLE
DAVID MAGOUYRK
FRANK RIKARD
MIKE RIVERS

AND,
DAVID, JENNIFER, GUY, BILL, STEVE, FRED,
KELLER, HAWG AND ALL OF THE JONES BOYS.

PUBLISHED BY: ALASTRA CORPORATION
EDITORS: REBECCA R. BURT
          ROZELLE LENTJES
          TINA BURT

PRODUCED BY: J. BURNS JOHNS & CO.
             BIRMINGHAM. ALABAMA

I love racing . . .

My entire family was born and reared in Talladega. As a young man my grandfather took me to watch the bulldozers clearing the land for the Talladega Superspeedway. My first racing memory, a couple of years later, is from that same place. From then on I've been hooked. Not as a racer but as a racefan.

I've often heard people say, "racing isn't a sport"; and in some ways they're right. It isn't a sport. It's a *Motorsport*. There's a world of difference.

Sports rely on an athlete, or a team of athletes, to compete on the basis of some type of physical skill and effort. Motorsports include all of that; plus there's the machine. Be it a car, a boat or a motorcycle, a motorsports team can perform only if the machine performs. And the machine can perform only if the team performs. This relationship between man and machine makes motorsports the most thrilling, and often the most frustrating, show in town. After all, how often does a football team have to pull out of a game, while leading late in the forth quarter, due to shoulder pad failure. Or how often does a professional golfer, leading a tournament, have to withdraw from the tournament because someone back in thirty-second place caused him to break his putter.

Also, there's a unique relationship between the competitors in motorsports. Drivers are constantly trying to beat one another and at the same time must take care of each other. When pushing a car to its limit, unplanned things happen. People make mistakes, and drivers are people; therefore drivers make mistakes. And it is up to the other drivers to help keep one small mistake from turning into twenty cars on *hooks*.

Not only does the nature of motorsports make for very exciting professional action; but it also allows for some of the best amateur action as well.

While the grass roots that gave rise to most professional sports have disappeared, the heritage that makes up Winston Cup racing is still alive and flourishing. Those so inclined still have the chance to form race teams of their own. Some of the original "privateers" are still driving. From dirt tracks to dragways, amateurs are able to not just *get a taste* of the sport they love; they are able to *eat it up*. The racing is as competitive as any, anywhere. It's also even possible to catch a current professional racing star driving in a Saturday Night feature.

Within the Motorsports community, NASCAR's Winston Cup Series has surpassed all in popularity growth. Indeed, it may have surpassed all sports in this category.

There are number of reasons for this success. First is the nature of the sport itself. Brightly colored cars, with equally colorful drivers, flying around the track . . . the sound of forty finely tuned, non-muffled engines roaring at more than 8,000 rpm . . . and the Action. Constant. All the time. Almost too much of it. Cars skirting next to each other at 200 mph . . . the fender banging of short track racing . . . the action is constant. The closest thing to a time out is a Yellow Flag. And at the racetrack, that's when the action really starts . . . in the pits . . . where a team's performance decides track position as much as 30-40 laps of hard racing.

And the racing schedule has a great impact, too. Unlike most sports where different teams play each week; in racing it's the same rivalries every week. After all, it's much more fun for a fan to say, "Wait till next *week*," instead of "Wait till next *year*."

Another reason for the success of stockcar racing is NASCAR, and the leadership it has provided over the last 30 years, focusing primarily on safety and a competitive racing environment. Safety is important for obvious reasons; however the importance of a competitive racing environment seems to have been overlooked by most other forms of racing where its rare to have even two cars on the lead lap at the end of a race, much less twenty. Sure the technology is advanced. But if only a few teams can afford it, you'll never see a pack of cars scrambling out of the last turn for the checkered flag after 500 miles of racing . . . an event which is not at all rare in Winston Cup racing.

While week in and week out there are some teams that are consistently strong, there is always a surprise car or two that have good runs and are capable of winning the race; and sometimes do. By keeping the car and pitting systems somewhat low-tech, NASCAR has ensured that consistent winning is more the result of consistency, attention to detail and to driver skill rather than the ability to buy technology. NASCAR has not only used this philosophy at the level of Winston Cup racing but all along the different levels of racing that they sanction. This not only provides a system through which drivers can gain experience and advance to the top levels; but it also ensures consistently exciting racing for the fans at the small tracks across the nation.

As this is being written, two major sports are on strike. Instead of bartering during the off season about how much is to be paid, in Winston Cup racing the drivers and the teams decide on the track who makes the big bucks . . . not in the lawyers offices.

As fans we should appreciate this unique guidance which has given us what is arguably the most competitive major sport in America.

I really do love racing . . .

W.M.B.

Dedicated to race teams and race fans, who together make our Saturday nights and Sunday afternoons so much fun.

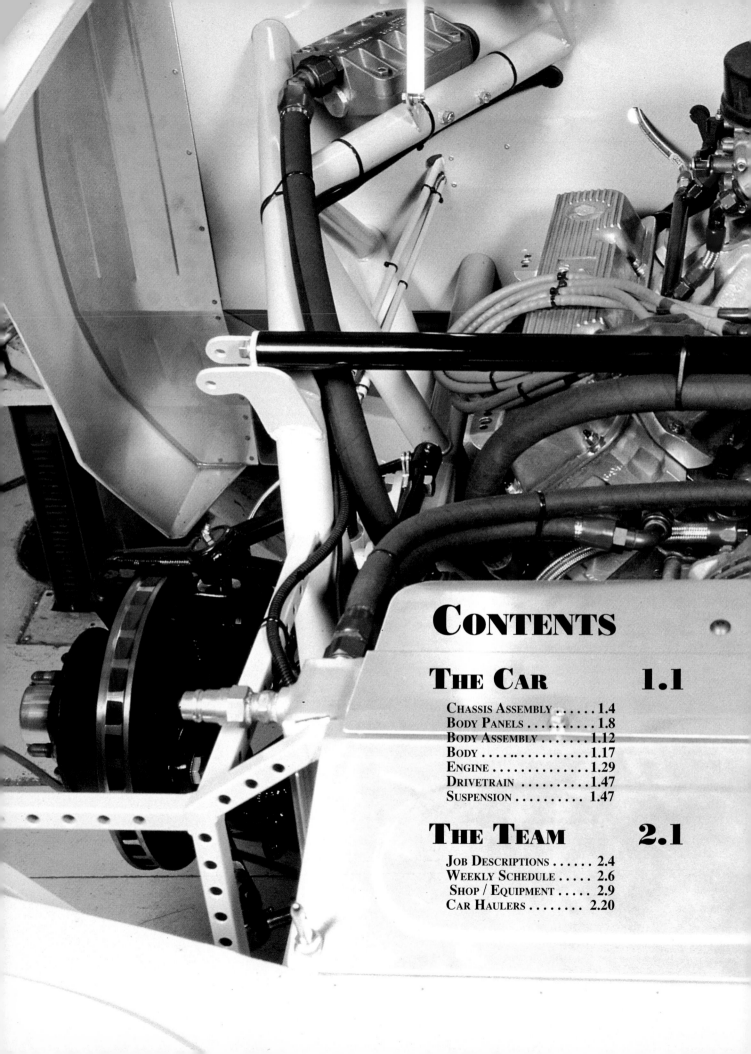

CONTENTS

THE CAR 1.1

THE TEAM 2.1

THE RACE   3.1

TRACKS   4.1

COMPETITORS   5.1

REFERENCE   6.1

THE CAR

While the Winston Cup cars that race today look somewhat like the production cars they are named after, they have very little in common other than the name. Today's Winston Cup cars are to some extent a paradox. It might be said that Winston Cup cars are on the cutting edge of "yesterday's" technology.

Winston Cup cars must be built within certain specifications established by NASCAR. These specifications eliminate many of today's exotic materials and designs for everything but the safety systems of the car.

Concepts and systems seen in other racing venues such as turbochargers, overhead cam configurations, advanced aerodynamics, in-car computer telemetry, and extensive use of materials --

carbon fiber, etc. -- are not allowed in Winston Cup racing. This forces the teams to rely on better engineering of old technology and more attention to the race set-up.

This is not to say that Winston Cup cars aren't exotic; they are. However, they are exotic in a different sense. Winston Cup teams make many small changes to the cars and engines that, when looked at alone, may not seem to help very much. But when all of these small changes are added up, they may be the difference between winning and being an "also ran."

Today's rules not only provide for safe and very competitive racing on the track; they also set the stage for another competition - the constant

race within the shops, practice sessions and wind tunnels - learning more and more about the forces that racecars encounter and the components on the cars that counter

those forces. By constantly "tweaking" and fine tuning each component and system on the racecar, the teams achieve more and more speed every year. Many times in the

past, the rules have been changed to slow the cars down, requiring the engineers to continue to search for changes that give that small but important advantage on the track.

Is it any wonder that many of the racing venues that relied heavily on expensive new technology have dropped in popularity, while Winston Cup's popularity has grown dramatically with few changes?

It is a shame, however, that while Winston Cup racing is enjoying its greatest popularity, there are fewer makes of cars running this year than there ever have been. Throughout the history of Winston Cup racing, Dodge, Plymouth, and AMC have competed; most have won races. In fact, until recently Hudson still held a record for consecutive wins. Perhaps with the rising popularity of Winston Cup racing, fans will be able to see more manufacturers reenter the competition.

The following chapter presents an overall look at the components that make up a modern Winston Cup racecar. The relationship of a Winston Cup car to the manufacturer is generally only skin deep. Taking away the

engine and sheet metal body, all cars are pretty much the same. In fact there is more than one car out there that has changed from Ford to Chevy or from Chevy to Ford and back again.

Building A
STOCK CAR

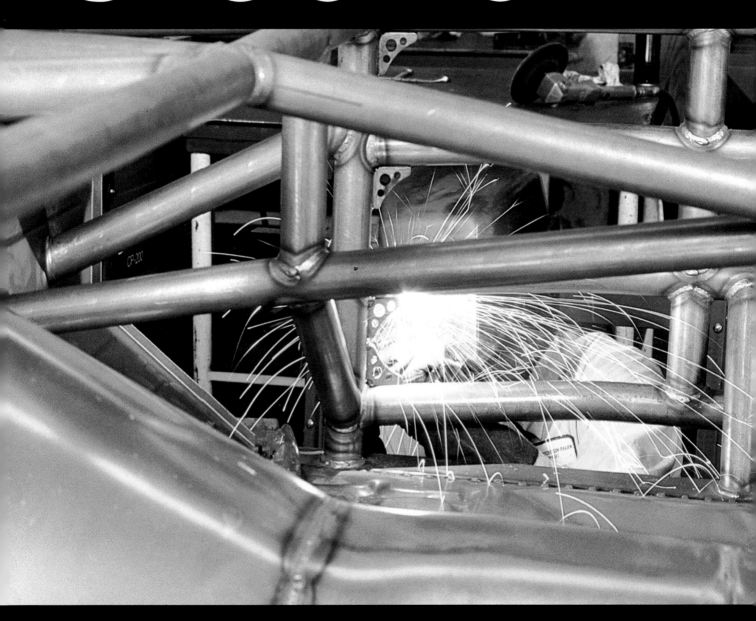

The days of starting with a production car and converting it to a racecar are long gone. Modern Winston Cup cars are hand built from metal tubing, fabrications, sheet metal and after-market racing products. The following pages show building the basic chassis, making and mounting the body panels, and a piece-by-piece description of the rest of the components that make up a modern Winston Cup racecar.

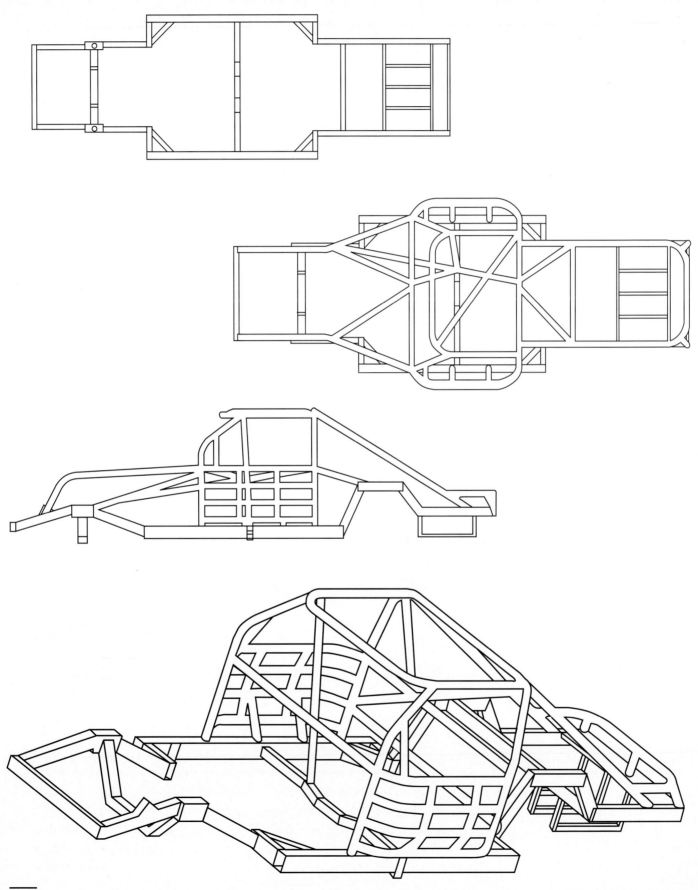

BUILDING THE CHASSIS

Frame rails, the innermost, bottom frame components, are made from square, carbon steel tubing. Frame rails must be built parallel with no offsets. The rocker panels, the outermost frame components, are 2" x 4" tubing, with a wall thickness of .120 inches. Cross members, the pieces that tie the frame together, and other frame pieces are 2" x 2" tubing (also .120 inch thick). All of the connections, attaching the frame pieces together, are welded.

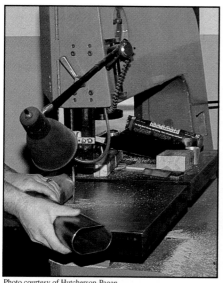

Photo courtesy of Hutcherson-Pagan

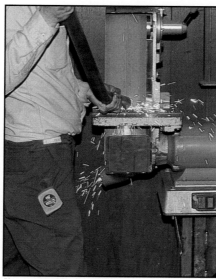

Photo courtesy of Hutcherson-Pagan

Chassis pieces must be cut and shaped; and all sharp edges deburred before being assembled. All of the individual pieces must be fitted precisely if the finished product is to be correct.

Pieces ready to be welded are clamped into place. The "jig" is the starting point of the chassis. Using it as a fixture to construct the chassis on, builders can build chassis after chassis almost exactly alike. Throughout the entire building process the chassis stays clamped to the jig. When a chassis is finished it is unclamped from the jig; and another chassis is begun.

Photo courtesy of Hutcherson-Pagan

Photo courtesy of Hutcherson-Pagan

Assembly starts at the bottom with the frame rails (clamped to the jig) and proceeds upwards. Major pieces, such as the main roll bar, are attached to the lower frame first. Connecting pieces are then welded into place between the major structural pieces.

The firewall, the floorpan, and the rear wheel wells are about the only sheet metal pieces added during the building of the chassis. Occasionally roll bars must pass through the sheet metal floor pan to the frame rails. All other sheet metal pieces are added after the chassis is completed.

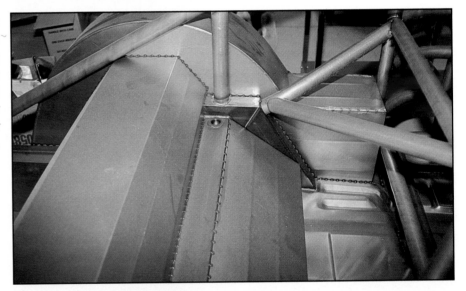

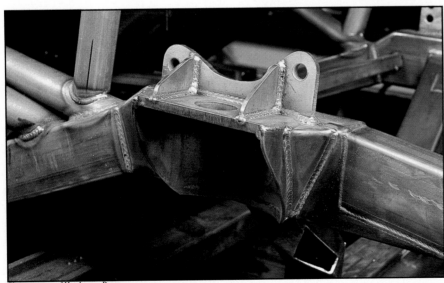

Photo courtesy of Hutcherson-Pagan

Suspension fittings are added to the frame rails. For the finished car to handle properly, all of these must be positioned correctly. A mistake at this point could mean a handling problem to overcome on the track. Wire-fed welders are used to make the connections.

Small flanges are added to provide extra strength around connections. All welded connections must be "clean," with no sharp edges.

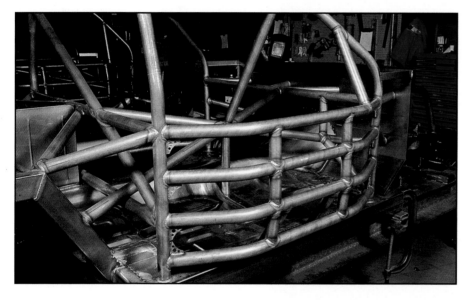

Built from the bottom up, the roll cage begins to take shape. Side bars give the entire car structural rigidity and integrity, and protect the driver in the event of an accident.

The finished product is delivered to the team. The chassis is now ready to have the body mounted and the other components added.

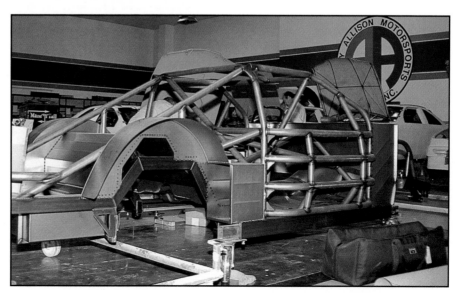

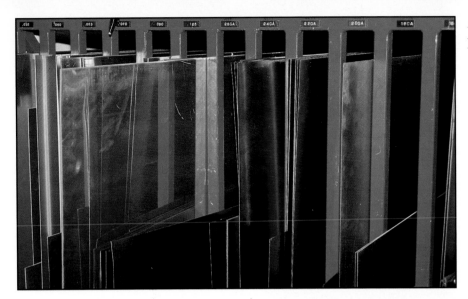

A body panel begins life as a standard piece of sheet metal.

A rough sketch is made directly onto the sheet metal with a marker.

A metal shear is used to cut the rough shape of the part.

BUILDING A BODY PANEL

More precise cuts are made with hand sheers and air-powered clippers.

Curves are then rolled into the piece. The compound curves (bending in more than one direction) are very difficult to make.

Once the fender begins to take shape, it is clamped into position to be checked. A steady process of mount-check-adjust begins. A fabricator may go through this routine many times to ensure proper fit.

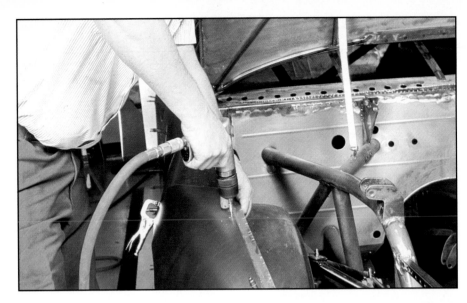

When the fender is ready to be mounted, holes are drilled along the mounting area for the rivets to pass through.

Many rivets are used to ensure a tight, secure fit. The body must withstand the tremendous air pressure of racing at 200 miles per hour, or the "fender banging" so common in short-track racing.

The entire side of a Winston Cup car is smooth, with no gaps between body panels. Where the sheet metal pieces meet, they are welded together.

BUILDING A BODY PANEL

Once all of the welding is done, the area is ground smooth.

The body is ready to go to the paint shop for further smoothing, priming, and then painting.

In the finished product none of the body panel connections is visible. The entire body appears to be one piece.

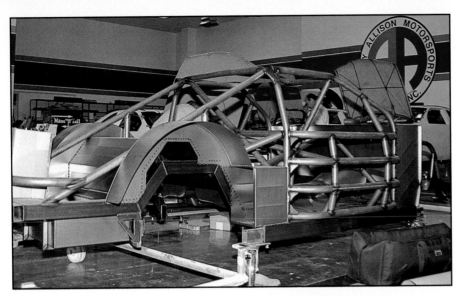

Most teams receive the chassis already built from a supplier. At this point in the construction process all Chevrolets, Fords, and Pontiacs are the same. As the bodies are built onto the chassis, their true color takes shape.

From the beginning of building until inspection before the race, the template rules the body. The template is a standardized aluminum pattern defining the profile of the roof. By already knowing how high the top of the car is supposed to be when completed, builders preset the template for use as a guide when building the body.

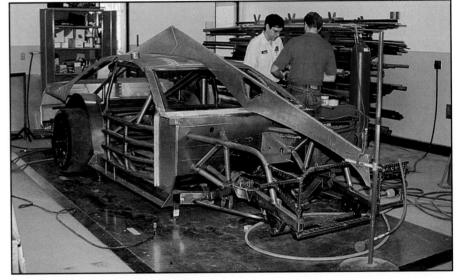

Beginning at the back, the rear facia and deck lid are mounted onto the chassis.

ASSEMBLING THE BODY

The rear roof pillars and rear window supports are added.

The roof comes next. The sheet metal roof, or roof skin, is the same as the one production cars use. The roof flap unit is added at this point. It must be properly aligned to fit well and to function properly.

At this point the top is taking shape without any sides. This "top down" construction method is the best way to make the finished product fit the template.

The cockpit is under construction. With such easy access, much of the inside work is done before the body is completed.

The front of the car is now ready to be put on. The template will be set up again to properly mount the hood and front facia.

The hood and front facia have been added and the sides are begun. Again, work begins in the rear and proceeds to the front.

ASSEMBLING THE BODY

Since the fenders have not yet been added, wooden spacers support the hood. At this point the windshield supports are welded into place.

Seams are welded and ground flush.

The "unpolished" finished product.

PAINTING

Extensive body work is necessary to make the body "slick." Before the final priming and painting is done, crews begin to "bolt-on" all of the car's cockpit and suspension systems.

On to the paint booth. Painters must make ten or twelve cars look exactly the same, so colors must be mixed to exacting standards to ensure consistency.

When the painting is complete, the job is far from finished. The engine and drive train must be installed and the set-up tuned in before the car can be raced.

Component Breakdown
BODY

Cars are required to weigh at least 3500 pounds with all fluids and without the driver. The right side weight must be at least 1600 pounds. If it is necessary to add weight to the car, it is added in the form of blocks weighing at least five pounds each. These blocks are bolted inside the body in an approved position. When weighed after the race, oil, water and gas may be added but the wheels cannot be changed. One-half of one percent of the car's weight will be added for the after-race weigh-in to compensate for wear experienced during the race.

Factory racing divisions of Ford and GM supply the front facias (or nose pieces); however, they are not the same as the front facias on production cars. Made of "kevlar," they are used only for racing purposes. The dimensions of the front facias are established before the season begins to ensure that no model gains an unfair advantage by converting the multiple piece production car facia to a one-piece racing facia. The front facias all have a serial number and their shape or contours cannot be altered to improve aerodynamic flow. The front facia is mounted on a frame of square tubing which is fabricated during the building of the chassis.

Openings are cut in the front of the facia to allow air to be ducted to various systems that require cooling. The grill openings used are covered by two layers of wire screen. This screen, used for protection from debris, is attached to the grill. No devices that direct air flow can be placed between the grill and the radiator.

The grill area is of critical importance and must do a number of things at one time. As the leading edge of the car, the facia is critical for good aerodynamic flow. Grills must allow enough air in to cool the engine, but too large an opening will create drag, lifting the front end of the car at high speeds. Grill openings are also used to duct air to the brake rotors when racing on tracks that are demanding on brakes. Air is ducted from the left grill opening to the oil cooler, which is mounted inside the left front fender in front of the left front tire. Overheating of these systems is likely if these openings are closed due to damage or debris.

Front facias are mounted before the fenders so that the rest of the car will fit their profile.

Viewed from the engine well, the backing structure supports the front facia and connects it to the chassis.

Front facia with the grill openings covered with wire screen to protect from debris.

HOOD

Factory-produced hood skins must be used. Original support panels holding the sheet metal hood rigid are replaced with custom supports. The hinges fold back to keep the hood open. When closed, the hood is locked into position with four positive pin fasteners. The fasteners are evenly spaced along the front of the hood. The air intake for the carburetor is located on the centerline of the car, between the back of the hood and front of the windshield.

A clean hood profile is necessary for good air flow over the car on longer tracks. If the hood is damaged, the disturbed air flow will slow a racecar. Short-track performance is usually not affected by cosmetic hood damage.

A clean hood is a must for good aerodynamic flow. Inset: close-up of pin fastener.

Hood being mounted during construction.

Open hood with hinges showing.

ROOF

Stock roof panels for the make and model car being raced are mandatory. The height, shape and size of the roof do not change. Two 1/2-inch pieces of aluminum angle must be mounted as far to the outside of the roof as possible, between the windshield and the rear glass. These are used to help stabilize the car at high speeds.

Air flow over the roof is of critical importance. How the air flows off the roof influences the way the air hits the rear spoiler, which in turn affects the way the car handles. Teams go to great lengths to make sure the air flow to the rear spoiler is optimized while still ensuring that the roof profile remains legal.

Roof flaps, which are made to deploy if the car gets sideways or backward in a spin, have become mandatory in Winston Cup racing. When the car gets sideways, the flaps are activated by the low pressure created by air flowing across the roof of the racecar. Much like an airplane wing, air moving fast across the top of the cars, creates a low pressure area. When the car gets sideways this low pressure sucks the roof flaps up. Once activated, the flaps "catch" the air under them and push the car down on the track. This minimizes the amount of air getting under the car and helps to prevent serious crashes, as air under a speeding car can cause it to flip.

Roof Rails.

Roof flaps in the deployed position.

Clean air flow over the roof is critical as this influences how the air hits the rear spoiler and thus affects the handling.

FIREWALL

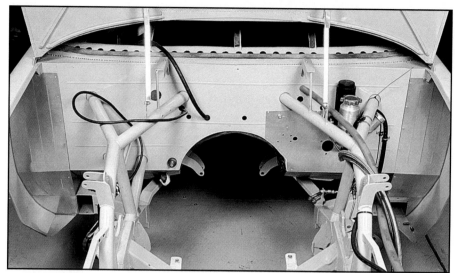

Firewalls are made of 22-gauge steel and must be welded into place. A tunnel is cut through the firewall for the transmission. The tunnel can be no wider than 17 inches at the bottom, and must be at least 10 inches below the leading edge of the windshield. The tunnel cannot be wider than 10 inches when it passes the driver's seat. Firewalls do just what their name implies. They act to protect the driver from the heat of the engine and provide protection during dangerous engine failures. "Crush panels" extend from the firewall to the fenders.

The firewall before engine installation.

DOORS & FENDERS

Doors don't really exist on modern Winston Cup cars, though the sides maintain the factory contours and accent lines. They are hand crafted from .025" sheet steel, in one piece, from about the center of the front wheel to the center of the rear wheel. They are riveted and welded in place with all of the weld seams smoothed. A short front fender and rear quarter panel are hand made and fill the area between the sides and the front and rear facias. Drivers get in and out of the car through the driver's side window.

As with all other body pieces on the car, great care is taken in producing the pieces to exacting tolerances. This is more easily said than done, considering the compound curves in the body of a Winston Cup car.

When measuring lap speeds down to one-hundredth or one-thousandth of a second, the slightest flaw can upset the aerodynamics of the car and slow it down or affect the handling. The best way to make these parts correctly is to have proper tools and years of experience.

Door panel under construction. Roll cage bars are visible behind the door.

Fenders are altered somewhat to allow for tire clearance. The stickers are located in precise positions if the car is competing for "manufacturers' awards."

Not really a door but a slick, aerodynamic, one-piece side. Numbers must be at least 18 inches high and located under the door window.

The fuel intake is located on the left quarter panel. A spring activated valve opens only when the fill tank nozzle is inserted.

DECK LID

Deck lids (or trunk lids) retain their stock shape, contours, and appearance. When closed they are held shut with two pin fasteners. Deck lids must have working hinges and a self-holding device to keep the lid up when it is open. The deck lid is one of the few "stock" parts used in a Winston Cup car. The stock deck lid backing structure is replaced with custom fabricated supports keeping the deck lid rigid at high speeds.

Deck lid before spoiler has been mounted.

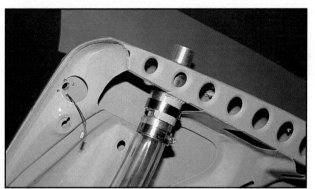

Fuel overflow spout exits through the left side of the deck lid.

Pin fastener in closed position.

Pin fastener in open position.

REAR FACIA

Manufactured much the same as the front facia, the rear facia standards are established by the original equipment manufacturer and NASCAR officials. While keeping the profile and shape roughly the same as that of a production car, the rear body pieces are one-piece construction and do not include a functional bumper.

Rear facia, just after mounting to the chassis.

Finished, with the decklid fitted.

FRONT AIR DAM

The front air dam must have a minimum ground clearance of 3-1/2 inches. All support brackets holding the air dam in place must be mounted on the back of the air dam. The leading edge of the air dam may not extend more than 1/2-inch forward of the bumper. The air dam's purpose is to keep as much air from going under the car as possible. The more air that goes under the car, the more lift the car will have. As the car goes faster, the lift increases. If the air dam is damaged, on longer, faster courses the result will be a slower car that is more difficult to drive.

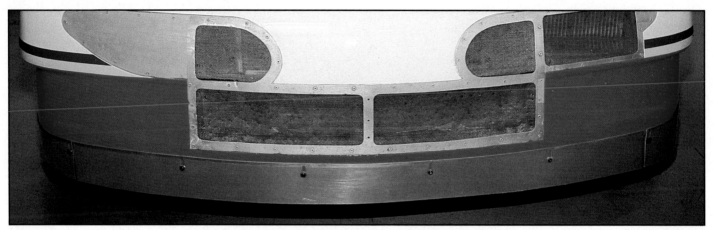

The front air dam, located along the bottom of the front facia.

REAR SPOILER

The air passing over the car and onto the rear spoiler is deflected upward, forcing the rear of the car down and improving the car's handling ability in the turns. This force is commonly referred to as "down force."

Rear spoilers are nonadjustable and must be attached to the rear deck lid. Spoilers are 57 inches wide, 6.5 inches high and 1/8-inch thick. The rear spoiler is made in two pieces and mounted with a thin gap on the center line of the body. This gap is necessary to allow inspection templates to be fitted directly on the car's body when checking the profile. All rear spoilers are made of aluminum and mounted so that they will not bend or flex under the air pressure encountered when racing. Rear spoilers must be mounted with at least six 1/4-inch or larger bolts across the back of the deck lid. Edges must be cut square and the corners can be rounded to no more than a 1/2-inch radius.

At Talladega and Daytona a predetermined angle setting is used. This setting is determined by officials before the race, insuring the angle is high enough to give the cars plenty of down force, making for safer racing.

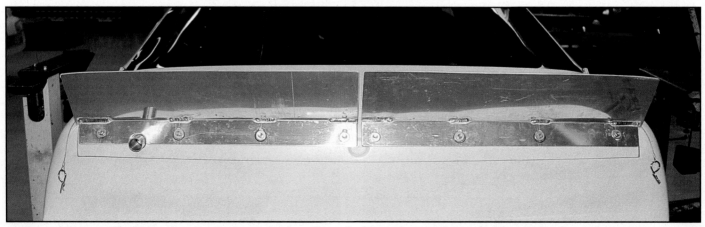

Rear spoiler (Note: the two-piece construction allows the inspection template to be placed directly on the body).

WINDSHIELD

All cars must use windshields made of hard-coated, polycarbonate material. Three metal braces must be used to support the windshield from the inside of the car and two metal reinforcements must be used on the outside. The inside reinforcements are bolted (using 1/4-inch bolts) to the roof or roll bar at the top of the support and to the dash panel at the bottom. The outside reinforcements must be directly in front of the outward, inside supports. The outside reinforcements are stainless steel, 1-inch wide strips with a rubber gasket between them and the windshield. Tinting windows any darker than the factory tinting is not allowed. A trailing driver must be able to see through the rear window and windshield of the car in front while racing.

All cars use polycarbonate racing windshields. At 200 miles per hour even a small piece of debris can still penetrate the windshield.

Braces prevent the windshield from popping out during accidents.

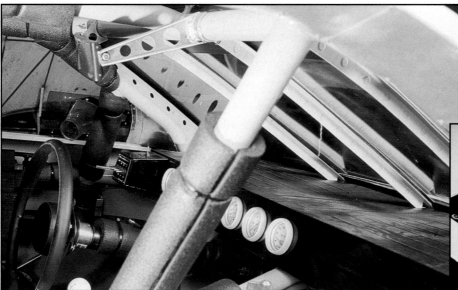

Internal braces support the windshield, adding strength.

Outside clamps allow for quick changes during pit stops.

SIDE WINDOWS

Tracks less than 1.5 miles and road courses - Side windows (or door windows) must be removed. A nylon web screen is installed in the driver side door window opening. Screens are made of 3/4-inch wide strips. The minimum screen size is 22 inches wide by 16 inches tall. Window screen mounts must be welded to the roll cage.

Tracks more than 1.5 miles - The same screen system is used on the driver's window. Cars must have a full window on the right side of the car. The window must be made of 1/4-inch safety glass. No tape is allowed on the side window glass.

No sharp edges are allowed after construction.

Right window glass keeps air out of the car if it gets sideways, helping reduce the risk of flipping.

Nets protect drivers from debris and prevent arms from being slung out the window during accidents.

QUARTER WINDOWS

Quarter windows (the small window directly behind the door window) remain located in their stock position. Only 1/4-inch "Lexan" is used for this window. These windows are not solid. Openings are cut into the windows; and when extra cooling is required, they are used to "pick up" air to cool the rear brakes and the oil reserve tank .

Quarter window ducts "pick up" air for cooling.

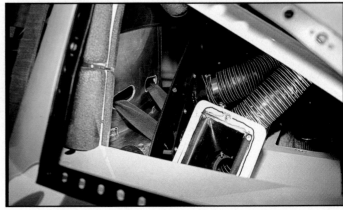

Quarter window removed, showing air ducts.

Support brackets under construction.

Polycarbonate glass, the same thickness and shape as the original glass, is used for the rear window. A light tint in the window is allowed, but the tint must be light enough to allow trailing drivers to see through. This ensures that driver's hand signals will be seen when waving or pointing to action taking place on the track, for example a pit stop or trouble with the cars ahead.

The rear window is secured by two metal straps, 1/8- inch thick (minimum) by 1-inch wide. These strips are bolted to the roof at the top and to the deck lid support panel at the bottom. Holes are drilled in both sides of the rear window to allow wrenches to be inserted through to the bolts which adjust the "wedge" or rear spring settings.

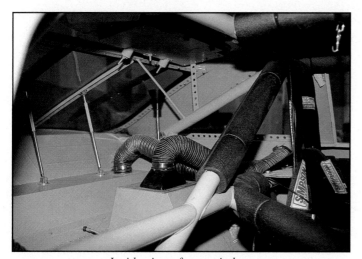

Inside view of rear window.

Hole for wedge adjustment wrench.

Rear window in place.

Safety and driver comfort are the main priorities when setting up the interior of the racecar. All gauges and controls must be positioned such that the driver can use them with the least distraction to his driving. Gauges are usually mounted so that when all of the needles are pointing straight up, everything is OK. Two ignition systems are mounted to the right of the driver. The backup ignition activator switch must be within easy reach.

All roll bars within the driver's reach are padded. This protects the driver during crashes. The driver's seating position is custom fit. Each driver has preferences for seat angle and height. Some drivers like to sit more upright, close to the steering wheel. Others sit low in the car in a more reclined position. Steering wheel size is also a matter of driver preference.

A complete fire extinguishing system is installed.

Safety and ergonomics are priorities when planning the cockpit.

Radio control button is mounted on steering wheel.

Pedals are closely spaced for "heel-toe" shifting

Oil lines are routed by the driver and into the oil reservoir.

Component Breakdown
ENGINE

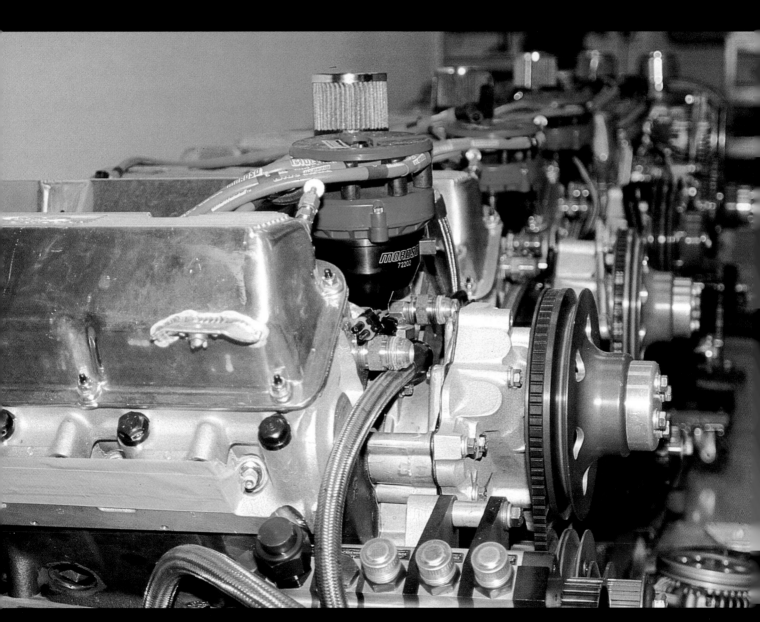

Only small block V-8 engines are allowed. The following blocks are considered "small blocks." Regardless of which is used, the engine must be built to have a displacement of between 350 and 358 cubic inches.

Chevrolet   307, 327, 350 and 400

Ford   302 and 351

MOTOR MOUNTS

The motor cannot be located farther back than the center line of the forward-most spark plug hole on the right side cylinder head, in line with the upper ball joint. Also, the center line of the crankshaft must be on the center line of the tread width (equidistant from both front wheels). A minimum of 10 inches ground clearance is mandatory from the center of the crankshaft to the ground. All motor mounts must be made of steel and are not adjustable.

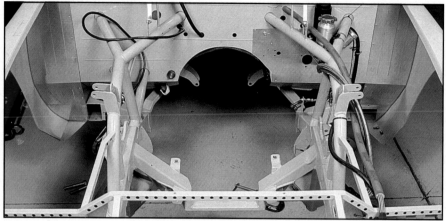
Mounting brackets are welded directly to the frame rails.

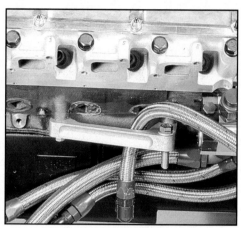
Motor mount bolted to block.

BLOCKS

Most blocks used in Winston Cup Racing are manufactured by the race divisions of General Motors and Ford. These blocks are made specifically for racing and do not appear in any production vehicle. Material is cast iron (aluminum blocks are not allowed). Engines must be between 350 and 358 cubic inches of displacement. Engines start with a longer stroke and smaller cylinder diameter (bore x stroke = displacement). As a block is worn and is bored out, the stroke is shortened as the bore increases to achieve the desired displacement. By using this method, blocks can be used for a relatively long period of time. Some two- and three-year-old blocks are still racing. Racing blocks differ from the production blocks in that they have thicker cylinder walls to eliminate distortion and give a better surface for the rings. Improved water passages increase the cooling ability. Adding bulkhead material to the main bearing bosses adds strength around the crankshaft. Increased strength around the deck surface where the heads bolt on increases engine stability. Blocks have 4-bolt main bearing caps.

The following may NOT be changed:

Material
Number of cylinders
Angle of cylinders
Number and type of main bearings
Integral or separate cylinder sleeves
Location of camshaft
Overall configuration

Cylinder head surface of a block.

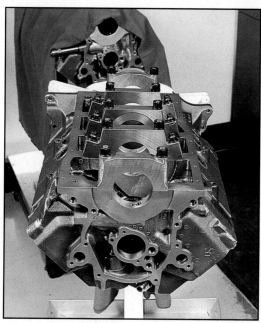

Bottom of block, showing main caps.

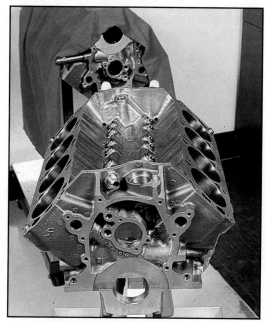

Top of block, showing valve lifter bores.

CRANKSHAFTS

Most crankshafts are 4340 alloy steel forgings, made by aftermarket sources; however, there are still a few billet machined crankshafts in use. Only steel crankshafts are allowed. Crankshafts may be lightened and balanced, and approved harmonic balancers (bolt-on balancing devices) are also allowed. The crankshaft lobes are tapered on the leading edges to reduce windage (drag created by the front edge of the crankshaft lobes passing through the air and oil in the block) allowing the engine to spin easier, increasing horse power.

Teams use various brands of high-quality bearings. Engine builders may take as long as a day to install main bearings, making sure of a tight, clean fit.

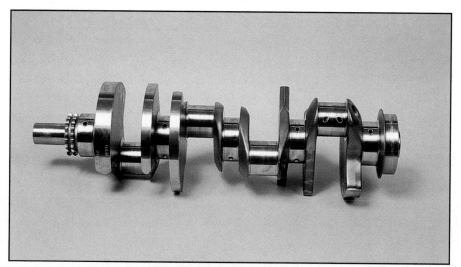

A Winston Cup crankshaft.

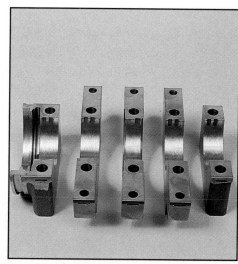

Heavy-duty "4-bolt" caps hold the crankshaft firmly in place.

CONNECTING RODS

Only steel connecting rods are allowed. Most are forged, H-beam style rods that are heavy and very strong. Engine builders tend not to give up much on the rods, not wanting to risk strength for a small performance gain. Heavy rod bolts are used to attach the rod caps. Many Chevys and Fords use identical rods. No stainless steel or titanium rods are allowed.

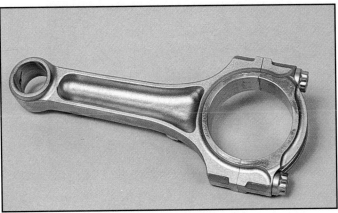

Typical connecting rod.

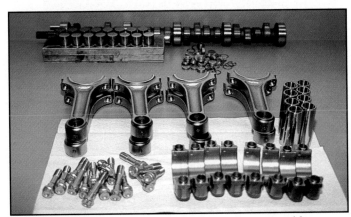

Connecting rods and hardware ready to assemble.

PISTONS

Winston Cup cars may use any type of piston. Most are forged aluminum of varying design. Pistons take an incredible pounding during 500 miles of racing. With the high compression and intense combustion pressures experienced in a racing engine, pistons will occasionally fail, usually burning a hole through the top of the piston or "burning a piston."

Pistons used in Winston Cup racing are not "flat topped." The crowns of the pistons have domes which help to increase compression. They must be "fly-cut" or "relieved" to provide clearance for the valves which share space in the combustion chamber with the piston domes. When the valves are off their seats, they cannot contact the rising piston or the engine will self-destruct.

After a run on the dyno, pistons are cleaned and checked for proper wear.

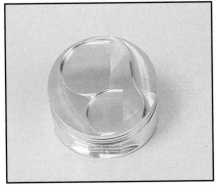

The top of a piston showing the valve location.

The ring grooves in the side of the piston.

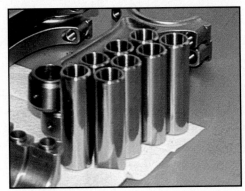

Wrist pins connect the pistons to the connecting rods.

CYLINDER HEADS

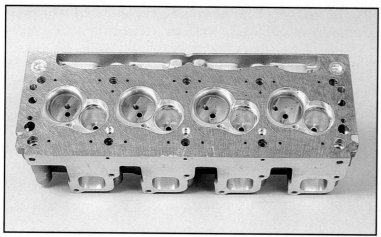

A Winston Cup head after machining and before assembly, showing the combustion surface.

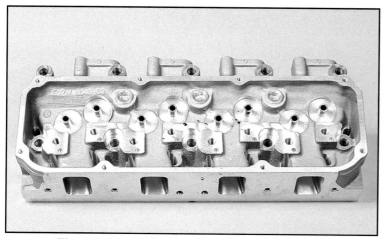

The top of the head where the valve train is located.

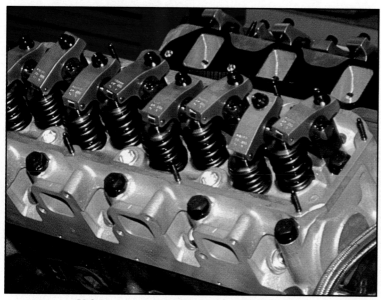

Valve train assembled on the cylinder head.

All Winston Cup heads are aluminum. Recent changes in the rules have limited the available heads to one Ford and one General Motors head design. Heads must be either:

Ford Cars- Ford: part number E3ZM6049C3 Dated 9/9/91 or later

GM Cars - Chevrolet: part number 10134364 Casting number 10134363

Valve location and angle must remain stock. Spacing between valves (center to center) is 1.935 inches for Chevrolet and 1.900 inches for Ford. Internal polishing and "porting" (custom machining the intake and exhaust ports on the cylinder head to match the manifold ports) are allowed. Before this rule there were many more types of cylinder heads available; and, as they were modified more and more, a team could easily have $20,000 to $30,000 in a set of heads. The new rules strictly limit the modifications allowed, which in turn ensures that the heads will be less expensive, more durable, and that racing will remain competitive.

Cylinder Head
The following may NOT be changed:

Material
Number of valves per cylinder
Type of combustion chamber
Location of spark plug
Orientation of spark plug
Arrangement of valves
Type of valve actuation
Number of intake ports
Number of exhaust ports
Center distances of intake ports
Center distances of exhaust ports
Shape of ports at mating surface of manifolds
Angle of port face relative to mating surface of head to block
Firing order

CAMSHAFTS

Teams look for a camshaft that is durable and provides an acceptable amount of power. The lobe designs of General Motors and Ford camshafts are similar; however, there are differences between the two. The Ford camshaft is shorter and thicker. This design is inherently stronger than the GM camshafts which are longer and narrower. Because of this design difference many times the Ford and GM camshafts are made using different manufacturing methods.

When camshafts break they tend to break at the rear, which is the longest section of the camshaft without support. Because of this, Chevrolet cams are usually made from 8620 alloy steel, with stellite (an extremely wear-resistant alloy) welded to lobes. The 8620 steel alloy gives the camshaft strength while the stellite on the lobe surfaces provides good wear resistance.

A camshaft has to be many things at once. A cam has to be hard in the lobe area for resistance to friction, but must be "soft" enough to flex a little and not snap and break.

It is very difficult to produce a camshaft that fits these requirements. Camshaft durability is so important that teams usually run the same camshaft at many different non-restricter plate tracks, relying on intake ports, headers and intake manifolds to change the "powerband" of the engine to fit the particular track.

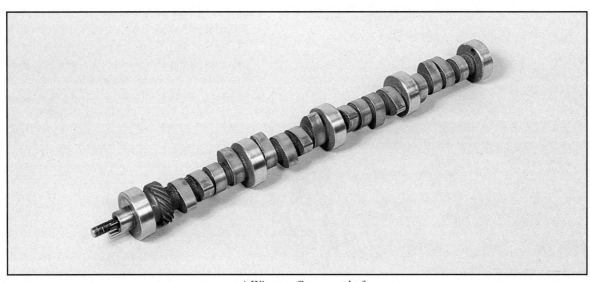

A Winston Cup camshaft.

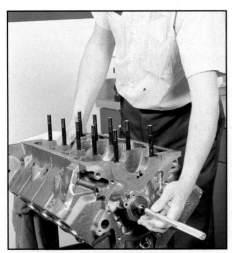

Camshaft installation.

Close-up of lobe surfaces.

Camshaft preparation.

LIFTERS & PUSHRODS

Valve lifters.

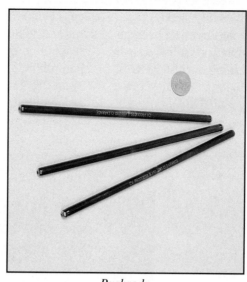

Pushrods.

Lifters ride on top of the camshaft lobes, transferring the "lift" of the lobe through the pushrod to the rocker arm. Only solid steel, or steel-hydraulic, flat-tappet, barrel-type lifters are allowed. This rule eliminates "roller lifters" which incorporate a rolling tip that rides against the cam, reducing friction and allowing much more radical lobe designs. Mushroom lifters, or any lifter that assists in closing the valve, are not allowed. Maximum lifter size allowed on both GM and Ford is .875-inch diameter.

Pushrods are a high quality racing type, able to withstand the tremendous force within the valve train.

ROCKER ARMS

Rocker arms mounted on cylinder head.

Rocker arms transfer the upward movement of the pushrod into the downward movement of the valve as it opens. Rocker arms that come as standard equipment on engines being used are allowed. Most teams use roller bearing rocker arms of a "split shaft" design which are much stronger than production rocker arms.

VALVE SPRINGS

Valves springs are made from a high quality steel. As engine speeds have increased, valve springs have become difficult parts to manufacture. Winston Cup engine speeds have increased to the point where turning over 9000 RPM is common. Harmonic problems at a particular RPM cause many valve train problems. Staying at an RPM where the point of bad harmonics occurs will increase the chances of engine failure. This is especially a problem at longer tracks where engines run a long time in one RPM range. Engine builders try to predict the point of bad harmonics, and design the engine so that these areas are in an RPM range that is not sustained. As the engine accelerates or decelerates through this range, harmonics are usually not a problem.

Valve springs.

Valve springs on heads.

VALVES

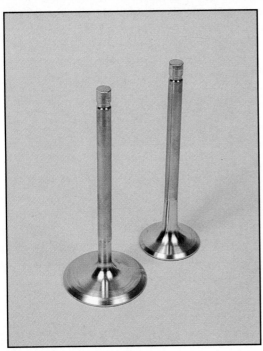

Valves.

Only steel and titanium valves are allowed in Winston Cup Racing. There is no restriction on either intake or exhaust valve size; however, the valve location and the valve angle must remain stock. As a practical matter, the specification of the "legal" cylinder head dictates the maximum size of the valve seats. There is little room to increase the valve size within these parameters.

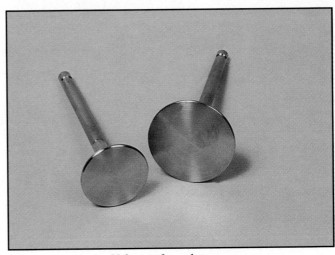

Valve surface close-up.

INTAKE MANIFOLD

High performance, aluminum intake manifolds are used in Winston Cup racing. The manifold used must be a model that has been approved by NASCAR officials. The distance from the gasket surface at the top of the manifold to the floor of the manifold "plenum" cannot exceed six inches. The plenum is the open area inside the manifold, where the fuel/air mixture is divided into eight parts or runners, one for each cylinder.

Different intake manifold modifications can make the same engine run very differently. Epoxy fillers may be added to the individual runners to change the flow characteristics of the manifold. Fillers may not be added to the plenum floor or walls. The intake opening size must be at least 3-9/16 inches when measured front-to-back, and 3-5/8 inches when measured side-to-side.

Typical intake manifold.

Intake manifold during "dyno" testing.

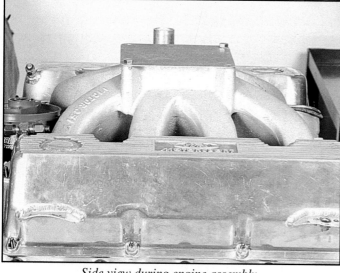

Side view during engine assembly.

CARBURETORS

Winston Cup cars run four-barrel, mechanically advanced, secondary venturi carburetors. Some polishing and other minor internal changes are allowed but no external alterations are made. Carburetor jets must be the same type as supplied by the manufacturer. Carburetors and their use are monitored closely by racing officials.

Restricter plates, mounted between the carburetor and the intake manifold, are used at Talladega and Daytona to limit the amount of fuel/air vapor to the engine. The result: less air, lower RPMs, less horsepower and lower speeds.

The following models are the only carburetors allowed.

**On all tracks except Talladega and Daytona:
Holley 4150 Series with 1-9/16 inch maximum venturi and 1-11/16 maximum throttle bore.**

**At Talladega and Daytona:
Holley 4150 Series with 1-3/8 inch maximum venturi and 1-11/16 maximum throttle bore.**

Carburetor with dust cover.

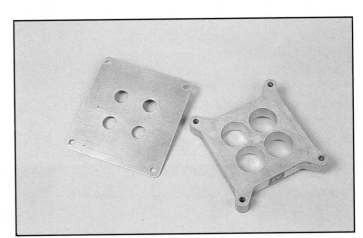

Restricter plate and carburetor spacer.

AIR FILTER

All Winston Cup cars use a round, dry-type air filter, much the same as the one used on production vehicles. The mandatory minimum diameter is 12 inches, and the maximum no more than 16 inches. Air filter housings are made of "Kevlar" or metal. The top and bottom pieces must be the same diameter and must be centered on the carburetor. The air filter element must be at least 1-1/2 inches high and no more than 4 inches high. Air filters may not be removed either during the race or during practice.

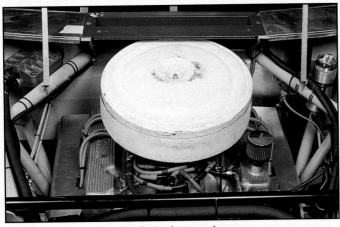

Mounted air cleaner element.

Air cleaner element is visible through back of housing.

EXHAUST SYSTEM

The exhaust system is made up of three main components: the headers, the collector pipe and the exhaust pipes.

Headers are made from pipe, bent to a custom fit. Each pipe runs from the exhaust port on the cylinder head to the collector pipe. By making each individual piece the same length, the exhaust system will help "pull" the exhaust gases from the cylinder, increasing engine efficiency. The shape, lengths, and configuration of the header pipes are adjusted to tune the powerband of the engine. This process allows crews to custom tailor the car's powerband to the track, building the maximum power where it is needed the most.

Collector pipes combine the four individual header runners on each side of the engine into a common pipe. Collector pipes are the links between the individual header runners and the single exhaust pipe.

Exhaust pipes begin at the collector pipe and must exit the car at the side between the front and rear wheels. They may exit the car on either side. Some teams locate both pipes on the left side of the car. This eliminates the chance that they might be "pinched" shut as the car pitches over in left hand turns or makes contact with the outside wall.

Exhaust pipes may have a maximum 3-1/2 inch inside diameter and must extend past the driver, under the frame and to the outer edge of the car. They cannot be fitted into a notched area in the rocker panel, quarter panel, or frame. They must be secured to the car with at least two 1/8-inch by 1-inch steel U-shaped brackets.

The exhaust pipes are not round. Instead they are "flattened", giving more ground clearance.

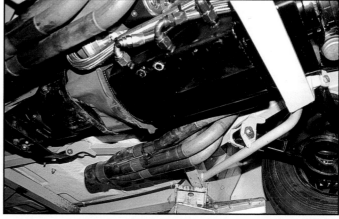

Collector.

Exhaust pipe tips.

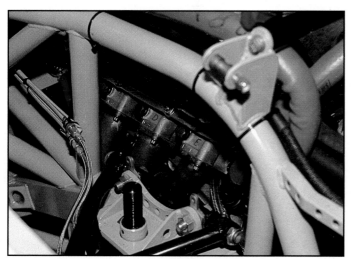

Headers.

Under-view of exhaust assembly.

OIL SYSTEM

Today's Winston Cup cars use a dry sump oil system. This type of oil system is not found on production vehicles. Instead of the oil flowing down to the pan to be recycled through the engine by a pump that picks up the oil from the bottom of the oil pan, the dry sump systems keep the oil in motion at all times. The pump is mounted on the outside of the engine (much the same as an alternator is mounted) and is driven by a belt. After the oil runs through the engine, it is quickly "picked up" and pumped through the oil system. During circulation the oil passes through many feet of hose, an oil tank mounted in the left rear of the car, and an oil cooler mounted in the left front of the car. The system runs at about 70 -- 80 p.s.i. and an acceptable range of oil temperature is 250 -- 270 degrees F.

OIL COOLER

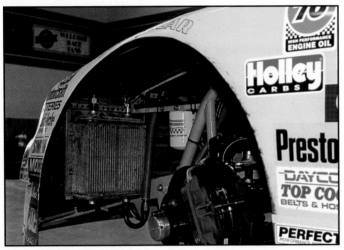

The mounted oil cooler with protective screen cover.

Placed behind the driver, the oil reserve tank must be encased in a 22-gauge metal, leakproof, insulated box. The tank holds approximately 18 quarts of oil. Oil reserve tanks are always located behind the driver, putting the weight in the middle and on the inside of the car. Due to this positioning, great care is taken to make the tank and protective shield as tough as possible. An extra oil temperature gauge is located on the oil reservoir tank so that crewmen can quickly get a read on the oil temperature.

OIL TANK

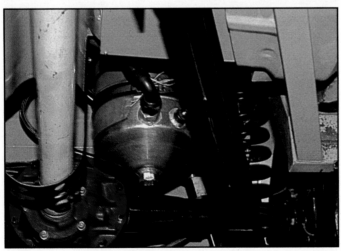

Oil reservoir tank in mounted position.

The oil cooler is a radiator used to keep engine oil cool. Oil constantly circulates through the cooler. As with a coolant radiator, the air (entering through the left front grill opening) is forced through the cooling fins; and the oil circulating through the passageways is cooled.

Mounted in the front of the car, the oil cooler is a fairly vulnerable piece of equipment. Often a Winston Cup car cannot survive impact to the left front that might be survivable to the right front because of the oil cooler.

With modern engine speeds, proper oil cooling is essential to be competitive on the track.

OIL FILTER & LINES

Winston Cup cars use oil filters very much like production cars do; but instead of being attached to the engine, the oil filter is mounted in the engine well at a very accessible position. Only high-quality stainless steel braided line is used for the oil system due to the high temperature and the consequences of a line failure.

Oil filter mounted and ready to go.

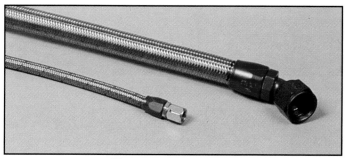

Close-up of braided line.

OIL PUMP

Winston Cup oil pumps are mounted onto the engine much in the same way that an alternator is mounted. Power is transferred to the oil pump by a wide heavy-duty belt running off of a special crankshaft pulley. These heavy-duty pumps have a high pumping output in order to push the oil quickly throughout the system.

Oil pump.

Oil pump manifold.

Mounted oil pump with drive belt.

COOLING SYSTEM

General Requirements: Winston cup cooling systems are similar to their production counterparts but with a few modifications. No special systems that use ice, freon or any other coolant can be used. Cooling is of critical importance to a Winston Cup engine.

With the 14:1 and 15:1 compression ratings being run and the high engine speeds being turned, much more heat is generated than in a production engine. Only high strength hoses are used in the cooling system. Lower radiator hoses are most often a one-piece, metal pipe. Other hoses are braided stainless steel with special high pressure fittings. Any hose failure on the track means a hazardous wet spot for drivers to go through, so hose integrity is of prime importance.

RADIATOR

Winston Cup cars all use aluminum radiators. Radiators are stock appearing and mounted in the stock position, not exceeding two inches from vertical. Dust screens to prevent debris from entering the radiator are allowed. Overflow pipes can be relocated to an alternate position.

One of the biggest problems with radiators is clogging as a result of small pieces of tire rubber ground off the cars during racing. These small gooey pieces become stuck inside the fins of the radiator, impairing its ability to pass air and cool the fluids.

Radiator.

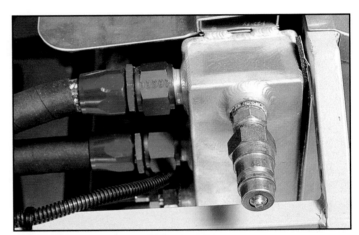

Filler nozzle.

WATER PUMP

Most Winston Cup cars run a specially built, custom-made water pump. Again, because of the heat generated in a Winston Cup engine, more water pump output is needed than a stock pump can provide. The impeller that does the actual pumping may be altered, changing the pitch and shape to change coolant flow rates. Changing impellers can greatly increase the pumping ability of the cooling system; and this increased circulation will improve the cooling efficiency of the entire system.

The racing water pump (at left) is driven by a belt and pulley, just as stock units.

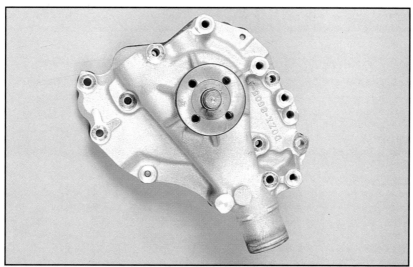

*While looking like a stock water pump on the outside,
a racing pump is different on the inside.*

COOLING FAN

Cooling fans used in Winston Cup racing must be steel, with no fewer than four blades. The pitch of the blade is changed to increase or decrease the air flow. All fans must have a diameter of at least 14 inches. Individual blades on the fan must be at least 3-1/2 inches wide. Fans must be operational and must be driven by a standard type belt from the crank shaft or by an electric motor. Today, teams run electric fans. These fans draw less energy from the engine by using a motor instead of a belt drive.

Cooling fan.

Cooling fan assembly viewed from beneath.

FUEL PUMP & LINES

Winston Cup cars use mechanical fuel pumps. Mechanical pumps get their pumping energy from a push rod riding on the camshaft. For safety reasons electric fuel pumps are not allowed in Winston Cup racing. If an engine with a mechanical pump quits running, the fuel quits pumping. However, in a car with an electric fuel pump the fuel may keep pumping even if the engine quits running. In a crash situation this could be disastrous.

High-quality stainless steel braided fuel line is used. Braided stainless line is rated to a much higher pressure than regular fuel line, and is much more resistant to damage and wear.

Fuel pump.

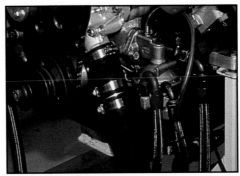

Mounted fuel pump.

Fuel line to carburetor.

FUEL CELL

Instead of a regular production gas tank, Winston Cup cars are required to use a "fuel cell." Fuel cells have a plastic body much stronger than a stock tank and much harder to damage. They are partitioned so that in the event of a rupture the fuel will not gush out of the opening.

Filler and overflow.

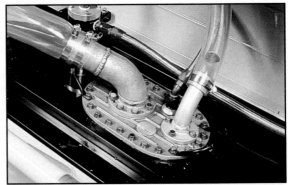

Filler and overflow at fuel cell.

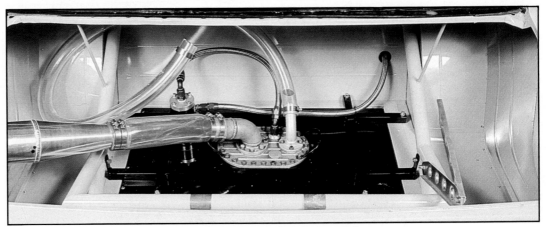

Fuel cell mounted in the "trunk."

DISTRIBUTOR & PLUGS

Distributors are mounted in the stock location and maintain the firing order of the stock model being raced. High quality after-market distributors and plug wires are used. These parts outperform their stock counterparts.

Distributor.

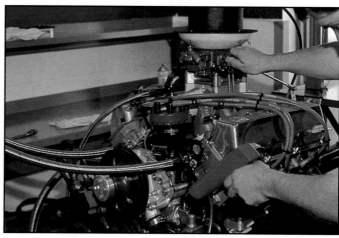

Mounted distributor during dyno testing.

COIL & IGNITION

Electronic ignition mounted inside the cockpit.

Electronic ignition systems are used in Winston Cup racing; however computerized systems are not allowed. The major ignition system components are located in the cockpit, to the right of the driver. This protects the equipment from debris and heat. All cars have two separate ignition systems. Two electronic ignition controls and two coils are mounted side by side. In the event of an ignition failure the driver can quickly flip a switch, changing to the backup system without having to make a pit stop.

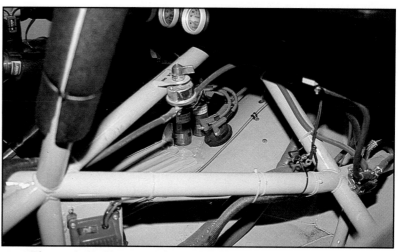

Electronic ignition controls are mounted to the right of the driver.

Backup coil switch.

ALTERNATOR

Mounted alternator with heavy-duty tension adjuster.

All cars have a functioning alternator. The alternators must work within preset specifications. Only standard drive belts are allowed.

The battery is located in a box mounted behind the driver. The compartment is accessed through a door in the front of the left rear wheel well. A standard, high quality, 12-volt battery is used.

STARTER

The mounted starter is visible between the exhaust collector and the oil pan.

Winston Cup cars all have working starters. After a race is underway a car may be "push started" in the pits, but a car can never be pushed onto the track.

Component Breakdown
DRIVETRAIN & SUSPENSION

Few things in Winston Cup racing are as important as a properly tuned suspension. How the individual suspension components are adjusted determines the "suspension set-up." These set-ups are the difference between the cars that handle well and those that don't handle so well. Its important to remember that horsepower will get you down the straights faster but the winning racecar is usually the one that gets through the corners the fastest.

FLYWHEEL & CLUTCH

Flywheels must be solid and made of steel. Drilling holes to lighten them is not allowed. The starter ring size must be the same size as the production starter ring gear.

Multiple-disc clutches are permitted in Winston Cup racing. The clutch housing assembly or cover can be aluminum or steel. Pressure plates and discs must be steel. The minimum clutch diameter allowed is 7-1/4 inches. Most teams use a 3- or 4-disc system with small diameter discs. Even though the discs are smaller than those in stock clutches, these multi-disc clutches have much more surface area; thus, they will stand up to the extreme strains of a 700 horsepower engine. Longer tracks can be hard on clutches, mainly when the car leaves the pits. Due to the rear gear ratios needed to reach the higher speeds experienced on the superspeedway, starting in first gear from a dead stop in a superspeedway car is like starting in second in a street car.

Teams may use only special clutch housings. A 3/8-inch steel scatter-shield is mandatory. The scatter-shield is an important piece of equipment. At the high RPM's that the engines turn, a broken clutch component or flywheel can become a very dangerous projectile -- not only dangerous to the driver in the car but also to the other drivers on the track. The scatter-shield works to contain any break-away components, preventing them from being released to do damage.

Flywheel and clutch components.

TRANSMISSION

Winston Cup cars use special, aftermarket, four-speed transmissions. All forward and reverse gears must be operational. If a gear in the transmission fails after the race begins, the car may continue racing. No automatic or semiautomatic transmissions are allowed.

Spare transmissions are prepared to go to the track.

Transmission viewed from under the car.

DRIVE SHAFT & REAR END

Drive shafts must be similar in design to standard production types. Two steel brackets are placed around the driveshaft and attached to the floor or crossmember, preventing the drive shaft from dropping to the track in case of failure. Drive shafts must be painted white so that if the brackets fail, the driveshaft can be seen by other drivers and the race spotters.

Any ring and pinion gear type may be used. Only one-piece, steel, rear-end housings are allowed. All cars usually have a 9-inch Ford rear-ends. Any rear axle ring and pinion gear ratio is allowed. Quick change rear ends are not used in Winston Cup racing. Only one-piece, single internal spline, steel axle shafts are permitted.

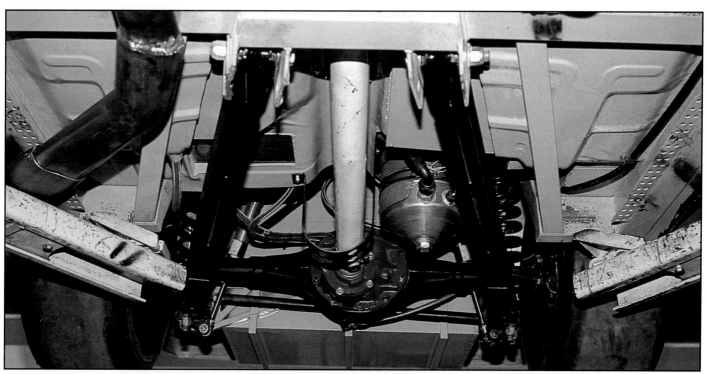

Driveshaft and rear end assembly. Oil reserve tank is visible to right of the driveshaft.

Work stands are used for driveshaft preparation.

Many rear end ratios are necessary for the different tracks.

Rear Gear Ratios by Track

Different tracks require different rear end gear ratios to ensure that all of the engine power available is optimized. An example of a rear gear ratio is 4.11 to 1 (or 4.11 : 1). This means that the driveshaft turns 4.11 revolutions for every 1 revolution of the tire.

Atlanta	*3.64 : 1*	*Indianapolis*	*4.20 : 1*	*Phoenix*	*4.22 : 1*
Bristol	*5.25 : 1*	*Martinsville*	*6.20 : 1*	*Pocono*	*3.89 : 1*
Charlotte	*3.70 : 1*	*Michigan*	*3.70 : 1*	*Richmond*	*4.86 : 1*
Darlington	*3.90 : 1*	*New Hampshire*	*3.60 : 1*	*Sears Point*	*5.30 : 1*
Daytona	*2.94 : 1*	*Rockingham*	*4.22 : 1*	*Talladega*	*2.94 : 1*
Dover Downs	*4.11 : 1*	*North Willksboro*	*5.67 : 1*	*Watkins Glen*	*3.89 : 1*

BRAKE MASTER CYLINDER

Master cylinders on Winston Cup cars are a simple, non-power-assisted type. They are mounted on the driver's side firewall, in roughly the same location as that of production cars.

Brake lines must be much stronger than their street counterparts. On short tracks, road courses, and some longer tracks, the demand on the brakes becomes critical. The heat generated at the rotor/pad contact dissipates through the caliper and into the fluid. The fluid, in turn, heats the brake lines. When subjected to such heat, production brake lines would become weak; and the pressure of applying the brakes would cause them to swell. This decreases the pressure at the pad and makes entire the brake system less efficient. The strength of braided stainless steel lines overcomes this problem.

Master cylinder mounted on firewall.

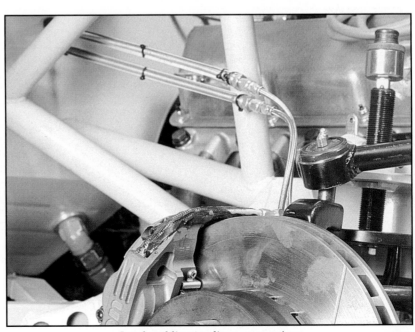

Insulated line / caliper connection.

BRAKE CALIPERS & PADS

Brake calipers respond to the pressure created by pressing the brake pedal, and squeeze the brake pads against the rotor. This is accomplished by the pressure from the master cylinder being transmitted through the brake line to the caliper. At the caliper, the brake fluid presses against pistons, which press against the brake pads, slowing the car down. Most street car calipers have one or two pistons per caliper while Winston Cup calipers have four pistons per caliper, allowing more pressure to be applied to the pads. Racing calipers must be built to stand up to the incredible heat generated when braking hard.

Brake pads are made especially for the purpose of racing. Due to the extreme heat encountered in racing brakes, normal street pads would wear out far too quickly. Instead of being made predominantly of an organic material, racing pads are a carbon/metal mix, which is much more heat and wear resistant.

Front brake caliper with pads installed.

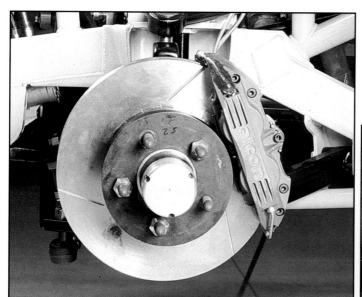

Front brake caliper.

Rear brake caliper.

Brake Rotors

Rotors used in Winston Cup racing must be made of steel. They must be able to stand up to extreme heat for long periods of time. Brake rotors will continue to work up to approximately 1200 degrees. At about this temperature they begin to glow. This can be seen at night races at Bristol as the cars brake, entering the turn. If the temperature continues to rise the heat is transferred into the caliper. When this happens the brake fluid will begin to boil, releasing air into the brake system. A driver will "lose" the pedal when air contaminates the system. Air released into the hydraulic brake system will result in the pedal going all the way to the floor when it is depressed.

Rotors are "vented" for cooling.

Rotors are grooved to keep pads smooth.

Lightweight rotor for superspeedways.

Nuts are locked into place with wire.

BRAKE COOLING DEVICES

Scoops "pick-up" air to cool brakes.

Flexible hose (3" dia.) carries air to brakes.

At some tracks, Talladega or Daytona for example, brake overheating is not a problem as brakes are seldom used other than in pitting. However, at tracks like Bristol or Martinsville, keeping the brakes cool is one of the most critical problems the teams must address. While all of the components making up the braking system are of the highest quality, they must still be cooled to work efficiently. This cooling is accomplished by ducting air through openings in the body onto the brake components.

Cars may have a maximum of three air scoops per brake. Each scoop directs air to the brakes with flexible hose (with a maximum diameter of 3 inches). A twenty-four square inch maximum scoop size is allowed. The scoops cannot extend forward of the leading edge of the air dam. Headlight openings may be used for brake cooling. Fans or blowers may be used to increase the air flow to the brakes. Liquid cooling of the brakes, which is used in some forms of auto racing, is not permitted.

Aluminum housing distributes air across caliper and rotor.

Rear brake ducting.

All Winston Cup cars must use a steering wheel with steel spokes supporting the rim. The wheels have a "quick release system" so that the wheel may be removed quickly. These quick release systems make it easier for a driver to get in the car and out of the car, especially in a crash situation. The wheel diameter is determined by the driver, who chooses the wheel size that gives him the best "feel" when driving the car. Steering wheels are usually marked so that the driver knows when the wheels are pointed exactly forward; with the tight fit between fender and tire, the tires will not come off during pit stops if the wheels are not straight forward.

Steering columns are made of steel. The center top of the steering post must have 2 inches of resilient material. A collapsible section must be made into the steering shaft for safety in the event of heavy front impact. Any universal joints used in the steering column, along with the collapsible section of the shaft, must be acceptable to racing officials.

A "worm type" gear is used in the steering system. A power steering pump assists the driver in turning the car. Without power steering, you might as well add another "0" to a 500 mile race.

Steering column is wrapped with protective foam inside cockpit.

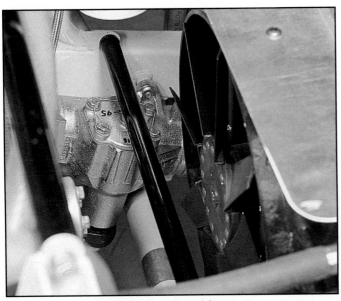

Steering gear, viewed from top.

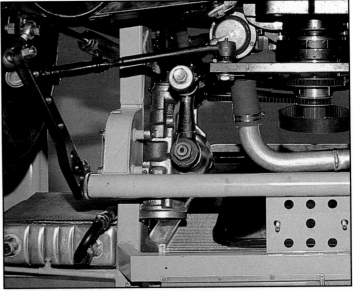

Steering gear, viewed from under car.

STEERING COMPONENTS

When the steering wheel is turned, it transfers the circular motion of the steering wheel, through the steering shaft, to the steering gear. One end of the steering gear is attached to the Pittman arm which changes the circular motion of the wheel into lateral motion. The other end of the Pittman arm is attached to the centerlink. As the centerlink moves back and forth the motion is transferred through tie rods to the steering knuckles, on which the front wheels are mounted. The idler arm, also attached to the centerlink, is used to stabilize the movement of the centerlink.

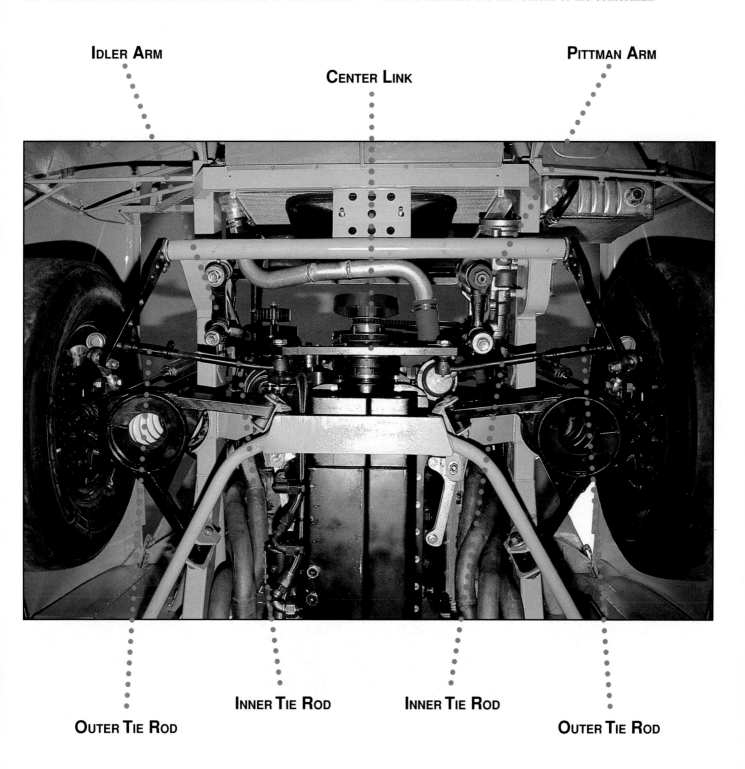

IDLER ARM

CENTER LINK

PITTMAN ARM

INNER TIE ROD

INNER TIE ROD

OUTER TIE ROD

OUTER TIE ROD

Winston Cup cars use coil springs made of heavy duty steel on both the front and rear suspensions. Springs must have a minimum diameter of 4-3/4 inches.

The front springs mount between the lower control arm and the frame. The bottoms of the springs ride in fittings attached to the lower control arms. The top spring mounts are welded to the frame rails. On the rear suspension the upper and lower coil spring mounts must be located between the rear frame side rails. The rear lower mounts must be located on either the rear axle trailing arms or on top of the rear axle housing. The upper mounts must be welded to the chassis directly above the lower mounts.

Springs are categorized by *spring rates*, which is the resistance a spring exerts when compressed, measured in pounds of force. Because of the importance of springs in making a car handle well, crews will test many combinations of spring rates on various corners of the car. On all tracks except road courses, a set-up will have a different spring rate at each corner of the car to counter the particular forces that that track applies to the car as it turns. For instance, at Daytona the force on the right front tire is about 3500 pounds, essentially the entire weight of the car.

Even after the team finds the right combination, their work is not done. Winston Cup cars are built with fixtures on the upper spring mount that allow teams to tune spring rates even finer. These devices are known as jack bolts or jack screws. As they are tightened or loosened they increase or decrease the spring rate. Fans will see this done during pit stops. It is most often called "putting wedge in the car" or simply "adjusting the wedge."

Special openings go through the rear window to allow the rear jack bolts to be turned very quickly during pit stops. However, the hood must be opened to adjust the front springs. Rubber inserts are allowed between the spring coils to add stiffness to the spring.

Front suspension showing coil springs.

Upper mount on frame rail.

Lower spring mount on control arm.

Jack bolt fitting without the spring.

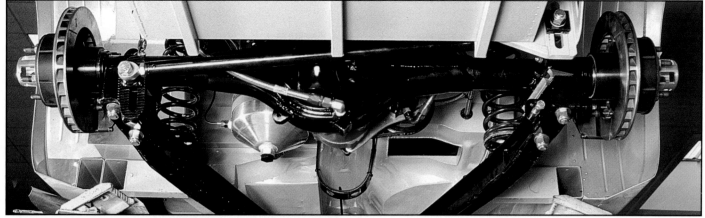

Rear suspension showing springs, as seen from under the rear of the car.

Rear spring.

Upper spring mount.

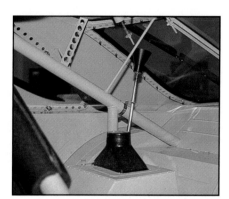

Spring adjustment access tube.

SHOCK ABSORBERS

Winston Cup cars use heavy duty shocks similar to the original shocks on the models being raced. The shocks used must be available to all competitors. Two shocks per wheel are allowed; but with the recent advances made in shock absorber technology, this is not seen any more. Modern shock absorbers handle the load with just one shock per wheel. Placing the shocks in the middle of the coil springs is not allowed.

Shock absorbers are tuned just like most other parts of the car. A "shock dyno" is used to test the shock rebound and handling characteristics. Teams can fine tune the shock to achieve the combinations they desire.

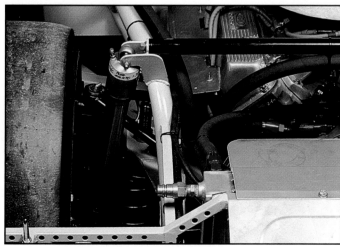

Front shock.

Rear shock.

SWAY BARS

Sway bars function to link the suspension and the chassis/body together. The stiffer the sway bar, the tighter the link between the chassis and the suspension. The tighter the link, the less movement between the suspension and the chassis, resulting in less "body roll" when the car is turning. However, if the sway bars are too stiff, control problems may result. Teams have many sway bar strengths available to allow them to tune the body roll to fit the track being raced.

Sway bar end links connect the swaybar to the control arm.

The sway bar is mounted in a sleeve which is attached to the frame.

STEERING KNUCKLES

Steering knuckles link the suspension and steering systems to the wheel. The upper and lower control arms are attached to the knuckle with ball joints. The wheel bearings ride on the spindle located on the outside of the knuckle.

Steering knuckle after machining.

CONTROL ARMS

Control arms are the main link between the chassis and the front suspension. The inside of the upper control arms are mounted to the frame using pivoting mounts with heavy duty bushings, and to the steering knuckles on the outside using ball joints. The lower control arms are attached to the frame and the steering knuckles. The front coil spring lower mounts are found on the lower control arms. Winston Cup cars use specially manufactured tubular control arms which are much lighter and stronger than their stock counterparts.

Upper control arm.

Lower control arm. The spring (yellow) is visible.

TRAILING ARMS

Trailing arms link the chassis and the rear suspension. The fronts of the trailing arms attach to the body with hinged fixtures just aft of the center of the car. The backs of the trailing arms attach to the rear axle and have fixtures to connect the rear shock absorbers and the rear springs which run from the frame to the trailing arms.

Rear trailing arms.

TRACK BAR

The track bar is used to keep the rear end "square" under the car. As the car goes through the turn the rear end will be twisted in relation to the body. Track or "panhard" bars are attached at one end to the frame and at the other end to the end of one of the trailing arms. Usually the bar runs from the left side of the body to the right rear trailing arm. This extra support is critical for stability through the turns.

The track bar is adjusted to refine the handling of the car during both practice and the race.

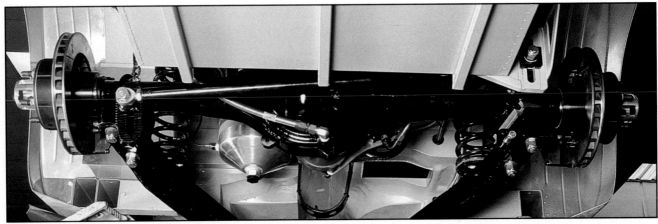

The left side of the track bar is connected to the trailing arm and the right side to the frame.

WHEELS & TIRES

Winston Cup cars run 9.5" x 15" steel wheels and specially produced racing tires.

In 1995 all Winston Cup tires are being supplied by Goodyear. Race tires are a radial design and made of a much softer rubber than even the most radical performance street tires. They have no tread pattern as they are to be used in dry conditions only.

The friction between the racing surface and the tire heats the rubber, making it even softer. It is this soft rubber as well as their heavy sidewall construction that allow the cars to achieve such high speeds in the turns.

Tire wear differs depending on the type of track being raced. For safety reasons tires incorporate an inner-liner, a small heavy duty innertube mounted on the rim inside the racing tire. In the case of a blowout this inner-liner should hold up, keeping the rim from digging into the pavement and causing the car to flip. At over a thousand dollars a set, a team's tire bill can be staggering in itself.

Two valve stems; one for inner-liners, and one for the tire.

Lug nuts are glued to wheels for quick pit stops.

A "scuff" tire. Scuffed tires have been run for a few laps to "work the tire in." Depending on the track conditions and the set-up of the car, teams may scuff new tires during practice to prepare them for use in the race.

"Sticker" tires are new, unused tires which still have the Goodyear factory sticker on the tire.

After a practice session, rubber cakes up in the engine well and the underside of the hood. After a short track race there may be pounds of shredded rubber all over the car.

THE TEAM

The best way to ensure success in Winston Cup racing is to have a fast car, a good driver, and a well tuned team (this is much easier said than done). Saying that one of these is more important than the other is like asking which is more important: your brain, your heart, or your lungs. Even if

you have the best of one, you won't last long if you don't have the other two. The best driver in the world may take twenty laps to gain track position that can be lost because of one extra second during a pit stop.

NASCAR teams do much more than what is evident during pit stops. Taking 4 tires off, putting 4 tires on, filling the car with fuel, adjusting the chassis, cleaning the air intakes, cleaning the windshield, and giving the driver whatever he needs in around eighteen seconds is only part of the job. Long before the season starts teams are hard at work.

To put a Winston Cup team together, a team owner or manager must not only assemble an experienced, compatible racing team; he must also have a sound business plan. Getting started can be difficult for new teams. Obtaining full sponsorship can be somewhat like the chicken and the egg. To get a sponsor who will supply the money, a team must be competitive. But in order to be competitive a team must have money. It's common to see cars in the race with no sponsorship. This is a gamble an owner must take, betting that his car

will run well enough to catch the eye of a potential sponsor.

New chassis and engines must be built, rented or bought, and tested.

Because teams are limited in the amount of testing they can do at the track, the testing that is done must be fully utilized. Modern Winston Cup racing also demands many hours of testing bodies in the wind tunnel and engines on the dyno. Supplier relationships are also critical, not just because of the necessity for dependable racing parts. The knowledge of the supplier helps solve problems that arise as cars are made to go faster and faster, with engines

turning ever increasing RPM's.

Once an owner has assembled a sponsor, parts, and people, his job is far from over. The team must have a shop with all the tools that they need to work with. As the sponsor's role in Winston Cup racing has grown, so have the standards for all of the equipment used by the team. While a team is made up of professionals who understand

the dynamics of a racecar they have another responsibility as well. They also represent the company that sponsors the car. Everything from the shop to the car, car haulers to uniforms, must be clean and attractive.

When the season finally starts there is more to be done. Transportation must be arranged for team and equipment for all 31 races. Hotel reservations, parking permits, track credentials, air fare, coordination of the sponsor's activities

at the track, down to small details such as having the driver's and the teams' medical histories on hand in case of an accident -- all of these must be taken care of. The importance of these arrangements cannot be overstated. If a team has logistics problems, their minds may not be 100% on racing, and performance could suffer.

A racecar will not win on the ability of the driver alone. Many things must happen correctly to give the driver the chance to show his ability. The winner is not always the team with the smartest people or the most money. Winning often is the product of endless compromise between team members. Ideas are presented, discussed and then carried out. It is this ability to communicate and work together

that often results in a winning racecar.

The nature of racing places intense demands on the teams. In any given race only one out of forty-two teams will

win. The others may spend a great deal of time and money only to tear up a racecar, be it their fault or someone else's. With all of this pressure, combined with being on the road thirty-five or so weeks a year, the modern team must have stamina as well as skill.

THE TEAM MEMBERS

The task of fielding a winning racecar has become so complex that it takes many people to compete. This extends from the person selling sponsorships on the car to the driver on the track. Many things have to happen just to get the car to the track. While all teams are set up differently, the following pages show general team job descriptions and schedules.

Monday

Work begins as the rig is unloaded from the previous Sunday's race. Truck drivers usually head out from the track immediately after the race, sometimes driving all night in order to get the rig and equipment back to the shop as soon as possible. Once the rig is back at the shop, all of the race gear must be unloaded, cataloged, and, if necessary, cleaned, rebuilt, replaced, or repaired. The rig itself is cleaned and serviced, making it ready to head out for the next race.

Tuesday & Wednesday

Depending on the outcome of the previous race, the work load differs. If the car managed to make it through the race undamaged, it may only need cosmetic work to prepare it for the next time it is to be raced. Cars that have been damaged must be fixed. This can range from relatively minor sheet metal work to major surgery requiring large sections to be repaired or replaced. If a car is totaled, it must be replaced with a new car. Teams may have many racecars available at any one time, and it is not usually necessary to race the same car two weeks in a row. The team concentrates on preparing the car for the next race; but if a damaged car is to be raced in the future, time must be found for repairing it.

The primary and backup cars and engines for the next race must be prepared. All the systems in the cars must be set up, checked and rechecked. Qualifying, race and backup engines must be built and tested on the dyno.

Once all of these preparations are completed, the rig must be restocked and inventoried to ensure that the team will have everything they will need at the track.

Thursday

The rig and team must be ready to head out so that they can reach their destination at some time on Thursday. In recent years the three-day race weekend has become popular, giving the teams more time to prepare cars and also giving them more time at home, a critical factor with thirty-one races in the year. Six to eight people may be enough to get the car through qualifying and practice, but on race day twelve to twenty people will be necessary to take care of all the jobs. Most teams bring people to the race only as they are needed, with the full race team not being assembled until late Saturday or early Sunday.

Friday

Schedules of events may vary from track to track. The following is an example of the typical race weekend. Registration and inspection begin early Friday morning (about 6:00 o'clock). Crews arrive at the track, park the rigs and begin to unload cars and equipment. Each team is assigned a single stall work area in the track garage area. This stall, combined with the rig, will be the team's base of operations during the race weekend.

A drawing is held to establish qualifying order. Practice begins at about 11:00 A.M. and continues until 2:00 P.M. Time trials or qualifying begin at 3:00 P.M., and determine starting positions 1 - 20. Some practice is usually allowed after time trials, if time and weather permit.

Saturday

Registration and inspection begin early in the morning. Practice is allowed from 10:30 A.M. until 12:00 P.M. Second day qualifying, determining the remainder of the starting field, is completed. All of the Winston Cup action then shifts back to the garage area as the Saturday event takes place (usually a Busch Grand National or an ARCA race). During this time the teams prepare for the last practice session before the race.

A one-hour practice period known as the "happy hour" is allowed after the Saturday event. Happy hour is one of the most critical times for a team. The set-up the car ends happy hour with is usually the setup it will start the race with. If the teams don't get the lap speeds they need to be competitive during happy hour, or can't practice because of a mechanical failure, the car will enter the race with an untested set-up. This is never considered an advantage, but races have indeed been won with untested set-ups. After happy hour the cars do not go back on the track until the race.

Sunday

All of the car preparations have taken place in the garage area, and it is not until Sunday morning that the teams set up the pit areas. At this time teams make final preparations, checking and rechecking the car's systems. Every nut and bolt is checked for tightness; all linkages, belts, hoses and other components are inspected to ensure that a small, ordinary part doesn't take the car out of the race. The cars are then pushed out to the starting grid, and after the pre-race festivities, the race finally begins. After the race, all equipment must be loaded back on the truck and made ready for the trip back to the shop, where on Monday morning it will all begin again.

Team Manager

Most teams designate one person to be team manager. The manager's primary responsibilities involve the business and logistics of the team. Day-to-day administrative duties are included, such as overseeing the accounting functions, making sure bills are paid and the payroll is met. General managers usually oversee the personnel functions of a race team, including hiring, dismissal, and salary distribution.

The manager must also address the long range plans for the team and take part in the marketing decisions.

Crew Chief

All Winston Cup teams have a crew chief who is usually responsible for all things related to the technical aspects of the racecar and the crew. This includes car preparation at the shop and at the track. Simply put, the crew chief's job is to make sure everything gets done and gets done properly. In Winston Cup racing the buck stops with the crew chief.

The track changes during the race, and as the car accumulates miles, the handling characteristics of the car change. One of the crew chief's primary jobs during practice and during the race is to communicate with the driver and try to understand and interpret his comments and descriptions on how the car is handling. He must evaluate suggestions from the crew and driver and decide what changes and adjustments are needed to make the car faster. If the car is running good, he decides how to maintain the existing handling characteristics. This ability to diagnose and adjust is one of the main ingredients in creating a winning race team.

Chassis Specialist

The chassis specialist is responsible for all things related to the car in terms of body set-up and suspension set-up. Long before the season starts, the chassis specialist is hard at work preparing the stable of cars necessary to run a Winston Cup team. The frames and roll cages must be built or purchased. Then bodies must be put on the car. Teams may buy cars assembled; however many teams choose to make their own bodies. As the cars are assembled they must be tested not only on the track but also in the wind tunnel. Teams build different cars for different types of tracks (speedways, short tracks and road courses). Chassis specialists must be able to understand the variety of tracks, to build cars for every category, and to refine a particular car to a particular track.

Engine Specialist

The engine specialist is responsible for the preparation of the engines at the shop, during the race set-up, and during the race. He is also responsible for rebuilding the engines between races. A number of engines will be prepared at the shop before heading out to the track. These engines will have been run on the dyno to ensure that they are building enough power and that the power comes on in the right RPM range for the track on which they will race. When the teams swap engines at the track, the new engine is usually ready to be run immediately. This advanced engine preparation is what makes it possible for teams to blow an engine at the end of practice Saturday and still be able to race competitively on Sunday with an engine that has not yet been run on the track.

Engine builders must evaluate similar components and decide which is best to use. Many hours of testing and retesting are required to make a sound decision. Engine builders must constantly look for the small changes that can be made to gain a quarter of a horsepower here and half a horsepower there. Engine builders know enough of these small refinements which, when accumulated, give an advantage on the track.

Public Relations Manager

As Winston Cup racing has grown and sponsorships have come to play such an important roll, many teams now have a public relations manager. Like any other product, a race team must be properly marketed. The public relations manager coordinates the sponsor with the race team to make sure that the needs of both are met.

Show car schedules must be arranged, and when sponsors have special events at races, the public relations manager must ensure that the sponsors and their guests have the full "racing experience." These activities, however, must not be allowed to distract the crews. While supporting the sponsor-team relationship, the public relations manager must also coordinate all of the media-related activities, from setting up driver appearances to supplying reporters and newspapers with information. The public relations manager is constantly striving to put the team and their sponsor in the spotlight.

Spotter

The spotter is the driver's and crew's extra set of eyes. Constantly watching the track, the spotter alerts the driver to situations on the track ahead of the driver's vision. Spotters warn of accidents, slower traffic, and pursuing cars. Spotters may also note how a competitor's car is handling on the track and may offer suggestions on passing techniques based on these observations.

Jack Man

The jack man must have strength and dexterity, and he must also have a very keen eye. The jack man must be quick enough to run around the car and all the other team members to place the jack. The jack man must also watch both of the tire changers to ensure that the tires are properly changed before he drops the car. If he drops it too soon, the resulting delay would be substantial as the car must be rejacked before the problem can be corrected.

Tire Specialist

The tire specialist is responsible for the preparation of the tires. Many times the tire set-up is changed during pit stops. For this to take place, the tires must be carefully prepared and analyzed. Tire pressure, rubber condition and stagger are all involved in fine tuning the car's handling characteristics. The crew chief must be able to rely on the tire specialist to provide the tires specifically called for in the desired set-up.

Gas Man

As with the jack man, strength and dexterity are required here. The physical aspects of the job are demanding. The gas man must climb over the pit wall, carrying the full gas can. Eleven gallons at roughly six pounds each makes for a ungainly 70 pounds or so. A gas man must carry the can high so that the fill nozzle can be immediately connected when he reaches the car. This eliminates any extra time required to lift the can to the car.

Catch-Can Man.

As the fuel flows into the fuel cell during the fueling process, the air in the fuel cell escapes through a vent hose which exits at the left rear of the deck lid. As the tank becomes full, fuel will escape up through this vent tube. The catch-can man's job is to ensure that no gas escaping from this vent sprays fuel where it could ignite.

This job was added after fuel overflow caused a number of fires during pit stops. The catch-can man can also assist the gas man in supporting the fill tank.

THE
SHOP & EQUIPMENT

A team must have a shop equipped with all the tools needed to build, prepare and maintain the cars. Building today's racecars takes much more than just bolting the pieces together. Specialized equipment is required, on site, to attain the precise tolerances required for today's competitive racing.

In the main shop teams work on many cars at once. Cars under construction are placed on rolling stands so that they can be moved easily. Lifts are used for easy access when working under the car. The main shop must be large enough for the cars, tools, and parts, and still have enough room for people to work efficiently.

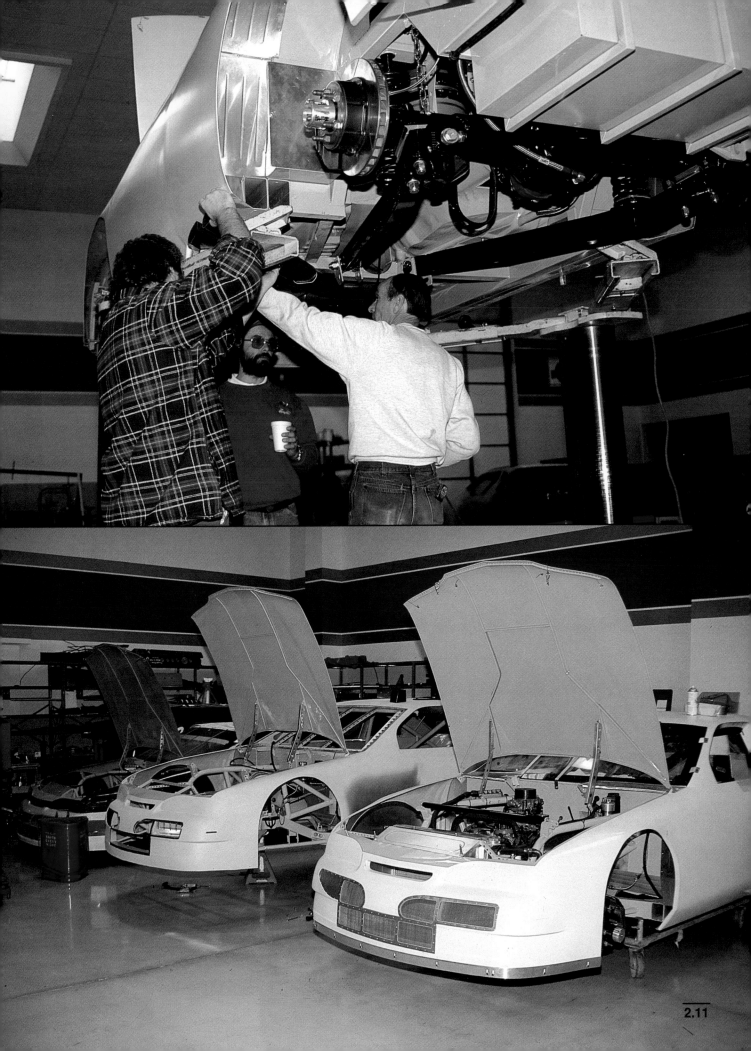

Parts, parts and more parts. Storage can become a problem with the incredible number of parts and tools a team must have. Mechanics use their own tools and boxes while special tools and equipment for the team to use are located throughout the shop. Special fixtures are used to store odd shaped components such as rear gears and axles.

A separate facility for building the car chassis and body. Welding and all other tools necessary for sheet metal work are provided. A large steel surface plate ensures a smooth and level base to build the cars on.

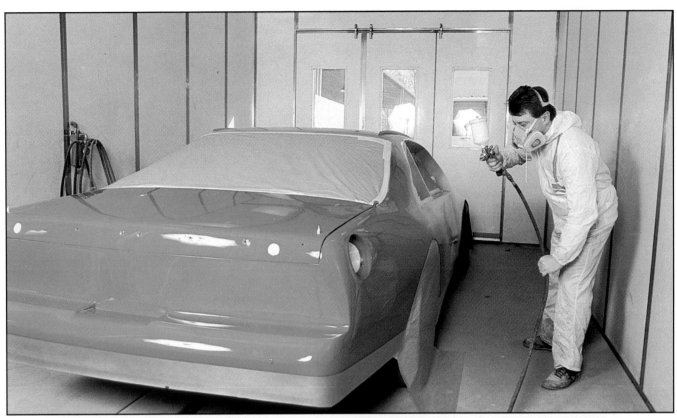

The paint booth. Cars must be painted not only when newly built or rebuilt after damage. Even if a car makes it through the race without contact with another car or the wall, many times it must be repainted due to the "sand blasting" effect of small debris hitting the car at high speed.

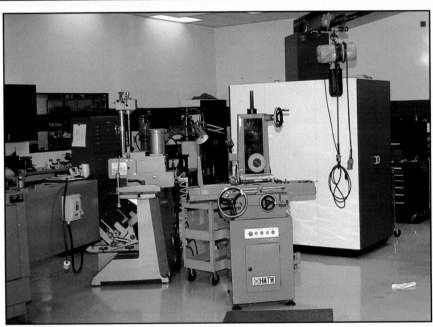

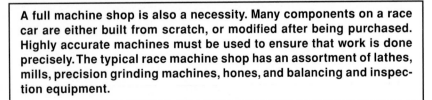

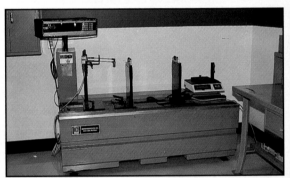

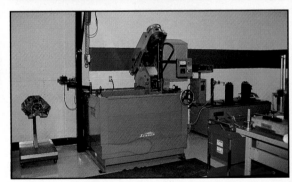

A full machine shop is also a necessity. Many components on a race car are either built from scratch, or modified after being purchased. Highly accurate machines must be used to ensure that work is done precisely. The typical race machine shop has an assortment of lathes, mills, precision grinding machines, hones, and balancing and inspection equipment.

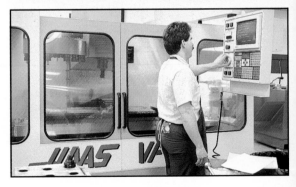

The engine assembly area is clean and organized, and kept as simple as possible. The machining work is completed in the machine shop before the components reach the engine room for assembly.

Before engines are ever put in a car they are tested on the "dyno." Through testing, teams learn how much power an engine will make and where in the powerband it will make it. The dyno facility has a control room and an engine room. The engine room has cooling systems, oil supply systems and fuel supply so that only the engine must be hooked up for testing.

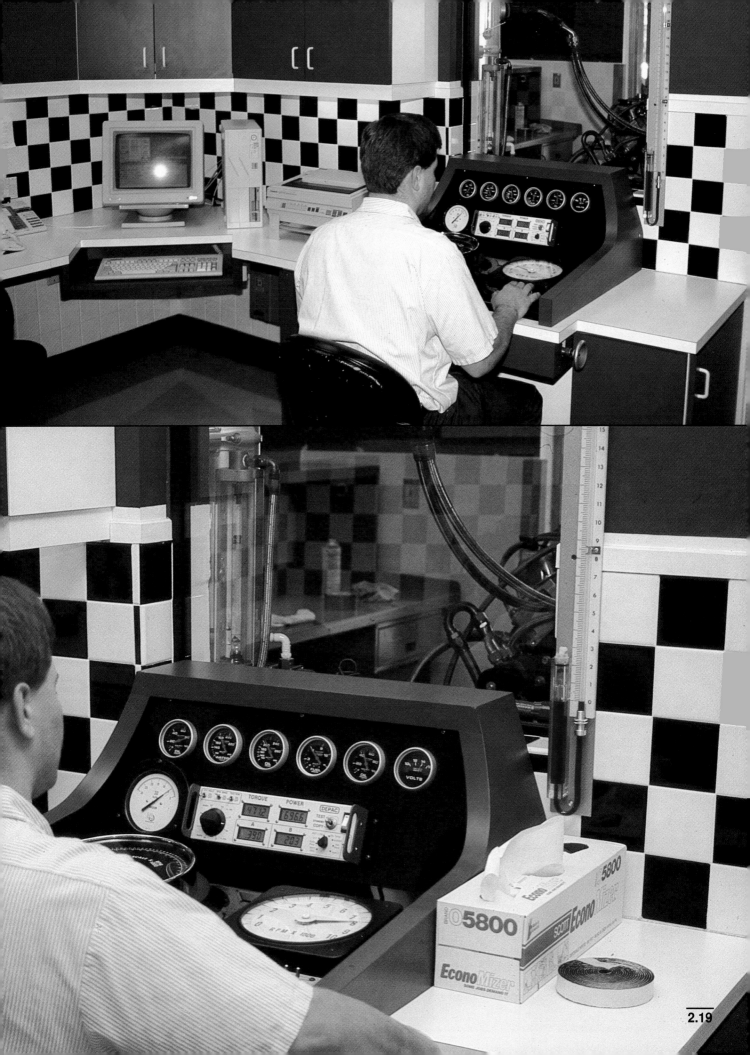

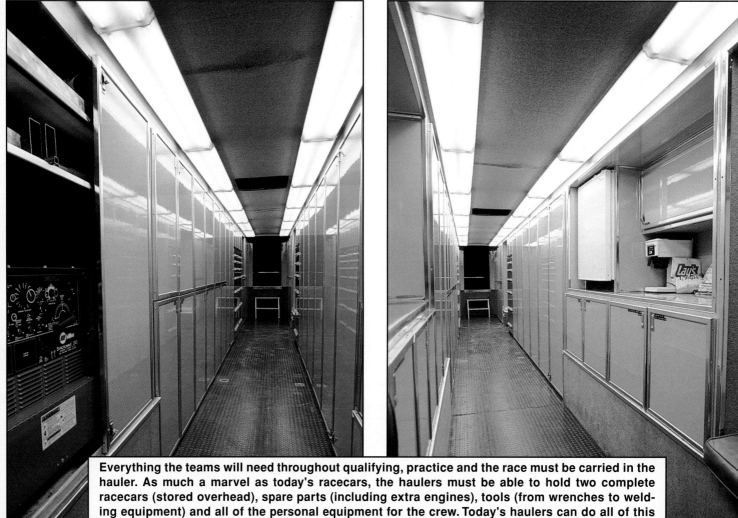

Everything the teams will need throughout qualifying, practice and the race must be carried in the hauler. As much a marvel as today's racecars, the haulers must be able to hold two complete racecars (stored overhead), spare parts (including extra engines), tools (from wrenches to welding equipment) and all of the personal equipment for the crew. Today's haulers can do all of this and still have enough room for a lounge in the front of the trailer.

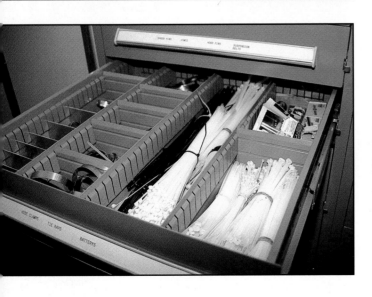

THE RACE

Much of the "race" is over by the time the team arrives at the track — the race to "dial in" the perfect set-up.

The set-up is a combination of engine power, handling ability, braking ability and aerodynamic qualities. Indeed, when cars and engines are built, the tracks on which they will run are the main influence on the design and building style. The goal of all of this preparation is to arrive at the track with the car ready to qualify and the race set-up already decided.

The engine set-up is worked out on the dyno before leaving the shop. Both the qualifying and race motors have been custom tuned for the track being raced. This ensures that the car will produce power when the driver needs it the most.

Engine power is an essential element in making a car go fast — but by far not the only element. In auto racing, three additional areas are important in producing a competitive car: good suspension set-up, good brakes and aerodynamic efficiency.

The tables below show typical set-up configurations used for of the four basic types of tracks.

Engine power increases the speed of the car only as long as the suspension can efficiently transfer that power. Additional power does not help if it cannot be controlled. *Smooth is fast, and an ill-handling car is not smooth.*

Many complex physical forces are at work on a moving racecar. Most of us have experienced some of these forces during our everyday driving, but not to the extremes encountered by the drivers on the tracks. A racecar's handling ability is ultimately determined by the team's ability to adjust the suspension to counter these forces, and by the driver's ability to find the best line around the track to push the car to its limit, but not over it.

The forces affecting the handling of a racecar vary with the position of the car in the track — whether the car is on a straightaway or on a turn. In a turn, centrifugal force will try to sling the car outward. Tracks are banked in varying degrees to counter this effect. As a rule, the higher the banking, the faster the cars can go. The thirty-eight degree banking at Bristol allows incredible speeds on one of the smallest tracks. The qualifying speeds at Bristol last year were only about 25 miles per hour slower than qualifying speeds at Indianapolis. The Indianapolis track is long — 2.5 miles — but it only has 4 degrees of banking in the turns while Bristol has 38 degrees. Centrifugal force is

---

SHORT TRACK SET-UP

SPRINGS

LF	RF
1100	1200

LR	RR
200	225

SHOCKS
RF: 380-180
LF: 325-125
RR: 275-110
LR: 275-110

SWAYBARS
FRONT: 1"
REAR: NONE

TIRE PRESSURE: LF: 18 LBS RF: 28 LBS
LR: 18 LBS RR: 28 LBS

SPOILER: 70 DEGREES

BODY ADJUSTMENTS: NO SPECIAL ADJUSTMENTS.

COOLING REQUIREMENTS: MAXIMUM COOLING FOR BRAKES AND REAR END.

INTERMEDIATE SET-UP

SPRINGS

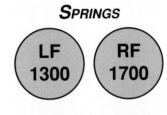

LF	RF
1300	1700

LR	RR
350	375

SHOCKS
RF: 480-180
LF: 420-180
RR: 325-125
LR: 325-125

SWAYBARS
FRONT: 1 1/16"
REAR: NONE

TIRE PRESSURE: LF: 30 LBS RF: 48 LBS
LR: 30 LBS RR: 43 LBS

SPOILER: 70 DEGREES

BODY ADJUSTMENTS: MORE ATTENTION PAID TO AERODYNAMIC FLOW.

COOLING REQUIREMENTS: MINIMUM COOLING FOR BRAKES. STANDARD REAR END COOLING.

more apparent to the race fan when the turns are not banked; but even with higher banking the force is still there and is simply being transferred elsewhere. Even though the turns are banked, teams must run stiffer springs on the right side to keep the car from *bottoming out*.

The suspension set-up for a road course car most closely resembles the suspension set-up on a production car. These are the only Winston Cup cars set up to turn right as well as left at speed, just as production cars are. However, all cars raced on a circle track, be it a half-mile short track or a two-and-a-half-mile superspeedway, are designed to turn well only to the left at speed. While turning, the right front tire carries the greatest amount of force. Next is the right rear, then the left front with the left rear carrying the least amount of weight. Teams must match the spring rates in all four corners of the suspension to compensate for these differences in pressure. Indeed, it would be impossible turn a Winston Cup car around and drive it clockwise around the track at anywhere close to the speeds reached going counterclockwise.

A suspension change is always a compromise. As with most things in life, when you get one thing you have to give up another. The better handling racecar is the one set up closest to the edge of the adjustment compromises.

On road courses and shorter tracks, having power and a good suspension won't help if the brakes won't slow the car when entering the turn. If a driver has brake problems, he must either slow down using the engine and transmission (which places additional strain on the transmission and the rear end) or he must reduce his speed in the straight so that he won't be carrying as much speed into the turn. Either way, brake problems can quickly turn an otherwise competitive car into an *also ran*.

Due to the variations in Winston Cup race tracks, the importance of each set-up adjustment varies from track to track. On the longer tracks aerodynamic efficiency becomes yet another area that must be considered. Some say it matters a great deal on shorter tracks also. Theoretically the only time aerodynamics don't matter is when the car is sitting still. Slight changes in the body work on the car can have dramatic effect on how efficiently the car cuts through the air.

A racecar's handling characteristics change during the race. The driver and the crew must work together during pit stops to make adjustments to the set-up that can change the handling of a car. The following pages will give an idea of the general handling problems that a team must overcome in order to be competitive during the race.

SUPERSPEEDWAY SET-UP

SPRINGS

LF 2000   RF 3200

LR 425   RR 475

SHOCKS
RF: 588-180
LF: 520-180
RR: 325-125
LR: 325-125

SWAYBARS
FRONT: 1 1/8"
REAR: NONE

TIRE PRESSURE: LF: 45 LBS   RF: 55 LBS
LR: 45 LBS   RR: 50 LBS

SPOILER: 40 DEGREES

BODY ADJUSTMENTS: *Hood and deck lid hinges are recessed. Fender edges are adjusted to provide good air flow around tire and wheel.*

COOLING REQUIREMENTS: *No cooling for brakes. Standard rear end cooling.*

ROAD COURSE SET-UP

SPRINGS

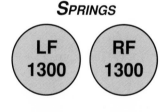

LF 1300   RF 1300

LR 250   RR 250

SHOCKS
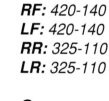
RF: 420-140
LF: 420-140
RR: 325-110
LR: 325-110

SWAYBARS
FRONT: 1 1/16"
REAR: 1/2"

TIRE PRESSURE: LF: 38 LBS   RF: 38 LBS
LR: 36 LBS   RR: 36 LBS

SPOILER: 70 DEGREES

BODY ADJUSTMENTS: *No special adjustments.*

COOLING REQUIREMENTS: *Maximum cooling for brakes, rear end, and transmission.*

OVERSTEER

Also known as being *loose*, oversteer is a condition during which the car turns or steers too much. The rear of the car wants to swing out to the right.

Most of us have experienced oversteer in our everyday driving. If while turning, you accelerated too much or hit a slick spot, the rear end of the car might have swung out, creating an oversteer situation. When this problem develops in a racecar, the driver must compensate, usually by slowing down, both entering and through the turns, to avoid oversteer and having the car spin out. The red car to the right illustrates a car oversteering, while the grey car illustrates a smooth, balanced turn.

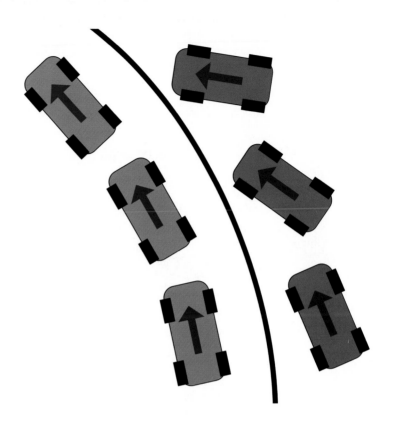

UNDERSTEER

Also known as *pushing*, or as the car *being tight*, understeer is the tendency for the car to go straight when the front wheels are being turned (to continue to "push" forward). If you have ever hit a patch of ice or wet leaves as you were turning and braking at the same time, you experienced a pushing condition. The car continues to go forward even though you are turning the wheel. When this develops in a racecar, the driver must slow down entering and going through the turns to avoid having the car push all the way into the wall. Obviously the ride to the next pit stop is a long one when the car is pushing. The yellow car to the right illustrates a *pushing* line through a turn (the grey car again showing the proper line).

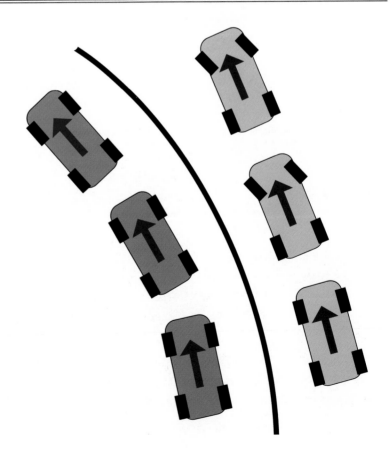

ALIGNMENT

Like a street car, a Winston Cup car has to be properly aligned to handle well. Street cars are aligned for proper "tracking" and for tire wear (50,000 miles or so). Racecars are aligned for proper tracking and maximum handling ability. All cars, street or race, have three basic alignment settings; toe, camber, and caster. Toe is the angle of the front of the tire and the rear of the tire relative to the centerline of the car. Camber is the angle of the top of the tire and the bottom of the tire relative to the vertical centerline of the tire. Caster is the angle between the ball joints and the vertical centerline of the tire.

The alignment is set before the teams leave for the track. At the track it may be refined to improve tire wear or handling. Problems can occur during the race if the car gets "knocked out of alignment." Contact with the wall or other cars, running over a piece of debris, or running off the track can all result in the alignment being knocked out of its proper setting.

Toe

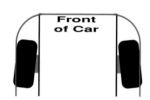

Toe-in condition: the front of the tire is pointed in while the back of the tire is pointed out.

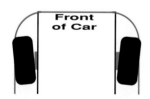

Toe-out condition: the front of the tire is pointed out while the back of the tire is pointed in.

Winston Cup cars run a slightly toed-in setting for good tracking.

Camber

Negative Camber: the tires are tilted with the top in and the bottom out.

Positive Camber: the tires are tilted with the top out and the bottom in.

Camber is set in a slightly negative position to improve handling.

Caster

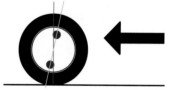

Negative Caster: the top of the ball joint is set behind the centerline.

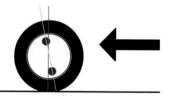

Positive Caster: the top of the ball joint is set in front of the centerline.

A slight positive caster setting allows for easier steering.

Aerodynamics

On longer intermediate tracks and superspeedways, the aerodynamic flow — the ability for the car to cut through the air — becomes critical. Teams go to great effort to maximize a car's aerodynamic efficiency, using wind tunnels for testing and learning which small changes to the body improve the speed of cars being run at longer tracks. For instance, the hinges for the hood and deck lid may extend outside the body work on short track and road course cars, but they would probably be recessed on superspeedway cars. The total resistance given by these hinges is roughly equivalent to that of a sewing thimble glued to the hood of the car. But every little bit counts. If a car has body damage, its ability to cut through the air will be lessened, especially if the front facia is damaged. Even minor dents can slow the car down on superspeedways. On short tracks aerodynamic flow is not as important and many battered racecars have made their way to victory lane, a few with no front body at all.

Brake Fade

Brake fade is mostly a concern on short tracks and road courses. On many of the longer courses the only time the brakes are used is when the car makes a pit stop. On road courses and short tracks, however, the driver may be *on the brakes* as much as the accelerator. When used this much, the brake rotors and pads become so hot that they transfer enough heat to the caliper to boil the brake fluid in the caliper. Boiling occurs when the rotor temperature gets above 1075 degrees F. When the fluid boils, air is released into the system causing the pedal to go to the floor when pressed. On tracks that place such a demand on brakes, the teams run extra cooling ducts to the brakes, cooling them as much as possible. When the brakes become too hot, the only way to fix the problem is to let the brakes cool by not using them as much, which inevitably means slowing down.

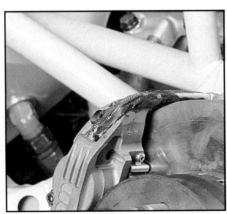

Brake lines are insulated where they come into contact with the caliper.

Tubing carries air from inlets at the front of the car to the brakes.

Wedge

Wedge is a name used to describe adjustments made to the coil springs to fine tune the suspension set-up. Wedge adjustments can be made on each corner of the suspension; however, only wedge adjustments to the rear can be made without opening the hood.

The rear spring is mounted under the frame and the rear trailing arm. This upward pressure that the spring exerts on the frame is critical to a car's handling ability. Wedge adjustments are made by turning a bolt that runs through the frame rail and is attached to a fixture holding the top of the coil spring. By tightening the bolt, the spring is squeezed tighter increasing the spring pressure or *spring rate*.

When wedge adjustments are necessary during pit stops, they are usually made on the rear springs. Tightening the left rear spring increases the spring rate and puts more pressure on the right front of the car. Likewise, lessening the spring rate on the left rear will take pressure off of the right front tire.

This sounds more complicated than it is. If you take a small spring and squeeze it between your thumb and forefinger, the further you squeeze the harder it becomes to continue to squeeze. That is, it takes much less strength to squeeze the first quarter-inch than the last quarter-inch. Wedge adjustments do the same thing to the car's coil springs. Now take a hardback book and balance it on a coffee cup so that the book is parallel to the table. If you barely lift on one corner, say the bottom left, then the top right corner will go down. Increasing the spring rate on the left rear of a racecar will put more upward pressure on the left rear of the frame and, just like with the book, a downward pressure will be exerted on the right front.

A general rule of thumb is:

> ***Pressure taken off the front corrects
> a loose condition.***

> ***Pressure taken off the rear corrects
> a tight condition.***

If too much of an adjustment is made to correct understeer, then an oversteer problem may be created. Added to this is the different result attained by adjusting the left side spring as opposed to the right side spring. Crews must use great care in making even the smallest of wedge adjustments.

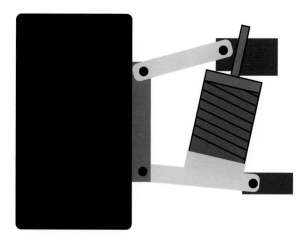

A typical coil spring suspension with jack bolts for wedge adjustments. The spring (purple) rides between the upper spring mount (orange) and the lower control arm on the bottom (yellow). The upper spring mount (orange) holds the top of the spring and is attached to the frame on top (blue) by the large jack bolt (black) which passes through a threaded fixture which is welded to the frame. When the jack bolt is tightened the upper spring mount moves down, away from the frame increasing the pressure on the spring and thus increasing the spring rate.

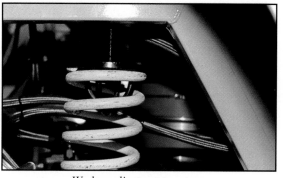

Wedge adjustment system.

Spoiler

The rear spoiler dramatically influences how the racecar handles. As air passes over the decklid on the car it hits the spoiler. The higher the angle, the more resistance the air meets and the more down force is created. A simple example of this principle can be experienced by holding your hand (flat, palm-down) out of a car window at speed. By rotating your hand down at varying degrees, the air resistance change can be felt. The more you tilt, the more the wind pushes your hand down. The same principle holds true for the spoiler. There is a fine line between speed and control on longer tracks. The lower the angle of the spoiler, the less resistance, allowing the car to go faster in the straightaways. On the other hand, the car will not have as much down force on the rear and is much more likely to be *loose*, and difficult to control in the turns. Too much spoiler and the car will have plenty of down force for the turns but will suffer on the straights.

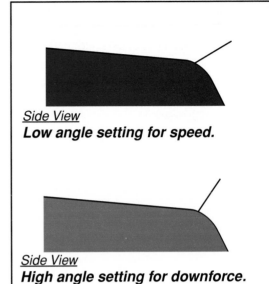

Side View
Low angle setting for speed.

Side View
High angle setting for downforce.

Grill Taping

A certain amount of air must pass through the front grill to cool the engine. This open grill area creates drag. The bigger the opening, the greater the drag and the lower the speed. Likewise, the smaller the opening the less the drag and the greater the speed. Teams may adjust the size of the openings by taping over some of the grill opening with duct tape, thus reducing the size of the opening. Taping over the grill can be used as an adjustment only when it will not critically affect engine cooling. It is often used in qualifying and toward the end of the race if circumstances permit pit stops.

Body Adjustments

Winston Cup cars have support rods that keep the fenders rigid. These rods have adjustable sleeves that can be lengthened or shortened. This is another aerodynamic adjustment that can affect speed and handling by changing the position of the edge of the fender in relation to the edge of the tire. A change in air flow around the fender wells and tires can have a substantial influence on speed at superspeedways. This adjustment is usually refined during wind tunnel testing and practice, and is seldom, if ever, changed during the race.

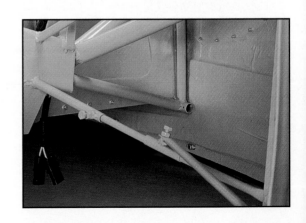

HANDLING ADJUSTMENTS

Stagger

Stagger is an adjustment made by using different sized tires on the car at the same time. Teams put tires on the outside of the car that have a slightly larger diameter than the tires on the inside of the car. This allows the car to turn more efficiently on circular tracks when the car makes only left turns. This principle can be seen by placing a light bulb next to a rolling pin on a flat surface and rolling both of them. The rolling pin rolls straight while the light bulb turns in a circle because of the difference in stagger between the inside and outside diameters.

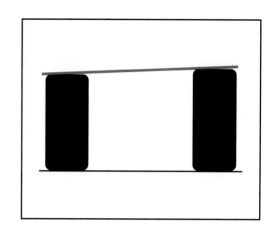

Tire Pressure

Adjusting tire pressure is a good example of how the smallest of changes can make a dramatic change in a car's handling. In a street car a couple of pounds of variation in tire pressure will not affect performance and will not be noticeable to the driver. However, in a racecar the handling characteristics of a car can be drastically changed by varying the tire pressure among the four tires. A few pounds more or less in a particular tire can fine tune the handling of a racecar. The more pressure in a tire, the stiffer the sidewall of a tire becomes. As with springs and shocks, this sidewall stiffness can be controlled and used to fine tune the set-up.

Changes in the temperature of the tire affect tire pressure. For every ten degrees of increased tire temperature the air pressure in the tire will increase one pound. This means that after a run, if a tire is seventy degrees hotter than when the run started, there will be seven more pounds of air pressure in the tire. Tire temperatures are monitored closely by the crews. Temperatures vary from track to track. Longer tracks with extended straightaways and gradual turns do not heat up tires nearly as much as the flatter short tracks where the car is turning more, and the scrubbing action between the tire and the track is more severe. When setting up the suspension, crews try to achieve diagonal balance between the tires. Diagonal balance is the relationship between the left rear and the right front, and the right rear and the left front. At the end of a run if the right front tire temperature is 200 degrees and the left rear is 190 degrees the car is said to have 10 degrees of push. Likewise is the right front is 190 and the left rear 200 the car is 10 degrees loose. The optimal set-up balances the tire temperature between these diagonal corners.

Overheating

A number of things can cause a racecar to overheat —
internal engine problems, for instance, or a small leak in a
head gasket or a cooling system problem such as a partial
or complete blocking of the front grill. Small pieces of
rubber, shredded from the soft race tires, often clog the
grill. If they get past the grill, they can clog the radiator,
reducing its ability to cool the engine. If a car encounters
debris, it can remain pressed against the grill and cut off
the air flow to the radiator and oil cooler.

If the overheating involves an internal engine problem,
chances are the team cannot correct it on the spot. All that
can be done is to make sure that as much coolant as
possible is kept in the cooling system. If the overheating is
caused by grill obstructions, the crew can try to clean out
the grill during pit stops. However, if the grill or radiator
has become clogged with tire rubber, the degree to which it
can be cleaned is limited.

Losing a Cylinder

When a car is said to have "lost a cylinder," the engine has
experienced some type of internal failure, causing it to quit
making power in one of its eight cylinders. While such a
failure may not be bad enough to completely stop an
engine, it is a most serious problem. Obviously the engine
has lost at least one-eighth of its ability to build power, and
it is running out of balance, far out of its design range.
These problems, as well as the possibility of a broken
component interfering with another component, can cause

further engine damage, often resulting in a lost cylinder
advancing to total engine failure.

A lost cylinder is usually the result of a valve train
problem. Either a rocker arm, valve spring or valve has
broken or otherwise stopped functioning. When a car has
lost a cylinder, there is very little a team may do to correct
the problem. The driver usually keeps the car on the track,
nursing it around and accumulating as many laps as
possible for championship points.

Ignition Failure

The electronic ignition system used in Winston cup racing
provides and controls the spark which fires the engine. If
this system fails, the engine will run poorly or quit alto-
gether. Winston Cup cars carry two ignition modules, both

mounted inside the car, next to the driver. If one fails, the
driver can switch to the backup. If the second unit fails, the
team must take a lengthy pit stop to install a new unit.

Burning a Piston

Pre-detonation is the most common cause of piston failure.
The typical modern production engine has a compression
ratio of 8.5 to 1. This ratio is calculated by dividing the
volume of the cylinder at the bottom of the stroke (the top
of the piston at the bottom of the cylinder) by the volume
of the cylinder at the top of the stroke (the top of the piston
at the top of the cylinder).

Winston Cup cars run compression ratios of around 15
to 1. In a properly functioning engine the mixture of air
and fuel in the cylinder is ignited or detonated (near the
top of the stroke) by the spark plug. Pre-detonation takes

place when the fuel/air mixture is ignited too soon by the
pressure of compression, before the piston is at the point of
the stroke where ignition of the fuel/air mixture should
take place. The piston then continues upward, further
compressing the exploding fuel air/mixture and causing
further detonations. Then the spark plug fires, re-detonat-
ing the whole mess. This series of detonations builds up
more heat than a proper, one-time firing at the top of the
stroke. As this heat builds, it can burn a hole all the way
through the top of the piston causing total engine failure.

ENGINE PROBLEMS

Catastrophic Engine Failures

With Winston Cup engines turning plus or minus 9000 RPM for 500 miles, it is surprising that more engines don't experience catastrophic failure.

Many things can go wrong with an engine causing it to quit or *blow*, but in reality, few in Winston Cup racing do. A list of all of the causes of engine failure would be quite a publication in itself. Most engine failures can be classified into of four types: ***random failure***, ***design growth failure***, ***support system failure***, or ***driver error***.

Random engine failure is caused by either a bad part, a part that was not properly installed, or a combination of the two. Improper heat treating, internal, non-visible manufacturing flaws, or parts that have been overstressed, can fail in an instant with no warning. If, during installation, a part is damaged, contaminated, or bolted or torqued too tight (or not tight enough), failure can be imminent.

Periodic design growth failures can affect more than one team during a season. As engine speeds increase, there is a period of time during which more stress is put on a particular component. Teams must then work with suppliers to redesign the part to withstand the new pressures being applied. For instance, for a while there were a number of engine failures due to the failure of valve springs. Engine speeds were too fast for the valve springs to consistently open and close without severely stressing their limits. Suppliers had to find new designs which could consistently withstand the new stresses. The problem was eventually solved, but in the process the engine was able to turn faster and inevitably the next weakest link in the engine will surface. Perhaps in this case it will be the pushrods. When the next problem surfaces, the whole process will begin again. The solution to one problem moves the teams closer to the next series of periodic design growth failures.

Support system failure is an engine failure as a result of a support system loss of efficiency or failure. For example, if the radiator becomes clogged, spectators may not notice it, but they will notice when the loss of cooling efficiency causes a cylinder head to crack. The failure was not caused by the cylinder head itself, or the man who installed it. It failed because it was put in a position of performing beyond its design criteria.

Drivers can also "blow" an engine. A missed shift can over-rev an engine, causing failure. Or, if a driver pulls in behind another car at 190 miles per hour, the reduced air resistance encountered in drafting can cause a slight increase in the RPM of the engine. If the motor is already red-lined, this may be all it takes to blow the motor.

BODY DAMAGE

Body damage impacts the performance of the car differently depending on where the damage occurs and on what type of track the race is being run. Slight dents along the side of the car will not have much of an impact on short tracks and road courses, but may ruin a car's competitiveness on longer tracks.

Some places on the car are more vulnerable than others. Damage to the left front of the car can be fatal, whereas the same damage could be done to the right front and the car could continue racing. The oil cooler is mounted just behind the sheet metal in the left front corner. If the cooler is damaged the engine will not last. If the cooler is punctured or supply lines are ripped loose, a nice patch of oil will drop on the track for all of the drivers to enjoy. Likewise, damage to the left rear can damage the fuel inlet, hindering refueling during pit stops. If the car is hit broadside against a wheel, the car may be knocked out of alignment.

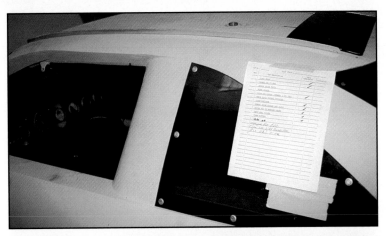

Preparing for a race begins long before arriving at the track. From practice sessions to dyno testing in the shop teams test and retest set-ups. All of the information gained during these tests will be used to decide on the way the car will be set-up when the team arrives at the track. The more preparation for the race that can be done before leaving for the track, the better. Most teams have delegated to different crew members the various jobs necessary to get the car ready. Each is responsible for a specific area, be it chassis, engines, wheels and tires, or loading the truck with the right equipment and parts for the race. Because of the large number of parts and equipment, teams use check lists to make sure that all of the jobs get done.

Engines are built and tested on the dyno, with the aim of preparing them so completely that they may be dropped into the car and run with little or tuning.

The chassis set-up is prepared with the springs, shocks, sway bars and other adjustments preset as much as possible. These settings are based on previous race or practice experience. Teams want to do only the finer tuning of the suspension during qualifying and practice.

Once the team and rig arrive, the temporary garage must be set up, the car unloaded, and everything made ready for qualifying and race practice. Then garage area becomes a bee hive of activity until the race begins.

Possibly the most important factor in a team's success is the ability of a driver and the crew to discuss the car's performance. A winning driver must have a competitive car; and the set-up is the greatest determining factor in having a competitive car. Good communication is very important in refining the set-up. The driver must be able to tell the crew exactly what the car is doing; then the crew and driver must evaluate the situation and decide on correcting adjustments. If the driver and the crew cannot communicate accurately when dialing in the car, hitting a good set-up will be difficult.

INSPECTION

All competing cars are inspected before each race; and may be inspected at any time during and after the race. Due to the fact that all racecars will be somewhat different, inspection procedures take place not only to catch premeditated cheating but also to ensure maximum competitiveness. Racecars are built by different people, in different places, at different times, with parts from different suppliers, all using the same rules.

These rules can be interpreted in a variety of ways. Indeed, just as teams must constantly look for an edge in their engine and chassis, they must constantly look for edges in the rule book, finding different ways to go faster while staying within NASCAR's rule specifications. In building the cars, teams interpret the rules in search of slight advantages that might provide the edge on the track. With the number of cars competing and the number of parts on a Winston Cup car, inspecting for violations is a difficult job for the officials.

It is impossible for the rule makers to think of everything, but the teams usually will. Inspection procedures ensure that the "spirit" of the rules is observed, again keeping the playing field as level as possible.

At the track the inspection area is used by all the teams before and during practice runs to ensure that changes made in the set-up don't take the car out of tolerance. These "self-inspections" ensure that the set-up being tested is legal and prevents any embarrassing moments during formal inspections. Cars may be sealed or impounded, and fines levied if rule violations are found.

The ever present template is mated to the car. The full length gauge insures proper body profile, critical when considering aerodynamics. Inset: Official templates for all models being run are available.

Officials calibrate the scales prior to inspection. Electric scales measure the entire car weight, and also the weight on each tire or "corner."

A car is rolled onto the scale for weighing.

Car height is measured using a "go/no-go" gauge. The red and green sections on the probe indicate whether the car is within specification.

If only green shows the car is legal. If red is visible the height is too low and the car will not pass inspection.

The height of the air dam is checked using a " block" gauge. The gauge must fit under the air dam.

The location of the air dam, relative to the bumper, is checked.

IN THE GARAGE

Throughout the pre-race activities the garage area is the center of action. Between practice runs on the track the car is adjusted and readjusted in the garage area. Although the cars are packed in (each team has one stall) the work done is pretty much limitless. Be it major body work or swapping motors or rear ends, the professionalism of the crew shows here, perhaps, more than anywhere else. Changing major components in just a few minutes is routine. With limited time for both qualifying practice and race practice, the less time spent in the garage means the more time spent on the track, and the better chance of dialing in the winning set-up.

QUALIFYING PRACTICE

The first order of business Friday is getting the car ready for qualifying. Most teams arrive at the track with a dedicated qualifying engine. Qualifying engines are set up a little more on the edge than the race engines. After all, they only have to last a few laps whereas the race engine must last 500 miles. The car arrives at the track with the qualifying engine in it and ready to go. During morning practice, teams try to "dial in" the suspension set-up.

The first set-up tried will most likely be based on previous experience at the track being raced. All previous set-ups are recorded and evaluated. Teams may start with the same set-up they ran well with at a previous race under basically the same track and weather conditions. As qualifying practice starts, lap times are tracked and the driver's observations about how the car is behaving are discussed. Qualifying practice usually consists of two lap runs, and then back to the garage for adjustments. Teams may change tire combination, tire pressure, spring rates, shock settings, wedge adjustments, sway bar combinations, spoiler angles and even rear-end gear ratios.

At superspeedways small body details such as the relationship of the fender to the edge of the tire, and air flow around the grill are refined; crews are always looking for slight aerodynamic improvements that could well mean a thousandth of a second during qualifying.

In past years many "qualifying only" parts were put on the cars. For instance, until recently a different dedicated qualifying radiator was used. Now the rules require that a car must race with the radiator that it qualified with, eliminating "qualifying radiators" which could not properly cool the engine for 500 miles.

Once the team feels that the car is running competitively enough to qualify, practicing stops and the wait for qualifying begins.

"Time-wise" most of the practice is spent in the garage area.

QUALIFYING

The number of cars in the race field varies from track to track. Longer tracks usually have a field of around 42 racecars. On short tracks the field size is usually around 32. Qualifying order is determined by a draw before qualifying begins.

Cars qualify one at a time. Normally, qualifying consists of a two-lap run, with the fastest of the two laps being the qualifying time. All qualifying runs start from a standstill, from the same point on pit road. The first lap time starts when the car has circled the track and crossed the start/finish line, already up to speed. If a car experiences a problem on the second qualifying lap, the first lap time may still be used. Usually only the first 20 positions are decided on the first day of qualifying. Positions 21 - 42 are decided on the second day of qualifying. Racecars that did not qualify for positions 1 - 20 may qualify again. The fastest time of the second session receives the twenty-first starting position, etc.

If a car does not qualify for the race in either session, it may still be able to race. "Provisional" starting positions are available, but are always at the end of the field. The recipients of these positions are decided by the points accumulated by the car owner. The longer an owner has raced a car, the more points he will have accumulated and the better his chance will be of obtaining a provisional starting position. The only other provisional qualifying positions are for past champions. Drivers who have won the Winston Cup Championship have a lifetime ticket for provisional starting positions.

Daytona - Initial qualifying is just as described above; however, only the front row (starting positions 1 & 2) is decided. The rest of the qualifying speeds are used to determine the starting order of two 125-mile qualifying races. The finishing orders of the 125-mile races determine positions 3-38. The remaining fastest qualifiers from initial qualifying and provisional starters complete the field.

SWAPPING MOTORS

Once qualifying is completed, teams shift gears and begin to set up the car for the race. The qualifying engine is taken out of the car and replaced with the race engine. Teams work quickly and usually have the car ready within an hour. Should the team run into problems with the race engine that can't be fixed, they can reinstall the qualifying engine and race with it or throw in another engine if they have one. Even if they don't, one can usually be rented, bought, or borrowed from another team.

RACE PRACTICE

After the motor is swapped teams change from the qualifying set-up to the race set-up. The race suspension must be fast and must also be comfortable for the driver for 500 miles. While qualifying practice runs are one or two laps long, the race practice runs are longer. A qualifying set-up must be fast as possible as quickly as possible; since a qualifying run is only two laps long, a set-up that is fast after eight laps does not help. However, a race set-up must be fast over long runs. A set-up that is fast for two laps and then fades may qualify well, but does not do much for you in the race. Over long runs during the race, the car changes. Tires progressively lose their grip the longer they are run. As the fuel is used, each gallon burned means around 6 pounds of weight out of the fuel cell. Twenty

gallons means around 120 pounds, which can make quite a difference in the handling.

Once all of these set-up changes have been made, the cars go back out and practice, recording lap speeds and adjusting the engine and suspension.

The most critical practice session comes after the Saturday main event. For one hour, Winston Cup cars are allowed to practice, doing their final tuning and set-up preparation. Known as *Happy Hour,* this is the last time cars are allowed to practice before the Sunday race. Any car that is wrecked beyond repair during practice may be replaced with a backup car, but the car forfeits its starting position and must start the race at the rear of the field.

Above: During practice sessions the road from the garage to the track is a busy one. Insets: Crews watch from the viewing platforms on the rigs and record lap times.

SETTING UP THE PIT

Sunday morning, teams begin to set up the pit stall. First the cart is pushed to the pit stall. The cart contains tools, parts, and the air tanks that provide the air for the air wrenches used while pitting. In recent years carts have come to have a video set-up to tape pit stops (the camera is extended over the pit area on a lightweight boom), and even small satellite dishes, enabling teams to monitor the television broadcast of the race.

A great deal of equipment must be crammed into the limited space available in each pit stall.

FUEL

Fuel for practice, qualifying, and the race is supplied by Unocal. The fuel used is a high octane racing gasoline rated at 104 octane. This allows teams to run the high compression engines seen in today's Winston Cup cars. Unocal operates a pump station throughout the race weekend. During practice the cars are pushed to the pump, and the gas is pumped directly into the car. Throughout the race, the fuel cans used to fill the car during pit stops are filled at the pump station and pulled to the pit, by the crews, on small carts.

Fuel cans are filled at the Unocal fuel facility.

During practice and qualifying, gas is pumped into the car.

Safety is the first priority at the fuel station.

TIRES

Teams buy race tires at the track from Goodyear, which sets up shop in the garage, mounting and balancing tires for the teams. The rubber compound used in the tires varies from track to track depending on the demands a particular track places on tires. Throughout the event a close eye is kept on tire pressures and tire wear. Because tire temperature has such an effect on tire pressure and tire wear, tire temperatures are measured after each run. Temperatures are taken from different spots on the tire to check the relationship of the inside and outside of the tires.

A huge tire inventory is necessary for a race weekend.

Goodyear employees mount and balance tires.

Tire temperatures are taken immediately after practice runs.

The temperatures are given to the driver for the crew to evaluate.

Wheels are cleaned and the lug nuts glued on.

Special weights hold the lug nuts in place until the glue dries.

Sunday morning finds many of the teams still at work. It is not uncommon to find many of the cars in varying states of repair. As the teams finish this preparation, the cars are pushed to their position on the starting grid. The cars, or at least the windshields, are covered to keep the interior cool.

A cart with a generator accompanies each car. The generator provides power for heaters which are used to keep the oil temperature up. Once the cars are on the starting grid, they will not be cranked until the race begins.

Over the last few years, pits stops and pit strategy have probably been as responsible for victories as any other factor. Three things can happen during a pit stop. A car can gain position, lose position, or stay in the same position.

Drivers who win races seem to be the ones who do a lot of "passing in the pits." Beating competitors in the pits means less work on the track. It may take twenty laps on the track to pass another car. A crew can pass that same car in the pits while the driver drinks a glass of water. If two cars are equally matched, they may be able to stay with each other on the track but not be able to pass each other. The pits may be the only place where one can gain an advantage on the other. This is why winning drivers typically compliment their crew when climbing out of the car in victory lane.

An extra second with the car on the jack can mean two or three cars to pass on the track. Even if these cars can be overtaken easily, the driver will use up a little more of his tires each time he passes one of them. This means his car will fade quicker than other cars that don't have to pass as much.

Performing the required work quickly and correctly is only part of the pit stop. Perhaps just as important as the work, if not more so, is the pit stop strategy.

First, the crew chief must communicate with the driver via radio and develop an understanding of how the car is handling. By using only the driver's descriptions, the spotter's observations and the lap speeds, the crew chief makes a decision as to how the set-up will be adjusted. Once the decision is made as to "what" will be adjusted, the crews must decide "how much." If a "loose" car is over adjusted, it may become tight, slowing the car even more. On a race afternoon, a crew chief's chain of thought may be something like this:

"The car's a little loose with new tires but after about twenty laps, as the fuel load lightens, it tightens up the car and lap times pick up. But it's killing the team on restarts because the car falls back and has to repass the same cars that passed us during those first twenty laps. Is it better to do nothing, and keep relatively the same track position, or make an adjustment to quicken the car on those first twenty laps and risk ruining the good handling characteristics we'll experience later in the run?"

This simple scenario is one of a myriad of situations that a crew chief may encounter during the race. Often the crew chief's problems are more complicated than this. Not only must he work to make his car faster around the racetrack, he must also watch the tactical actions of the competition, and be prepared to develop an entirely new plan at a moment's notice in case of a change in the situation. With so many problems to evaluate, sometimes the crew chief's best tool is his ability to listen to and evaluate suggestions from the driver and the other crew members.

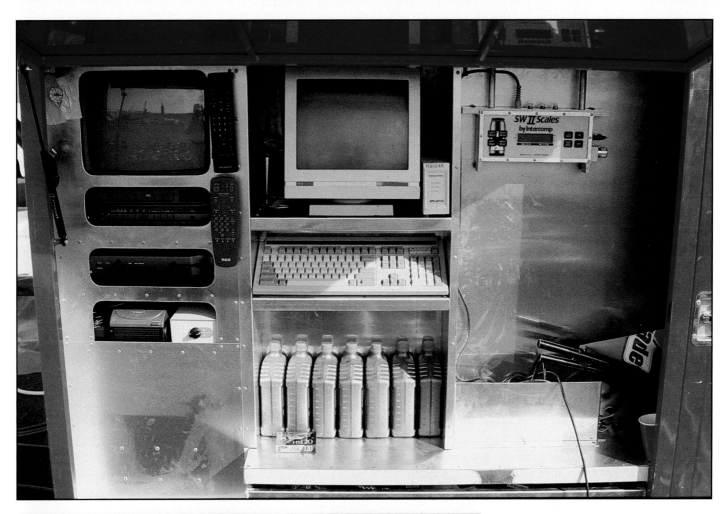

Pit equipment has become as sophisticated as the cars. From lightweight jacks to pit carts with satellite dishes, the variety of tools used in the pits continues to grow. The equipment used in making pit stops can be as important as equipment on the car. More than one race has been lost when a jack or air wrench malfunctioned.

The crew chief keeps an eye on the action from his seat atop the tool cart.

Primary and backup jacks are made ready. A plethora of special tools are laid out for easy access.

Air guns are made ready with air hoses coiled to prevent tangles.

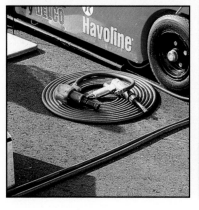

Left: Air chisels are close by in case of an accident which requires sheet metal to be cut away.
Right: A good supply of "quick dry" is kept handy.

PIT STOP CHOREOGRAPHY

In recent years, with the introduction of speed limits on pit road, the distance lost on the track while pitting is much greater. Teams must carefully choose when to pit in order to minimize the track position lost. Caution flags provide the best time for pitting; however inevitably teams will be forced to pit during *green flag racing*, or while the racing remains at full speed. For every second a cars sits in the pits, it loses distance on the track relative to the race speed.

The chart on the right shows the distance lost in relation to the time in the pits and the speeds on the track.

During pit stops only seven men are allowed over the wall. A crew member may not come back over the wall during a stop and be replaced with another. If the driver breaks the speed limit, runs over an air hose or in some other way pits incorrectly, he will be given a stop and go penalty; being forced to come back into the pits to have the penalty accessed. With the slow pit road speed limits, a stop and go penalty will almost always result in a lost lap.

The following diagrams show pit stops broken down with each crew member's movements and responsibilities.

					SPEED						
	100	**110**	**120**	**130**	**140**	**150**	**160**	**170**	**180**	**190**	**200**
1	147	161	176	191	205	220	235	249	264	279	293
2	293	323	352	381	411	440	469	499	528	557	587
3	440	484	528	572	616	660	704	748	792	836	880
4	587	645	704	763	821	880	939	997	1056	1115	1173
5	733	807	880	953	1027	1100	1173	1247	1320	1393	1467
6	880	968	1056	1144	1232	1320	1408	1496	1584	1672	1760
7	1027	1129	1232	1335	1437	1540	1643	1745	1848	1951	2053
8	1173	1291	1408	1525	1643	1760	1877	1995	2112	2229	2347
9	1320	1452	1584	1716	1848	1980	2112	2244	2376	2508	2640
10	1467	1613	1760	1907	2053	2200	2347	2493	2640	2787	2933
11	1613	1775	1936	2097	2259	2420	2581	2743	2904	3065	3227
12	1760	1936	2112	2288	2464	2640	2816	2992	3168	3344	3520
13	1907	2097	2288	2479	2669	2860	3051	3241	3432	3623	3813
14	2053	2259	2464	2669	2875	3080	3285	3491	3696	3901	4107
15	2200	2420	2640	2860	3080	3300	3520	3740	3960	4180	4400
16	2347	2581	2816	3051	3285	3520	3755	3989	4224	4459	4693
17	2493	2743	2992	3241	3491	3740	3989	4239	4488	4737	4987
18	2640	2904	3168	3432	3696	3960	4224	4488	4752	5016	5280
19	2787	3065	3344	3623	3901	4180	4459	4737	5016	5295	5573
20	2933	3227	3520	3813	4107	4400	4693	4987	5280	5573	5867
21	3080	3388	3696	4004	4312	4620	4928	5236	5544	5852	6160
22	3227	3549	3872	4195	4517	4840	5163	5485	5808	6131	6453
23	3373	3711	4048	4385	4723	5060	5397	5735	6072	6409	6747
24	3520	3872	4224	4576	4928	5280	5632	5984	6336	6688	7040
25	3667	4033	4400	4767	5133	5500	5867	6233	6600	6967	7333
30	4400	4840	5280	5720	6160	6600	7040	7480	7920	8360	8800
40	5867	6453	7040	7627	8213	8800	9387	9973	10560	11147	11733
50	7333	8067	8800	9533	10267	11000	11733	12467	13200	13933	14667
60	8800	9680	10560	11440	12320	13200	14080	14960	15840	16720	17600

SECONDS (left axis) — DISTANCE (IN FEET)

GAS ONLY PIT STOP

● WEDGE ADJUSTMENT POINT.

● FUEL FILL POINT.

▭ JACK PLACEMENT POINT.

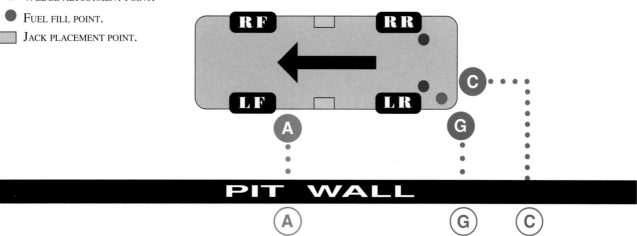

A **Assistant** - Watches fueling and signals driver when to go.

G **Gas Man** - Adds as much fuel as required.

C **Catch-Can Man** - Places catch can at fuel overflow nozzle.

Note: During Gas Only pit stops additional crewmen may be used to make handling adjustments. During two and four tire pit stops, the signal for the driver to go varies.

TWO TIRE PIT STOP

Step 1

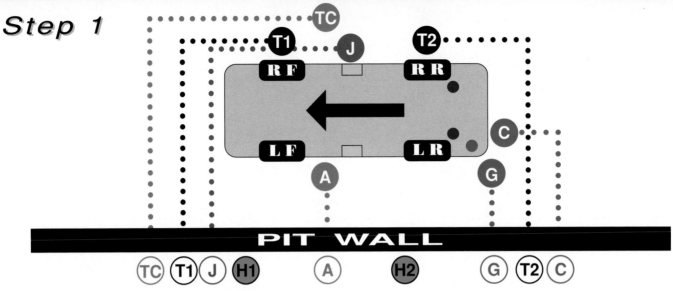

J   **Jack Man** - Runs around front of car, jacks up right side.

T1   **Tire Changer** - Follows Jack Man. Takes off worn right front tire and puts on new right front.

T2   **Tire Changer** - Runs around rear of car. Takes off worn right rear tire and puts on new right rear.

A   **Assistant** - Cleans windshield or makes adjustments.

TC   **Tire Carrier** - Runs around front of car with new right side tires and hands them to the tire changers.

G   **Gas Man** - Carries 11 gallon fuel can to left rear and fills.

C   **Catch-Can Man** - Places catch-can at fuel overflow nozzle.

H1   **Helper 1** - Cleans grill with extended brushes from behind the pit wall.

Step 2

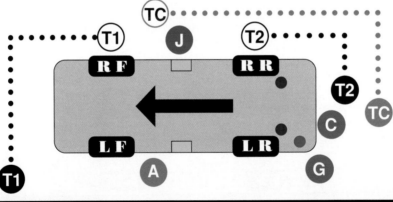

J   **Jack Man** - Drops the jack when all lug nuts are on, and allows driver to pull away before returning to the wall.

T1   **Tire Changer** - Runs back around front of car making sure air line is out of the way.

T2   **Tire Changer** - Runs back around rear of car making sure air line is out of the way.

A   **Assistant** - Continues making adjustments if necessary, or helps other crewmen.

TC   **Tire Carrier** - Helps other crewmen where necessary.

G   **Gas Man -** Continues to add fuel until car pulls away.

C   **Catch-Can Man -** Continues until car pulls away.

H1   **Helper 1 -** Continues until completed.

FOUR TIRE PIT STOP

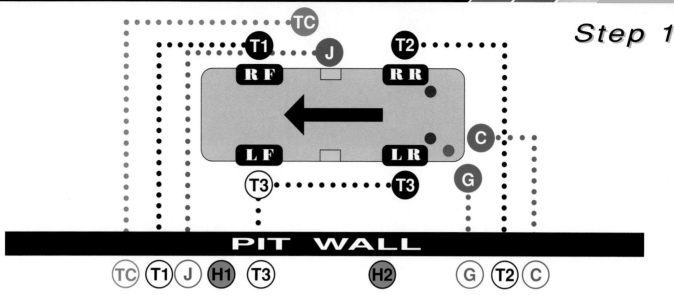

Step 1

J   **Jack Man** - Runs around front of car, jacks up right side. Drops the car when 2 lug nuts on each wheel are on.
T1   **Tire Changer** - Follows Jack Man. Takes off worn right front tire and puts on new right front.
T2   **Tire Changer** - Runs around rear of car. Takes off worn right rear tire and puts on new right rear.
T3   **Tire Changer** - Loosens left front tire and left rear tire.
TC   **Tire Carrier** - Runs around front of car with new right side tires and hands them to the tire changers.
G   **Gas Man** - Carries 11 gallon fuel can to left rear and fills.
C   **Catch-Can Man** - Places catch-can at fuel overflow nozzle.
H1   **Helper 1** - Cleans grill with extended brushes from behind the pit wall.
H2   **Helper 2** - Gets left side tires ready to be handed over the wall.

Step 2

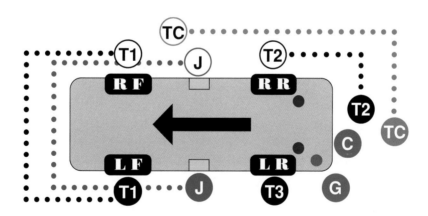

J   **Jack Man** - Runs back around front of car, jacks up left side. Drops the jack when all lug nuts are on.
T1   **Tire Changer** - Follows Jack Man back around car. Puts on new left front tire.
T2   **Tire Changer** - Assists other crewmen.
T3   **Tire Changer** - Puts on new left rear tire and tightens.
TC   **Tire Carrier** - Assists other crewmen.
G   **Gas Man** - Finishes emptying the first can of fuel and starts the second 11 gallon can.
C   **Catch-Can Man** - While keeping the catch-can in place, helps the gas man start the second fuel can.
H1   **Helper 1** - Continues until completed.
H2   **Helper 2** - Rolls the left side tires to the tire changers.

TRACK SIGNAL FLAGS

GREEN FLAG

Displayed to **Start**, or **Restart** the race. When the race is started the cars must maintain their positions until the start/finish line is crossed. On restarts the racing begins as soon as the flag is displayed.

YELLOW FLAG

Displayed immediately after a cause for **Caution**. Cars may "race back" to the flag, as the order they finish the lap during which the flag was displayed will determine the restart order. Cars line up single file on the track behind the pace car until time to restart.

BLACK FLAG

Displayed to **Order a particular car to the pits Immediately**, usually because the car may not be safe or because of driver actions. If ignored, the Black flag is crossed by the White flag, indicating scoring of the car has been suspended.

RED FLAG

Displayed to **Stop** the race when conditions make it unsafe to race. Cars are lined up in a designated area and no work may be done to them until the race is restarted.

PASSING FLAG

Displayed to indicate a **Passing Situation**. Cars on the track about to be passed by faster cars are shown this flag letting them know what is happening. This flag is usually displayed to cars about to be overtaken by the race leaders.

WHITE FLAG

Displayed to indicate that the race leader has started the **Last Lap** of the race. If the Yellow and White flags are both displayed, then the race will end under caution.

CHECKERED FLAG

Displayed at **Completion of the Race**. All cars on the track receive the Checkered flag on the last lap, their final positions all being relative to the race winner.

LICENSES

Drivers, car owners, and crew members must have a current NASCAR license in order to take part in Winston Cup Series events. The license recognizes the person as a participant only in a specific capacity. Licenses are obtained through the NASCAR general headquarters. To obtain a license a person must be at least 16 years of age, must meet the physical fitness requirements set by NASCAR, and, in the case of drivers, may have to pass a driving test. A car owner must also obtain a license from NASCAR for a car to be eligible to compete. It is during this licensing process that cars are given their numbers. Drivers aren't issued numbers, nor do they own them. The car number is issued to and owned by the car owner.

ENTRY PROCEDURE

Each race requires filling out an entry form before competing. The entry form lists, among other things, the date, total purse, pay-off per finishing position, and bonus awards (television awards, qualifying awards, and manufacturer's prize money). The entry form also lists the eligibility requirements, qualifying rules and any other special conditions that exist at a particular track. The names of the drivers and car owners, the license number and type of car, the car sponsor, and appropriate signatures are required. There are two sections of the entry application. One is sent to the race promoter, the other to NASCAR.

RESPONSIBILITY

The crew chief is the sole spokesman for the car owner and driver, and during the event must assume responsibility for the actions of the driver and the crew. If problems arise, the crew chief is subject to disciplinary action.

Drivers are responsible for being on time for all required events. Should they be late or miss a drivers' meeting, they can be sent to the rear of the starting line, or not be allowed to race at all. If the driver on a team is to be changed, officials must be given advance notice.

STARTING ORDER DETERMINATION

Drivers can attempt to qualify only one car. The qualifying time is accredited to the car, not the driver. In the event the approved driver is changed, the car's qualifying position is not changed. If a car is wrecked beyond repair during practice, after it has qualified, then a backup car may be used. The backup car brought to the track cannot be unloaded from the truck unless approved. Backup cars start at the rear of the field as they did not qualify.

The fastest qualifier, or *pole car*, is usually given the choice of the inside or outside position on the first row, and is used as the control car on starts. The fastest qualifier must lead the first lap of the race. Any car passing the pole car before it crosses the start/finish line will be penalized; usually a "stop and go" penalty is assessed.

If qualifying is rained out, the order is determined by the current Winston Cup point standings.

STARTING THE RACE

At the beginning of the race the pace car leads the field through a couple of laps. During these "pace laps," cars on the starting grid can resume their place if they drop out of position. After one or two pace laps a driver can duck into the pits, top off the fuel supply and resume position before the race starts. This may give a car one more lap under green flag racing, which might come in handy later.

If a car drops out completely on the first lap, its finishing position is determined by its starting position in relation to the starting position of the other cars that dropped out on the first lap.

In order for the initial driver of a car to receive points, that driver must start the race. If the initial driver does not start the race, the relief driver accumulates the points and winnings. This is why an injured driver may start the race and quickly switch to a backup driver.

STOPPING THE RACE

If the track becomes unfit for racing, the race must be stopped. This can be a result of weather, a bad accident, or damage to the track that creates unsafe conditions for the drivers and fans. Cars are stopped and lined up in the order in which they were running after the completion of the last lap. If a race is stopped, cars cannot be worked on. If a car is already in the pits or garage area being worked on, all work must stop until the race is resumed.

Should a race event be stopped, it can be re-started as long as time permits. Should the race be stopped and racing can not be resumed, then the event will be rescheduled for a later date. If half or more of the race has been completed when stopped, and racing cannot be resumed, then the race will be declared official and the running order at the time of the race stoppage will be the final finishing order. This is why it is so critical to be at the front of the pack when rain is threatening.

SETTLING UP

After the race, prize money is the first order of business. Each event has a payoff per finishing position. These amounts are listed on the entry form and do not change once they are announced. Each race has a different purse. Big races, at the big tracks, usually have the biggest payoffs. Below is a list of purses for all 1994 Winston Cup events.

RACE	TRACK	PURSE
DAYTONA 500 BY STP	DAYTONA	$2,756,845
GOODWRENCH 500	ROCKINGHAM	939,289
PONTIAC EXCITEMENT 400	RICHMOND	850,947
PUROLATOR 500	ATLANTA	1,037,763
TRANSOUTH FINANCIAL 400	DARLINGTON	814,857
FOOD CITY 500	BRISTOL	821,387
FIRST UNION 400	N.WILKESBORO	703,912
HANES 500	MARTINSVILLE	729,631
WINSTON SELECT 500	TALLADEGA	1,065,261
SAVE MART SUPERMARKETS 300K	SEARS POINT	894,167
COCA-COLA 600	CHARLOTTE	1,304,918
BUDWEISER 500	DOVER	931,186
UAW-GM TEAMWORK 500	POCONO	916,208
MILLER GENUINE DRAFT 400	MICHIGAN	1,002,168
PEPSI 400	DAYTONA	1,033,162
SLICK 50 300	NEW HAMPSHIRE	1,078,662
MILLER GENUINE DRAFT 500	POCONO	926,933
DIE HARD 500	TALLADEGA	1,060,486
BRICKYARD 400	INDIANAPOLIS	3,213,849
BUD AT THE GLEN	WATKINS GLEN	841,651
GM GOODWRENCH DEALER 400	MICHIGAN	994,487
GOODY'S 500	BRISTOL	825,404
MOUNTAIN DEW SOUTHERN 500	DARLINGTON	857,420
MILLER GENUINE DRAFT 400	RICHMOND	840,631
SPLITFIRE SPARK PLUG 500	DOVER	958,261
GOODY'S 500	MARTINSVILLE	770,919
TYSON HOLLY FARMS 400	N.WILKESBORO	752,800
MELLOW YELLOW 500	CHARLOTTE	1,144,850
A C DELCO 500	ROCKINGHAM	949,610
SLICK 50 500	PHOENIX	940,436
HOOTERS 500	ATLANTA	1,043,451

In addition to the main purse, special prizes and bonuses are also available. If the race is televised each position will receive a "television award." The first five qualifiers usually receive a "qualifying award." Manufacturer awards are another way to bring home more money from the track. This prize money is contingent on a car's use of products and the displaying of decals. This is why the decals on so many cars are arranged the same way. Their location is predetermined, and the teams are given a drawing showing where each decal is to be placed. Because all cars do not take part in the manufacturer award system, it is possible for a car to take home more money than a car that finished in a better position in the race.

Once the prize money has been paid, it's time to worry about points. There are three main point races going on through the year. First is driver points. A driver is awarded a number of points based on each race performance. At the end of the year prize money is awarded to each driver based on his position in the point rankings. The driver with the most points is the Winston Cup Champion.

Listed below is the driver and car owner point determination system used in each race.

FINISHING POSITION	POINTS	FINISHING POSITION	POINTS
1	175	21	100
2	170	22	97
3	165	23	94
4	160	24	91
5	155	25	88
6	150	26	85
7	146	27	82
8	142	28	79
9	138	29	76
10	134	30	73
11	130	31	70
12	127	32	67
13	124	33	64
14	121	34	61
15	118	35	58
16	115	36	55
17	112	37	52
18	109	38	49
19	106	39	46
20	103	40	43

For additional cars subtract three points per position

Add: 5 Bonus points for leading any one lap in a race
5 Bonus points for leading the most laps

The second race is for owner points. This works much the same as the driver points, but the payoff is for the owner.

The third points race is for the car manufacturers. All automobile manufacturers taking part in the season are in the manufacturer points race. Now down to Chevrolet, Ford and Pontiac, the manufacturers compete for the bragging rights of being the most successful make in Winston Cup racing.

Manufacturer points are rewarded as follows:

FINISHING POSITION	POINTS
1	9
2	6
3	4
4	3
5	2
6	1

Upon completion of the season the point funds are distributed. This takes place at the season ending banquet. The Driver Champion, Owner Champion, Rookie of the Year and the Manufacturer Champion are presented. The driver and owner funds are distributed as follows.

DISTRIBUTION OF DRIVER AND OWNER POINT FUNDS

1st	20%	11th	2.9%
2nd	10%	12th	2.8%
3rd	9%	13th	2.7%
4th	8%	14th	2.6%
5th	7%	15th	2.5%
6th	6%	16th	2.4%
7th	5%	17th	2.3%
8th	4%	18th	2.2%
9th	3.5%	19th	2.1%
10th	3%	20th	2.0%

ATLANTA MOTOR SPEEDWAY · BRISTOL INTERNATIONAL
RACEWAY · DAYTONA INTERNATIONAL SPEEDWAY · DOV
MOTOR SPEEDWAY · MARTINSVILLE SPEEDWAY · MICHI
INTERNATIONAL RACEWAY · NORTH CAROLINA MOTOR S
INTERNATIONAL RACEWAY · POCONO INTERNATIONAL R
POINT RACEWAY · TALLADEGA SUPERSPEEDWAY · WAT
BRISTOL INTERNATIONAL RACEWAY · CHARLOTTE MOTO
INTERNATIONAL SPEEDWAY · DOVER DOWNS INTERNATI
MARTINSVILLE SPEEDWAY · MICHIGAN INTERNATIONAL
NORTH CAROLINA MOTOR SPEEDWAY · NORTH WILKESBO
POCONO INTERNATIONAL RACEWAY · RICHMOND INTERN
SUPERSPEEDWAY · WATKINS GLEN INTERNATIONAL · AT
RACEWAY · CHARLOTTE MOTOR SPEEDWAY · DARLINGT
DOVER DOWNS INTERNATIONAL SPEEDWAY · INDIANAPOL
MICHIGAN INTERNATIONAL SPEEDWAY · NEW HAMPSHIR
SPEEDWAY · NORTH WILKESBORO SPEEDWAY · PHOENIX
RACEWAY · RICHMOND INTERNATIONAL RACEWAY · SE
WATKINS GLEN INTERNATIONAL · ATLANTA MOTOR SPE
MOTOR SPEEDWAY · DARLINGTON RACEWAY · DAYTONA
INTERNATIONAL SPEEDWAY · INDIANAPOLIS MOTOR SPE
INTERNATIONAL SPEEDWAY · NEW HAMPSHIRE INTERNA
NORTH WILKESBORO SPEEDWAY · PHOENIX INTERNATIO
RICHMOND INTERNATIONAL RACEWAY · SEARS POINT R
INTERNATIONAL · ATLANTA MOTOR SPEEDWAY · BRIST
SPEEDWAY · DARLINGTON RACEWAY · DAYTONA INTERN
SPEEDWAY · INDIANAPOLIS MOTOR SPEEDWAY · MARTIN
NEW HAMPSHIRE INTERNATIONAL RACEWAY · NORTH CA
· PHOENIX INTERNATIONAL RACEWAY · POCONO INTERN
SEARS POINT RACEWAY · TALLADEGA SUPERSPEEDWAY
SPEEDWAY · BRISTOL INTERNATIONAL RACEWAY · CHA
DAYTONA INTERNATIONAL SPEEDWAY · DOVER DOWNS
SPEEDWAY · MARTINSVILLE SPEEDWAY · MICHIGAN IN

THE TRACKS

ATLANTA MOTOR SPEEDWAY

Area	Length	Banking
Total Track	1.522 *miles*	
Front Straight	1320 *feet*	5 *degrees*
Turn 1	1349 *feet*	24 *degrees*
Turn 2	1349 *feet*	24 *degrees*
Back Straight	1320 *feet*	5 *degrees*
Turn 3	1349 *feet*	24 *degrees*
Turn 4	1349 *feet*	24 *degrees*

Pit Road Layout: 42 Pits - All on front
First Winston Cup Race: 1960
Qualifying Record: 185.830 mph (Greg Sacks 1994)
Fastest Race: 156.849 mph (Dale Earnhardt 1990)
Slowest Race: 110.052 mph (Darrell Waltrip 1977)

THE TRACK

Very fast. Of all the tracks we go to, you get the most sensation of speed at Atlanta. Two quarter-mile straightaways and two half-mile corners; so you're talking about being in the corner an exceptional amount of time. The track has been repaved and has good grip; but it's still a little rough - has some seams and stuff. Starting with qualifying, you're looking for one lap almost flat out. You're just barely rolling out of the throttle, getting in the corners -- really manipulating the race car there. It's very demanding. Once you get qualified and are running the race, you have to give up getting into the corner in order to get off the corner. You're in the corner so long and you build up so much tire heat, you try to give up getting in; get the car directional and then get off the corner with as much exit speed as you can. Atlanta is one of those race tracks where typically there are two areas to run. You can run a low groove or high groove. Usually, the middle to the bottom of the track is where most of the rubber is laid down; so the upper groove has to be worked in most of the time. As the race progresses, if your race car gives up a certain way then you have to search for an avenue to accommodate the race car; and typically that's the higher portion of the race track.

SPEED CHART

Sec.	MPH	Sec.	MPH	Sec.	MPH	Sec.	MPH
27.00	202.933	28.00	195.686	29.00	188.938	30.00	182.640
27.05	202.558	28.05	195.337	29.05	188.613	30.05	182.336
27.10	202.185	28.10	194.989	29.10	188.289	30.10	182.033
27.15	201.812	28.15	194.643	29.15	187.966	30.15	181.731
27.20	201.441	28.20	194.298	29.20	187.644	30.20	181.430
27.25	201.072	28.25	193.954	29.25	187.323	30.25	181.131
27.30	200.703	28.30	193.611	29.30	187.003	30.30	180.832
27.35	200.336	28.35	193.270	29.35	186.685	30.35	180.534
27.40	199.971	28.40	192.930	29.40	186.367	30.40	180.237
27.45	199.607	28.45	192.591	29.45	186.051	30.45	179.941
27.50	199.244	28.50	192.253	29.50	185.736	30.50	179.646
27.55	198.882	28.55	191.916	29.55	185.421	30.55	179.352
27.60	198.522	28.60	191.580	29.60	185.108	30.60	179.059
27.65	198.163	28.65	191.246	29.65	184.796	30.65	178.767
27.70	197.805	28.70	190.913	29.70	184.485	30.70	178.476
27.75	197.449	28.75	190.581	29.75	184.175	30.75	178.185
27.80	197.094	28.80	190.250	29.80	183.866	30.80	177.896
27.85	196.740	28.85	189.920	29.85	183.558	30.85	177.608
27.90	196.387	28.90	189.592	29.90	183.251	30.90	177.320
27.95	196.036	28.95	189.264	29.95	182.945	30.95	177.034

TOP PERFORMERS

	Driver	Starts	Wins	Top Five	Top Ten	Winnings	Multiple Race Winners	
1	Dale Earnhardt	33	6	20	22	$974,820	Cale Yarborough	7
		100%	18.18%	60.61%	66.67%		Richard Petty	6
2	Bill Elliot	36	5	11	15	$751,260	Dale Earnhardt	6
		100%	13.89%	30.56%	41.67%		Bobby Allison	5
3	Darrell Waltrip	45	3	18	28	$649,350	David Pearson	4
		100%	8.70%	26.09%	43.48%		Fred Lorenzen	4
4	Rusty Wallace	23	2	6	10	$516,420	Bill Elliott	5
		100%	6.67%	40.00%	62.22%		Darrell Waltrip	3
5	Morgan Shepherd	26	3	7	16	$482,825	Neil Bonnett	3
		100%	11.54%	26.92%	61.54%		Morgan Shepherd	3
6	Ricky Rudd	34	2	7	16	$443,705	Rusty Wallace	2
		100%	5.88%	20.59%	47.06%		LeeRoy Yarborough	2
7	Geoff Bodine	25	0	4	9	$389,885	Panch	2
		100%	0.00%	16.00%	24.00%		Buddy Baker	2
8	Mark Martin	17	2	4	7	$385,595	Mark Martin	2
		100%	11.76%	23.53%	41.18%			
9	Terry Labonte	33	0	6	18	$377,785		
		100%	0.00%	18.18%	54.55%			
10	Ernie irvan	13	1	4	5	$314,292		
		100%	7.69%	30.77%	38.46%			

BRISTOL INTERNATIONAL SPEEDWAY

Area	Length	Banking
Total Track	0.533 *mile*	
Front Straight	650 *feet*	16 *degrees*
Turn 1	379 *feet*	36 *degrees*
Turn 2	379 *feet*	36 *degrees*
Back Straight	650 *feet*	16 *degrees*
Turn 3	379 *feet*	36 *degrees*
Turn 4	379 *feet*	36 *degrees*

Pit Road Layout: 38 Pit Stalls (19 front and 19 back)
First Winston Cup Race: 1961
Qualifying Record: 124.946 (Chuck Bown 1994)
Fastest Race: 101.074 mph (Charlie Glotzbach 1971)
Slowest Race: 61.826 mph (Ned Jarrett 1965)

SPEED CHART

Sec.	MPH	Sec.	MPH	Sec.	MPH	Sec.	MPH
14.00	137.057	15.00	127.920	16.00	119.925	17.00	112.871
14.05	136.569	15.05	127.495	16.05	119.551	17.05	112.540
14.10	136.085	15.10	127.073	16.10	119.180	17.10	112.211
14.15	135.604	15.15	126.653	16.15	118.811	17.15	111.883
14.20	135.127	15.20	126.237	16.20	118.444	17.20	111.558
14.25	134.653	15.25	125.823	16.25	118.080	17.25	111.235
14.30	134.182	15.30	125.412	16.30	117.718	17.30	110.913
14.35	133.714	15.35	125.003	16.35	117.358	17.35	110.594
14.40	133.250	15.40	124.597	16.40	117.000	17.40	110.276
14.45	132.789	15.45	124.194	16.45	116.644	17.45	109.960
14.50	132.331	15.50	123.794	16.50	116.291	17.50	109.646
14.55	131.876	15.55	123.395	16.55	115.940	17.55	109.333
14.60	131.425	15.60	123.000	16.60	115.590	17.60	109.023
14.65	130.976	15.65	122.607	16.65	115.243	17.65	108.714
14.70	130.531	15.70	122.217	16.70	114.898	17.70	108.407
14.75	130.088	15.75	121.829	16.75	114.555	17.75	108.101
14.80	129.649	15.80	121.443	16.80	114.214	17.80	107.798
14.85	129.212	15.85	121.060	16.85	113.875	17.85	107.496
14.90	128.779	15.90	120.679	16.90	113.538	17.90	107.196
14.95	128.348	15.95	120.301	16.95	113.204	17.95	106.897

TOP PERFORMERS

Driver	Starts	Wins	Top Five	Top Ten	Winnings	Multiple Race Winners	
1 *Dale Earnhardt*	31 100%	9 29.03%	16 51.61%	23 74.19%	$714,575	*Darrell Waltrip*	12
2 *Darrell Waltrip*	40 100%	12 30.00%	24 60.00%	30 75.00%	$691,875	*Dale Earnhardt*	9
3 *Rusty Wallace*	22 100%	5 22.73%	10 45.45%	15 68.18%	$527,365	*Cale Yarborough*	9
4 *Ricky Rudd*	33 100%	0 0.00%	10 30.30%	21 63.64%	$358,940	*David Pearson*	5
5 *Terry Labonte*	32 100%	1 3.13%	13 40.63%	22 68.75%	$352,575	*Rusty Wallace*	5
6 *Bill Elliot*	24 100%	1 4.17%	6 25.00%	12 50.00%	$334,360	*Bobby Allison*	4
7 *Mark Martin*	16 100%	1 6.25%	7 43.75%	9 56.25%	$324,695	*Richard Petty*	3
8 *Geoff Bodine*	25 100%	0 0.00%	6 24.00%	9 36.00%	$300,271	*Alan Kulwicki*	2
9 *Ken Schrader*	20 100%	0 0.00%	4 20.00%	8 40.00%	$247,980		
10 *Kyle Petty*	26 100%	0 0.00%	2 7.69%	7 26.92%	$234,866		

THE TRACK

Probably the second race track in sensation of speed to Atlanta. Very high bank, 38 degrees. Steepest of all the places we go. A concrete race track, entirely concrete. Has been shaved a lot. To the point where we're seeing a lot of rocks; halves of rocks that are surrounded by concrete. Very abrasive race track. As of late it's been wearing on the compound tires. Seems to wear the tires out. Real manipulative type of racetrack. You have to drive the car into the corner fairly hard. You have to tell yourself the car is going to turn. You get back on the throttle before the car actually becomes turned, and gets directional. Otherwise you're definitely too late on the throttle, and you won't have a quick lap time. It's one of those race tracks where it's mind over matter. You have to make sure that you feel like the car is going to turn and get directional; and get back on the gas before it happens. Then you drive the car off the corner. A lot of undulations in the concrete of the racetrack. The cars get up, off the racetrack. You get airborne off Turn Two. The car actually leaves the ground a little bit. It's a very difficult racetrack. Very demanding. Both on the driver, from fatigue, and the racecar as far as wear on the car and components. There's a big difference between the night race and the day race. Typically, the day race is the easiest of the races. The night races, you really have a problem there, because you can't see a long way ahead of yourself. When you're driving in that corner, all you can see is banking. You have to look out of the upper portion of the windshield to look over off Turn Two. It's a real different look out of the windshield at Bristol. We're traveling at such high speeds there now, there is absolutely no margin for error. If somebody causes a problem, you're collected in it. Plus the weather is usually very humid when we run there. We wait all day. We're down in a hole. The racetrack is set beneath all the stands. You basically have no air down there. It's very stagnant. It becomes a very humid, hot, demanding race from the driver's standpoint, and very tough on the racecar.

CHARLOTTE MOTOR SPEEDWAY

Area	Length		Banking	
Total Track	1.5	miles		
Front Straight	1152	feet	5	degrees
Turn 1	1152	feet	24	degrees
Turn 2	1953	feet	24	degrees
Back Straight	1360	feet	5	degrees
Turn 3	1152	feet	24	degrees
Turn 4	1152	feet	24	degrees

Pit Road Layout: 42 Pits - All on front
First Winston Cup Race: 1960
Qualifying Record: 184.759 mph (Ward Burton 1994)
Fastest Race: 154.537 mph (Ernie Irvan 1993)
Slowest Race: 104.207 mph (Buddy Baker 1968)

THE TRACK

Charlotte's the show palace. One of the major platforms to showcase Winston Cup racing. A dynamite facility. The home of the Winston Select, a unique racing format. A chance for the Winston Cup "winners" to compete in a high dollar, old time, Saturday Night Shootout. Two preliminary events and a 10 lap main, with more money going to the winner than in any race of the year except the Daytona 500. With points not being a factor, the action is fast, aggressive, controversial, and sometimes just plain ugly. The only race of its kind on the Winston Cup circuit. A great look for both the race people and the spectators. The racetrack's been repaved recently and the lighting is spectacular. A very different racetrack with two very diverse corners. You have one corner in Turn One when the car typically stays tight; and you can feel a little bit of a hump getting in. So you can't really attack the corner quite as well as you'd like. Turn Three and Four the car is typically looser. You carry a lot more speed into that corner. Trying to get off that corner, trying to get the car in as hard as you can, trying to get the car directional, without the car being real loose or real tight, is a major chore. Then you have the dogleg and front straightaway which set you up to position yourself to get ready to go back into Turn One. It's a difficult race track; and very demanding on the crew chief and the driver to come up with a compromise in the chassis for both corners. It's a racetrack where you can race your competitor, and you can race fiercely. A good handling racecar will really show up there, if you can find a compromise for both corners.

SPEED CHART

Sec.	MPH	Sec.	MPH	Sec.	MPH	Sec.	MPH
25.00	.... 216.000	26.00	.... 207.692	27.00	.... 200.000	28.00	.... 192.857
25.05	.... 215.569	26.05	.... 207.294	27.05	.... 199.630	28.05	.... 192.513
25.10	.... 215.139	26.10	.... 206.897	27.10	.... 199.262	28.10	.... 192.171
25.15	.... 214.712	26.15	.... 206.501	27.15	.... 198.895	28.15	.... 191.829
25.20	.... 214.286	26.20	.... 206.107	27.20	.... 198.529	28.20	.... 191.489
25.25	.... 213.861	26.25	.... 205.714	27.25	.... 198.165	28.25	.... 191.150
25.30	.... 213.439	26.30	.... 205.323	27.30	.... 197.802	28.30	.... 190.813
25.35	.... 213.018	26.35	.... 204.934	27.35	.... 197.441	28.35	.... 190.476
25.40	.... 212.598	26.40	.... 204.545	27.40	.... 197.080	28.40	.... 190.141
25.45	.... 212.181	26.45	.... 204.159	27.45	.... 196.721	28.45	.... 189.807
25.50	.... 211.765	26.50	.... 203.774	27.50	.... 196.364	28.50	.... 189.474
25.55	.... 211.350	26.55	.... 203.390	27.55	.... 196.007	28.55	.... 189.142
25.60	.... 210.937	26.60	.... 203.008	27.60	.... 195.652	28.60	.... 188.811
25.65	.... 210.526	26.65	.... 202.627	27.65	.... 195.298	28.65	.... 188.482
25.70	.... 210.117	26.70	.... 202.247	27.70	.... 194.946	28.70	.... 188.153
25.75	.... 209.709	26.75	.... 201.869	27.75	.... 194.595	28.75	.... 187.826
25.80	.... 209.302	26.80	.... 201.493	27.80	.... 194.245	28.80	.... 187.500
25.85	.... 208.897	26.85	.... 201.117	27.85	.... 193.896	28.85	.... 187.175
25.90	.... 208.494	26.90	.... 200.743	27.90	.... 193.548	28.90	.... 186.851
25.95	.... 208.092	26.95	.... 200.371	27.95	.... 193.202	28.95	.... 186.528

TOP PERFORMERS

	Driver	Starts	Wins	Top Five	Top Ten	Winnings	Multiple Race Winners	
1	Dale Earnhardt	36	5	12	14	$1,166,188	Bobby Allison	6
		100%	13.89%	33.33%	38.89%		Darrell Waltrip	6
2	Darrell Waltrip	45	6	19	29	$1,080,862	Dale Earnhardt	5
		100%	13.33%	42.22%	64.44%		David Pearson	4
3	Bill Elliot	37	2	10	18	$988,136	Buddy Baker	4
		100%	5.41%	27.03%	82.22%		Fred Lorenzen	4
4	Rusty Wallace	26	2	5	11	$672,750	Richard Petty	3
		100%	7.69%	19.23%	42.31%		LeeRoy Yarborough	3
5	Geoff Bodine	23	1	5	10	$616,000	Cale Yarborough	3
		100%	4.35%	21.74%	43.48%		Neil Bonnett	2
6	Ken Schrader	21	1	5	9	$608,910	Benny Parsons	2
		100%	4.76%	23.81%	42.86%		Bill Elliott	2
7	Mark Martin	18	1	4	6	$541,370	Rusty Wallace	2
		100%	5.56%	22.22%	33.33%		Junior Johnson	2
8	Kyle Petty	30	1	5	10	$533,760	Jim Paschal	2
		100%	3.33%	16.67%	33.33%		Davey Allison	2
9	Ricky Rudd	37	3	5	19	$513,415		
		100%	8.11%	13.51%	51.35%			
10	Terry Labonte	33	3	4	13	$475,030		
		100%	9.09%	12.12%	39.39%			

DARLINGTON RACEWAY

Area	Length	Banking
Total Track	1.366 *miles*	
Front Straight	1228 *feet*	2 *degrees*
Turn 1	NA	23 *degrees*
Turn 2	NA	23 *degrees*
Back Straight	1228 *feet*	2 *degrees*
Turn 3	NA	25 *degrees*
Turn 4	NA	25 *degrees*

Pit Road Layout: 42 Pits - All on front
First Winston Cup Race: 1960
Qualifying Record: 166.998 mph (Geoff Bodine 1994)
Fastest Race: 139.958 mph (Dale Earnhardt 1993)
Slowest Race: 76.260 mph (Johnny Mantz 1950)

SPEED CHART

Sec.	MPH	Sec.	MPH	Sec.	MPH	Sec.	MPH
27.00	182.133	28.00	175.629	29.00	169.572	30.00	163.920
27.05	181.797	28.05	175.316	29.05	169.281	30.05	163.647
27.10	181.461	28.10	175.004	29.10	168.990	30.10	163.375
27.15	181.127	28.15	174.693	29.15	168.700	30.15	163.104
27.20	180.794	28.20	174.383	29.20	168.411	30.20	162.834
27.25	180.462	28.25	174.074	29.25	168.123	30.25	162.565
27.30	180.132	28.30	173.767	29.30	167.836	30.30	162.297
27.35	179.803	28.35	173.460	29.35	167.550	30.35	162.030
27.40	179.474	28.40	173.155	29.40	167.265	30.40	161.763
27.45	179.148	28.45	172.851	29.45	166.981	30.45	161.498
27.50	178.822	28.50	172.547	29.50	166.698	30.50	161.233
27.55	178.497	28.55	172.245	29.55	166.416	30.55	160.969
27.60	178.174	28.60	171.944	29.60	166.135	30.60	160.706
27.65	177.852	28.65	171.644	29.65	165.855	30.65	160.444
27.70	177.531	28.70	171.345	29.70	165.576	30.70	160.182
27.75	177.211	28.75	171.047	29.75	165.297	30.75	159.922
27.80	176.892	28.80	170.750	29.80	165.020	30.80	159.662
27.85	176.575	28.85	170.454	29.85	164.744	30.85	159.404
27.90	176.258	28.90	170.159	29.90	164.468	30.90	159.146
27.95	175.943	28.95	169.865	29.95	164.194	30.95	158.889

THE TRACK

As of now, even with the repaving, it's the same old Darlington except with a facelift. Every aspect of that racetrack is the same, except you just have more grip; even though it becomes more greasy during the race. You still have the narrow corners. Very much a give-and-take racetrack. It's very difficult to run two abreast around there with any real speed. If you get position on somebody there, it's a necessity for that person to give up the ghost and allow you to pass. You really race that racetrack. It's not a real racer's racetrack, as far as racing a competitor. Out of all the tracks, probably the most focus has to be put on Darlington because it's so narrow. The speeds are elevated so extensively that you really have to battle that racetrack to avoid the "lady in black" putting a stripe on you.

TOP PERFORMERS

	Driver	Starts	Wins	Top Five	Top Ten	Winnings
1	Dale Earnhardt	32	9	14	19	$900,020
		100%	28.13%	43.75%	59.38%	
2	Bill Elliot	34	5	18	28	$748,685
		100%	14.71%	52.94%	82.35%	
3	Darrell Waltrip	43	5	18	23	$642,185
		100%	11.63%	41.86%	53.49%	
4	Mark Martin	17	1	10	13	$431,330
		100%	5.88%	58.82%	76.47%	
5	Ricky Rudd	36	1	6	18	$425,875
		100%	2.78%	16.67%	50.00%	
6	Terry Labonte	32	1	9	16	$388,295
		100%	3.13%	28.13%	50.00%	
7	Rusty Wallace	22	0	8	12	$355,125
		100%	0.00%	36.36%	54.55%	
8	Geoff Bodine	26	0	3	14	$352,447
		100%	0.00%	11.54%	53.85%	
9	Dave Marcis	50	0	9	16	$292,592
		100%	0.00%	18.00%	32.00%	
10	Ken Schrader	20	0	4	7	$288,980
		100%	0.00%	20.00%	35.00%	

Multiple Race Winners

David Pearson	10
Dale Earnhardt	9
Cale Yarborough	5
Bobby Allison	5
Darrell Waltrip	5
Bill Elliott	5
Fireball Roberts	4
Harry Gant	4
Richard Petty	3
Herb Thomas	3
Buck Baker	3
Buddy Baker	2
Fred Lorenzen	2
Joe Weatherly	2
Nelson Stacy	2
LeeRoy Yarborough	2
Curtis Turner	2

DAYTONA INTERNATIONAL SPEEDWAY

Area	Length	Banking
Total Track	2.5 *miles*	
Front Straight	3800 *feet*	18 *degrees*
Turn 1	1500 *feet*	31 *degrees*
Turn 2	1500 *feet*	31 *degrees*
Back Straight	3600 *feet*	6 *degrees*
Turn 3	1500 *feet*	31 *degrees*
Turn 4	1500 *feet*	31 *degrees*

Pit Road Layout: 42 Pits - All on front
First Winston Cup Race: 1959
Qualifying Record: 210.364 mph (Bill Elliot 1987)
Fastest Race: 177.602 mph (Buddy Baker 1980)
Slowest Race: 124.740 mph (Junior Johnson 1960)

THE TRACK

A unique racetrack. Out of all the places you go, the most incredible atmosphere for the Daytona race. Very difficult race. So many variables. The racetrack is worn. It's actually sunken in certain portions of the track, where they have some major dips. Turn One and Two, a major dip in the bottom of the race track. You're wide open a majority of the time. But with certain tires, the differences in the radial tire, and the aerodynamics of the car, the cars have become a lot more violent. With the air coming off the other cars, the cars will take off. You can turn all you want to the left and the cars just take off to the right and won't stop because of the air being manipulated off the cars ahead of you. There's a whole different driver's concept at Daytona. The draft plays such an incredible part. It's so different. The transition and the banking are very abrupt from a very flat straightaway to probably 31 degrees of banking in a very short period of time. It's like a roller coaster ramp. The cars get into the G force getting into the corner very quickly. The cars get loose getting into the corners. The air plays a big factor, as the wind blows exceptionally hard from side to side. Then it changes. It can change within a lap. You have to keep an eye on the flag. There's just no constant. Everything changes. If the sun is out the cars will pick up speed. It's one of those races that has a great mystique and a lot of history. It's a great feel to go there. So many things. You're there for thirteen days or so. All the functions and activities. The history behind the race. All the greats of racing there. The greats who haven't won it; those who have. Coming back there is such a special time. Before the new airport was there, they brought the steps to the plane, and as you stepped off the airplane you could see the racetrack. You can just feel the racetrack the moment you step off the plane. I almost wish the old airport was still there. Typical "days of thunder" morning, the sun coming up over the speedway thing, an incredible moment. Anytime you're around Daytona, there's such an air about it, like no other race.

SPEED CHART

Sec.	MPH	Sec.	MPH	Sec.	MPH	Sec.	MPH
44.00	204.545	45.00	200.000	46.00	195.652	47.00	191.489
44.05	204.313	45.05	199.778	46.05	195.440	47.05	191.286
44.10	204.082	45.10	199.557	46.10	195.228	47.10	191.083
44.15	203.851	45.15	199.336	46.15	195.016	47.15	190.880
44.20	203.620	45.20	199.115	46.20	194.805	47.20	190.678
44.25	203.390	45.25	198.895	46.25	194.595	47.25	190.476
44.30	203.160	45.30	198.675	46.30	194.384	47.30	190.275
44.35	202.931	45.35	198.456	46.35	194.175	47.35	190.074
44.40	202.703	45.40	198.238	46.40	193.966	47.40	189.873
44.45	202.475	45.45	198.020	46.45	193.757	47.45	189.673
44.50	202.247	45.50	197.802	46.50	193.548	47.50	189.474
44.55	202.020	45.55	197.585	46.55	193.340	47.55	189.274
44.60	201.794	45.60	197.368	46.60	193.133	47.60	189.076
44.65	201.568	45.65	197.152	46.65	192.926	47.65	188.877
44.70	201.342	45.70	196.937	46.70	192.719	47.70	188.679
44.75	201.117	45.75	196.721	46.75	192.513	47.75	188.482
44.80	200.893	45.80	196.507	46.80	192.308	47.80	188.285
44.85	200.669	45.85	196.292	46.85	192.102	47.85	188.088
44.90	200.445	45.90	196.078	46.90	191.898	47.90	187.891
44.95	200.222	45.95	195.865	46.95	191.693	47.95	187.696

TOP PERFORMERS

	Driver	Starts	Wins	Top Five	Top Ten	Winnings	Multiple Race Winners	
1	Dale Earnhardt	33	2	13	24	$1,527,786	Richard Petty	10
		100%	6.06%	39.39%	72.73%		Cale Yarborough	8
2	Bill Elliot	35	4	12	18	$1,412,700	David Pearson	6
		100%	11.43%	34.29%	51.43%		Bobby Allison	6
3	Darrell Waltrip	43	1	13	17	$1,155,338	Fireball Roberts	4
		100%	2.33%	30.23%	39.53%		Bill Elliot	4
4	Geoff Bodine	27	1	6	12	$1,059,795	A.J. Foyt	3
		100%	3.70%	22.22%	44.44%		Davey Allison	2
5	Terry Labonte	32	0	7	17	$1,029,340	Ernie Irvan	2
		100%	0.00%	21.88%	53.13%		Dale Earnhardt	2
6	Sterling Marlin	25	1	6	12	$939,065	Buddy Baker	2
		100%	4.00%	24.00%	48.00%		LeeRoy Yarborough	2
7	Ken Schrader	20	0	5	12	$780,410		
		100%	0.00%	25.00%	60.00%			
8	Ernie Irvan	13	2	5	6	$765,195		
		100%	15.38%	38.46%	46.15%			
9	Ricky Rudd	36	0	4	15	$715,817		
		100%	0.00%	11.11%	41.67%			
10	Rusty Wallace	22	0	0	7	$546,682		
		100%	0.00%	0.00%	31.82%			

DOVER DOWNS INTERNATIONAL SPEEDWAY

Area	Length	Banking
Total Track	1 *mile*	
Front Straight	1076 *feet*	9 *degrees*
Turn 1	782 *feet*	24 *degrees*
Turn 2	782 *feet*	24 *degrees*
Back Straight	1076 *feet*	9 *degrees*
Turn 3	782 *feet*	24 *degrees*
Turn 4	782 *feet*	24 *degrees*

Pit Road Layout: 42 Pits - All on front
First Winston Cup Race: 1969
Qualifying Record: 152.840 mph (Geoff Bodine 1994)
Fastest Race: 125.945 mph (Ricky Rudd 1987)
Slowest Race: 100.820 mph (David Pearson 1975)

SPEED CHART

Sec.	MPH	Sec.	MPH	Sec.	MPH	Sec.	MPH
22.00	163.636	23.00	156.522	24.00	150.000	25.00	144.000
22.05	163.265	23.05	156.182	24.05	149.688	25.05	143.713
22.10	162.896	23.10	155.844	24.10	149.378	25.10	143.426
22.15	162.528	23.15	155.508	24.15	149.068	25.15	143.141
22.20	162.162	23.20	155.172	24.20	148.760	25.20	142.857
22.25	161.798	23.25	154.839	24.25	148.454	25.25	142.574
22.30	161.435	23.30	154.506	24.30	148.148	25.30	142.292
22.35	161.074	23.35	154.176	24.35	147.844	25.35	142.012
22.40	160.714	23.40	153.846	24.40	147.541	25.40	141.732
22.45	160.356	23.45	153.518	24.45	147.239	25.45	141.454
22.50	160.000	23.50	153.191	24.50	146.939	25.50	141.176
22.55	159.645	23.55	152.866	24.55	146.640	25.55	140.900
22.60	159.292	23.60	152.542	24.60	146.341	25.60	140.625
22.65	158.940	23.65	152.220	24.65	146.045	25.65	140.351
22.70	158.590	23.70	151.899	24.70	145.749	25.70	140.078
22.75	158.242	23.75	151.579	24.75	145.455	25.75	139.806
22.80	157.895	23.80	151.261	24.80	145.161	25.80	139.535
22.85	157.549	23.85	150.943	24.85	144.869	25.85	139.265
22.90	157.205	23.90	150.628	24.90	144.578	25.90	138.996
22.95	156.863	23.95	150.313	24.95	144.289	25.95	138.728

TOP PERFORMERS

	Driver	Starts	Wins	Top Five	Top Ten	Winnings
1	Dale Earnhardt	32	3	15	19	$693,415
		100%	9.38%	46.88%	59.38%	
2	Bill Elliot	25	4	11	16	$594,155
		100%	16.00%	44.00%	64.00%	
3	Darrell Waltrip	43	2	14	21	$535,360
		100%	4.65%	32.56%	48.84%	
4	Ricky Rudd	33	3	10	17	$494,445
		100%	9.09%	30.30%	51.52%	
5	Rusty Wallace	22	3	7	11	$462,050
		100%	13.64%	31.82%	50.00%	
6	Ken Schrader	20	1	8	12	$424,020
		100%	5.00%	40.00%	60.00%	
7	Geoff Bodine	25	1	5	9	$379,935
		100%	4.00%	20.00%	36.00%	
8	Terry Labonte	32	0	7	12	$344,365
		100%	0.00%	21.88%	37.50%	
9	Mark Martin	16	0	8	9	$319,360
		100%	0.00%	50.00%	56.25%	
10	Kyle Petty	27	0	4	9	$310,960
		100%	0.00%	14.81%	33.33%	

Multiple Race Winners

Bobby Allison	7
Richard Petty	7
David Pearson	5
Bill Elliot	4
Harry Gant	4
Dale Earnhardt	3
Rusty Wallace	3
Cale Yarborough	3
Ricky Rudd	3
Neil Bonnett	3
Darrell Waltrip	2
Benny Parsons	2

THE TRACK

A special racetrack. Unique. New all-concrete surface. Like the Bristol track. A one-mile racetrack, unique because of the degree of banking all the way around the racetrack. The straightaways are banked. You drive off this banking into a hole in Turn One, that is very steeply banked also. Very rough, abrasive, a lot of seams. The car has to get directional rather quickly. It's a lot tighter corner than you think and then you come off Turn Two and you climb the hill back out of the hole. A very narrow exit off of Turn Two, still climbing out of a hole and driving on a banked straightaway, all the way back down into Turn Three where you feel like you go a little bit down hill again into a less severely banked corner. Getting the car in a little easy; getting the car directional quickly; driving back to the bottom; and then driving back up out of that hole, straight up the banking again to the wall coming down the front straightaway. It's one of those real rhythm racetracks. Where if your car's working well, it changes. Very susceptible to change. Very difficult to keep a car constant throughout the entire race. They used to seal the racetrack. You'd wear the sealer off, and there would be one groove. Then they quit sealing it, and repaved it. It's one of those racetracks, where if you got into a rhythm and the car was working well, you felt like you were just hauling the mail down that corner. It almost felt like the car just got airborne as it went down in that hole, and boy, you get to the bottom, about the time the car hits the bottom, and it bottoms out and you're back on the throttle, flat out. The car just groans and the motor just grunts; and you drive back up that hill. Very demanding, both on the car and the driver. Demands a lot of torque from the motor. The racecars bottom out getting in the corner. It has to be very difficult on the tires. You can really manipulate a racecar there.

Indianapolis Motor Speedway

Area	Length	Banking
Total Track	2.5 *miles*	
Front Straight	3300 *feet*	0 *degrees*
Turn 1	1650 *feet*	9 *degrees*
Turn 2	1650 *feet*	9 *degrees*
Back Straight	3300 *feet*	0 *degrees*
Turn 3	1650 *feet*	9 *degrees*
Turn 4	1650 *feet*	9 *degrees*

Pit Road Layout: 42 Pits - All on front
First Winston Cup Race: 1994
Qualifying Record: 172.414 mph (Rick Mast 1994)
Fastest Race: 131.977 mph (Jeff Gordon 1994)
Slowest Race: 131.977 mph (Jeff Gordon 1994)

The Track

A racetrack where you really have to focus, because you lose sight of where you are on the track. There are so many corners. It's like a big square. You almost have two corners per corner. You drive down the front straightaway, coming off Turn Four, and you're heading for the start/finish line. It looks like a cone, wide where you are, but so far down the straightaway. It looks like it's a point down there. As you come down the straightaway, the wider that point becomes. It just flares open. It's like the doors opening. You get to the start/finish line, and you see the first corner. You start trying to go to the bottom of the racetrack which is the wrong thing to do. You have to make yourself drive alongside the wall and turn the car as late as possible into Turn One to try to get an angle for the car to get off the corner. Then you drive for the center of the wall of that square again. By the time you get to that point, you're set up for the next corner. You have to stay wide again and make that late apex to the center of that corner. Then you're edging out again, out to the edge of the wall. It's kind of a drift at that point. Then you have the same concept again, a long straightaway where you can vaguely see the end. The car carries so much speed down the straightaway. Great feeling. You have so much time to relax, to feel the car underneath you, and build momentum. Then, the same thing happens again. You have to take a wide turn into Turn Three. You want to feel like you're done with that corner, but then all of a sudden you're out to the wall and there's the next corner again. You have to know where you are on the racetrack, which corner you're on and what your needs are for the next corner. If you lose sight of any one portion of that racetrack, if you miss one corner there, it sets you up to lose an enormous amount of time. Exit speed is crucial. Getting the car directional in the center of the corner, and getting off the corner. But at a place like Indy where it's so flat, there's absolutely no banking, you have to carry exit speed off the corners. You have to make sure the car gets turned, gets pointed coming off the corners.

Speed Chart

Sec.	MPH	Sec.	MPH	Sec.	MPH	Sec.	MPH
50.00	180.000	51.00	176.471	52.00	173.077	53.00	169.811
50.05	179.820	51.05	176.298	52.05	172.911	53.05	169.651
50.10	179.641	51.10	176.125	52.10	172.745	53.10	169.492
50.15	179.462	51.15	175.953	52.15	172.579	53.15	169.332
50.20	179.283	51.20	175.781	52.20	172.414	53.20	169.173
50.25	179.104	51.25	175.610	52.25	172.249	53.25	169.014
50.30	178.926	51.30	175.439	52.30	172.084	53.30	168.856
50.35	178.749	51.35	175.268	52.35	171.920	53.35	168.697
50.40	178.571	51.40	175.097	52.40	171.756	53.40	168.539
50.45	178.394	51.45	174.927	52.45	171.592	53.45	168.382
50.50	178.218	51.50	174.757	52.50	171.429	53.50	168.224
50.55	178.042	51.55	174.588	52.55	171.265	53.55	168.067
50.60	177.866	51.60	174.419	52.60	171.103	53.60	167.910
50.65	177.690	51.65	174.250	52.65	170.940	53.65	167.754
50.70	177.515	51.70	174.081	52.70	170.778	53.70	167.598
50.75	177.340	51.75	173.913	52.75	170.616	53.75	167.442
50.80	177.165	51.80	173.745	52.80	170.455	53.80	167.286
50.85	176.991	51.85	173.578	52.85	170.293	53.85	167.131
50.90	176.817	51.90	173.410	52.90	170.132	53.90	166.976
50.95	176.644	51.95	173.244	52.95	169.972	53.95	166.821

Top Performers

	Driver	Starts	Wins	Top Five	Top Ten	Winnings	Multiple Race Winners
1	Jeff Gordon	1	1	1	1	$613,000	None
		100%	100.00%	100.00%	100.00%		
2	Brett Bodine	1	0	1	1	$203,575	
		100%	0.00%	100.00%	100.00%		
3	Bill Elliot	1	0	1	1	$164,850	
		100%	0.00%	100.00%	100.00%		
4	Rusty Wallace	1	0	1	1	$140,600	
		100%	0.00%	100.00%	100.00%		
5	Dale Earnhardt	1	0	1	1	$121,625	
		100%	0.00%	100.00%	100.00%		
6	Darrell Waltrip	1	0	0	1	$82,600	
		100%	0.00%	0.00%	100.00%		
7	Ken Schrader	1	0	0	1	$77,400	
		100%	0.00%	0.00%	100.00%		
8	Michael Waltrip	1	0	0	1	$72,300	
		100%	0.00%	0.00%	100.00%		
9	Todd Bodine	1	0	0	1	$63,600	
		100%	0.00%	0.00%	100.00%		
10	Morgan Shepherd	1	0	0	1	$67,350	
		100%	0.00%	0.00%	100.00%		

MARTINSVILLE SPEEDWAY

Area	Length		Banking	
Total Track	0.526	*mile*		
Front Straight	800	*feet*	0	*degrees*
Turn 1	295	*feet*	12	*degrees*
Turn 2	295	*feet*	12	*degrees*
Back Straight	800	*feet*	0	*degrees*
Turn 3	295	*feet*	12	*degrees*
Turn 4	295	*feet*	12	*degrees*

Pit Road Layout: 18 on front, -- 18 on back
First Winston Cup Race: 1956
Qualifying Record: 94.129 mph (Ted Musgrave 1994)
Fastest Race: 79.078 mph (Rusty Wallace 1993)
Slowest Race: 56.440 mph (Lee Petty 1959)

SPEED CHART

Sec.	MPH	Sec.	MPH	Sec.	MPH	Sec.	MPH
18.50	102.357	19.50	97.108	20.50	92.371	21.50	88.074
18.55	102.081	19.55	96.859	20.55	92.146	21.55	87.870
18.60	101.806	19.60	96.612	20.60	91.922	21.60	87.667
18.65	101.534	19.65	96.366	20.65	91.700	21.65	87.464
18.70	101.262	19.70	96.122	20.70	91.478	21.70	87.263
18.75	100.992	19.75	95.878	20.75	91.258	21.75	87.062
18.80	100.723	19.80	95.636	20.80	91.038	21.80	86.862
18.85	100.456	19.85	95.395	20.85	90.820	21.85	86.664
18.90	100.190	19.90	95.156	20.90	90.603	21.90	86.466
18.95	99.926	19.95	94.917	20.95	90.387	21.95	86.269
19.00	99.663	20.00	94.680	21.00	90.171	22.00	86.073
19.05	99.402	20.05	94.444	21.05	89.957	22.05	85.878
19.10	99.141	20.10	94.209	21.10	89.744	22.10	85.683
19.15	98.883	20.15	93.975	21.15	89.532	22.15	85.490
19.20	98.625	20.20	93.743	21.20	89.321	22.20	85.297
19.25	98.369	20.25	93.511	21.25	89.111	22.25	85.106
19.30	98.114	20.30	93.281	21.30	88.901	22.30	84.915
19.35	97.860	20.35	93.052	21.35	88.693	22.35	84.725
19.40	97.608	20.40	92.824	21.40	88.486	22.40	84.536
19.45	97.357	20.45	92.597	21.45	88.280	22.45	84.347

TOP PERFORMERS

	Driver	Starts	Wins	Top Five	Top Ten	Winnings
1	Darrell Waltrip	40	11	26	28	$788,180
		100%	110.00%	260.00%	280.00%	
2	Dale Earnhardt	32	5	12	17	$629,020
		100%	15.63%	37.50%	53.13%	
3	Rusty Wallace	22	4	10	12	$613,265
		100%	18.18%	45.45%	54.55%	
4	Geoff Bodine	27	4	9	10	$518,520
		100%	14.81%	33.33%	37.04%	
5	Ricky Rudd	31	2	9	14	$369,265
		100%	6.45%	29.03%	45.16%	
6	Terry Labonte	33	0	9	21	$339,760
		100%	0.00%	27.27%	63.64%	
7	Bill Elliot	24	0	2	9	$293,435
		100%	0.00%	8.33%	37.50%	
8	Mark Martin	18	1	5	11	$281,170
		100%	5.56%	27.78%	61.11%	
9	Kyle Petty	29	0	5	10	$257,640
		100%	0.00%	17.24%	34.48%	
10	Morgan Shepherd	27	1	4	6	$225,755
		100%	3.70%	14.81%	22.22%	

Multiple Race Winners

Richard Petty	15
Darrell Waltrip	11
Cale Yarborough	6
Fred Lorenzen	5
Dale Earnhardt	5
Rusty Wallace	4
Geoff Bodine	4
Harry Gant	3
Junior Johnson	2
Rex White	2
Fireball Roberts	2
Buck Baker	2
Bob Welborn	2
Bobby Isaac	2
Ricky Rudd	2

THE TRACK

Martinsville. A unique little racetrack. Great scenery around the racetrack, very well groomed. Half-mile in length. Ducks and geese abundant. A pond. It's a pretty little racetrack, pleasant surroundings. It's like a football field with curves. You have a racetrack that has asphalt straightaways and concrete corners, so you have a transition where you come off the asphalt onto the concrete. There's an abrupt transition there. The cars have a tendency to come off the racetrack a little bit and you have a tendency to get some wheel hop. There are a lot of little washboards through the corners, so the car's shocks become very important. The car has to settle in. You still have to get in hard enough to get position on people; but the car has to make the cut. Very tight corners. The car has to get in tight enough, but be free enough, to make the transition and get directional very quickly. Then you have to use a lot of throttle to get off the corner. Again, it demands a lot. If you're hooked up pretty well, it takes a lot from the motor. Takes good throttle response, good torque. The car needs to move hard off the bottom and stay hooked up. It's one of those racetracks where later in the race, brakes become a major problem. You have such a short period of time to cool the brakes that if you ride the brakes or you have to use excessive brakes, they'll heat up, glow red, and then ultimately blow the fluid; and you'll lose brakes. So it's a real driver's racetrack. Again, a short track that's ruled by the bumper. But it is absolutely a racetrack where the driver has to use enough brake to get the car in the corner as hard as he can, but not use enough brake to lose them. It's a difficult racetrack from those standpoints. Also, it changes as rubber builds up. It balls up there. You actually have strips of rubber that ball up on the racetrack and cause even more of a washboard effect. It's just a long 500 laps around Martinsville; and a lot of pushing and shoving. If you're not boogered up there, you probably haven't been in the race.

MICHIGAN MOTOR SPEEDWAY

Area	Length	Banking
Total Track	2 *miles*	
Front Straight	3600 *feet*	12 *degrees*
Turn 1	1180 *feet*	18 *degrees*
Turn 2	1180 *feet*	18 *degrees*
Back Straight	2242 *feet*	5 *degrees*
Turn 3	1180 *feet*	18 *degrees*
Turn 4	1180 *feet*	18 *degrees*

Pit Road Layout: 42 Pits - All on front
First Winston Cup Race: 1969
Qualifying Record: 181.082 mph (Geoff Bodine 1994)
Fastest Race: 157.704 mph (Rusty Wallace 1989)
Slowest Race: 107.583 mph (Richard Petty 1975)

THE TRACK

Very deceiving. Two miles long. Relatively smooth. Gradual transition into the banking -- 18 to 24 degrees. Very smooth. Very wide, both from the straightaway standpoint and the corners. Two places to race: on the bottom or way up top. You can make it work on either of those areas. The bottom seems to bog the motor down and you can't get off the corner. So running up off the bottom in Turn One and Two is the most accommodating place for the motor and the car. Up high, if you get the car working well up there and the car is free, you can make the high side work for you and gain a lot of momentum coming off the corners. You come off Turn Two; it narrows up a little bit there. You need to keep your eyes peeled there. You have to really watch because the racetrack sort of comes back in at you coming off Turn Two a little. You carry a lot of extra speed off there. So smooth you don't realize just how fast you're going. You drive down the back straightaway so smooth, and you get ready to start to turn the car on the corner there, and the banking's so gradual. It's very accommodating. It almost sucks you in. You get a false sense of security, like you really can drive this thing all the way through there wide open. You drive in there and all of a sudden you're almost in too far; and the car starts to get out from underneath you. Or, the car won't hang on and you just roll out of the throttle a little bit. Then you're back in the throttle again. You carry a lot of extra speed. Incredible feeling. Real accommodating for speed there. It's got all the things you need to go fast. It's smooth. Gradual in the transition. Everything you think about there is staying in the throttle and going fast. You can bust your butt real quick, or you slow your car down because you overdrive the racetrack. You've got to slow down to go fast. Smooth is fast. If you overdrive the car, you wait too long to get in the throttle. Being smooth, getting in a little easier, getting back on the throttle quicker is definitely the way to get around Michigan.

SPEED CHART

Sec.	MPH	Sec.	MPH	Sec.	MPH	Sec.	MPH
37.50	192.000	38.50	187.013	39.50	182.278	40.50	177.778
37.55	191.744	38.55	186.770	39.55	182.048	40.55	177.559
37.60	191.489	38.60	186.528	39.60	181.818	40.60	177.340
37.65	191.235	38.65	186.287	39.65	181.589	40.65	177.122
37.70	190.981	38.70	186.047	39.70	181.360	40.70	176.904
37.75	190.728	38.75	185.806	39.75	181.132	40.75	176.687
37.80	190.476	38.80	185.567	39.80	180.905	40.80	176.471
37.85	190.225	38.85	185.328	39.85	180.678	40.85	176.255
37.90	189.974	38.90	185.090	39.90	180.451	40.90	176.039
37.95	189.723	38.95	184.852	39.95	180.225	40.95	175.824
38.00	189.474	39.00	184.615	40.00	180.000	41.00	175.610
38.05	189.225	39.05	184.379	40.05	179.775	41.05	175.396
38.10	188.976	39.10	184.143	40.10	179.551	41.10	175.182
38.15	188.729	39.15	183.908	40.15	179.328	41.15	174.970
38.20	188.482	39.20	183.673	40.20	179.104	41.20	174.757
38.25	188.235	39.25	183.439	40.25	178.882	41.25	174.545
38.30	187.990	39.30	183.206	40.30	178.660	41.30	174.334
38.35	187.744	39.35	182.973	40.35	178.439	41.35	174.123
38.40	187.500	39.40	182.741	40.40	178.218	41.40	173.913
38.45	187.256	39.45	182.510	40.45	177.998	41.45	173.703

TOP PERFORMERS

	Driver	Starts	Wins	Top Five	Top Ten	Winnings	Multiple Race Winners	
1	Bill Elliot	35	7	15	22	$823,750	David Pearson	9
		100%	20.00%	42.86%	62.86%		Cale Yarborough	8
2	Darrell Waltrip	39	2	17	25	$656,903	Bill Elliott	7
		100%	5.13%	43.59%	64.10%		Richard Petty	4
3	Dale Earnhardt	30	2	10	19	$641,613	Bobby Allison	4
		100%	6.67%	33.33%	63.33%		Davey Allison	3
4	Rusty Wallace	22	3	11	14	$580,825	Rusty Wallace	3
		100%	13.64%	50.00%	63.64%		Darrell Waltrip	2
5	Ricky Rudd	36	1	7	17	$475,937	Dale Earnhardt	2
		100%	2.78%	19.44%	47.22%		Mark Martin	2
6	Geoff Bodine	25	1	6	11	$461,280		
		100%	4.00%	24.00%	44.00%			
7	Mark Martin	18	2	7	11	$447,355		
		100%	11.11%	38.89%	61.11%			
8	Terry Labonte	32	0	4	7	$370,735		
		100%	0.00%	12.50%	21.88%			
9	Morgan Shepherd	27	0	5	11	$362,150		
		100%	0.00%	18.52%	40.74%			
10	Kyle Petty	28	0	3	9	$346,775		
		100%	0.00%	10.71%	32.14%			

Area	Length	Banking
Total Track	1.058 *miles*	
Front Straight	1500 *feet*	0 *degrees*
Turn 1	647 *feet*	12 *degrees*
Turn 2	647 *feet*	12 *degrees*
Back Straight	1500 *feet*	5 *degrees*
Turn 3	647 *feet*	12 *degrees*
Turn 4	647 *feet*	12 *degrees*

Pit Road Layout: 42 Pits - All on front
First Winston Cup Race: 1993
Qualifying Record: 127.197 mph (Ernie Irvan 1994)
Fastest Race: 105.947 mph (Rusty Wallace 1993)
Slowest Race: 87.599 mph (Ricky Rudd 1994)

NEW HAMPSHIRE INTERNATIONAL SPEEDWAY (LOUDON)

SPEED CHART

Sec.	MPH	Sec.	MPH	Sec.	MPH	Sec.	MPH
28.00	136.029	29.00	131.338	30.00	126.960	31.00	122.865
28.05	135.786	29.05	131.112	30.05	126.749	31.05	122.667
28.10	135.544	29.10	130.887	30.10	126.538	31.10	122.469
28.15	135.304	29.15	130.662	30.15	126.328	31.15	122.273
28.20	135.064	29.20	130.438	30.20	126.119	31.20	122.077
28.25	134.825	29.25	130.215	30.25	125.911	31.25	121.882
28.30	134.587	29.30	129.993	30.30	125.703	31.30	121.687
28.35	134.349	29.35	129.772	30.35	125.496	31.35	121.493
28.40	134.113	29.40	129.551	30.40	125.289	31.40	121.299
28.45	133.877	29.45	129.331	30.45	125.084	31.45	121.107
28.50	133.642	29.50	129.112	30.50	124.879	31.50	120.914
28.55	133.408	29.55	128.893	30.55	124.674	31.55	120.723
28.60	133.175	29.60	128.676	30.60	124.471	31.60	120.532
28.65	132.942	29.65	128.459	30.65	124.268	31.65	120.341
28.70	132.711	29.70	128.242	30.70	124.065	31.70	120.151
28.75	132.480	29.75	128.027	30.75	123.863	31.75	119.962
28.80	132.250	29.80	127.812	30.80	123.662	31.80	119.774
28.85	132.021	29.85	127.598	30.85	123.462	31.85	119.586
28.90	131.792	29.90	127.385	30.90	123.262	31.90	119.398
28.95	131.565	29.95	127.172	30.95	123.063	31.95	119.211

TOP PERFORMERS

	Driver	Starts	Wins	Top Five	Top Ten	Winnings	Multiple Race Winners
1	Ricky Rudd	2	1	2	2	$117,250	None
		100%	50.00%	100.00%	100.00%		
2	Rusty Wallace	2	1	2	2	$116,475	
		100%	50.00%	100.00%	100.00%		
3	Mark Martin	2	0	2	2	$108,425	
		100%	00.00%	100.00%	100.00%		
4	Dale Earnhardt	7	0	1	1	$83,300	
		100%	00.00%	50.00%	50.00%		
5	Dale Jarrett	2	0	1	1	$57,625	
		100%	00.00%	50.00%	50.00%		
6	Ernie Irvan	2	0	0	0	$53,650	
		100%	00.00%	00.00%	00.00%		
7	Sterling Marlin	2	0	0	2	$50,675	
		100%	00.00%	00.00%	100.00%		
8	Kyle Petty	2	0	0	2	$46,675	
		100%	00.00%	00.00%	100.00%		
9	Davey Allison	1	0	1	1	$44,725	
		100%	50.00%	50.00%	50.00%		
10	Bill Elliot	2	0	0	1	$42,725	
		100%	00.00%	00.00%	50.00%		

THE TRACK

A little bit of Phoenix, a little bit of Pocono, a lot of Indianapolis. Relatively smooth. Problems with asphalt breaking up. You're hooked up so good it tears the asphalt out of the ground. Very narrow racetrack. From the standpoint of wrecks off either corners, you're gonna get collected because it's so narrow. You don't have a real escape route. Extremely flat. No real security getting in either of the corners. You gotta be able to get in the corner relatively hard. The car has to make a rapid cut to get directional again; and you drive back to the very bottom of the racetrack. The racetrack feels like its camber is the opposite way. The car lays over a great deal, like you're running on two tires. Coming off Turn Two, down the very narrow back straightaway, you carry a lot of speed. There are no real visuals for getting in the corners. Nothing to give you a feeling about when you should be in or out of the throttle. It's a "feel" thing. You really have to mind yourself getting in Turn Three. It's slick up there. Typically, oil's coming out of the racetrack. It's worn and very flat. But like Phoenix, it's almost like you're driving past a dogleg but you're not. You're still turning, getting in that corner. You almost want to drive it straight in the corner and let the car diamond the corner. Try to carry a lot of entry speed and drive straight to the top of the racetrack, almost out of the groove; and the tail of the car will swing and the car will get pointed, like a big diamond. You shoot straight back to the bottom. You're out of the gas as you get in the corner. Let the car roll. You have to carry a lot of roll speed through these corners to the top of the race track. You tap the brakes again. It acts like a pendulum. The car will swing the tail, and you're back in the throttle. You drive straight to the bottom of the racetrack and try to make it a long drag strip, all the way down that front straightaway. You can't do much in One and Two, but Three and Four are much like Phoenix, you diamond the racetrack. Get in really hard. Use up a lot of the racetrack. Get the car turned. Drive straight back to the bottom. Make it a long, long drag strip.

NORTH CAROLINA SPEEDWAY
(ROCKINGHAM)

Area	Length	Banking
Total Track	1.017 *miles*	
Front Straight	1005 *feet*	8 *degrees*
Turn 1	676 *feet*	22 *degrees*
Turn 2	676 *feet*	22 *degrees*
Back Straight	1030 *feet*	8 *degrees*
Turn 3	676 *feet*	25 *degrees*
Turn 4	676 *feet*	25 *degrees*

Pit Road Layout: 42 Pits - All on front
First Winston Cup Race: 1965
Qualifying Record: 157.099 mph (Ricky Rudd 1994)
Fastest Race: 130.748 mph (Kyle Petty 1992)
Slowest Race: 97.865 mph (Richard Petty 1977)

THE TRACK

Long, long race. Much like Dover. You feel like you're there forever. Very diverse corners. Repaved. There's an enormous amount of grip. All the asphalt was down below the rocks, so you're just dancing there after the tires give out ...very loose. Now it has grip. But, same old racetrack. Same corners. Just a facelift, much like Darlington. The track gives you a lot of different looks during the day. One of those tracks where you can move the groove up. If you get loose, you can move the groove to the top, run on the high side and be very fast. You drive down the front straight. You're banked ... away from the wall. You drive back to the wall ... set up for Turn One, trying to get as high as you can to turn the car into the corner. A flat spot in Turn One ... enter just a little wide of the flat spot or the car unloads and drives up the racetrack. You stay a little wide, you get the caught down in the bottom, it sets, and you're back in the throttle again; and you can run the bottom. A bit of a dip off Turn Two sends the car to the right. The track narrows up, comes back at you; and the wall's there. So when you're wanting to carry a lot of speed, there's a tendency for the car to drift more off that corner. You need more room, but there is none. You have to pinch the car off sometimes getting off that corner. You have to make the turn and get the car directional at the right point and not get in the gas too soon. If you throttle it too soon, the car starts to push and you run out of track. Narrow back straight. You run into Turn Three, where if you charge the corner, you're going to go up the racetrack. There's another flat spot there, and an abrupt transition in the banking -- severe banking. If you overdrive that corner, the car has a tendency to shove up the racetrack. Get out of position there and you can't get a lot of exit speed. Getting in that corner a little bit on the wide side, getting the car turned very quickly, and then running right to the bottom again. Running the bottom until you start driving up the racetrack. About the start/finish line, the wall comes back to you, and you're back up against it again, ready to go into Turn One.

SPEED CHART

Sec.	MPH	Sec.	MPH	Sec.	MPH	Sec.	MPH
22.00	166.418	23.00	159.183	24.00	152.550	25.00	146.448
22.05	166.041	23.05	158.837	24.05	152.233	25.05	146.156
22.10	165.665	23.10	158.494	24.10	151.917	25.10	145.865
22.15	165.291	23.15	158.151	24.15	151.602	25.15	145.575
22.20	164.919	23.20	157.810	24.20	151.289	25.20	145.286
22.25	164.548	23.25	157.471	24.25	150.977	25.25	144.998
22.30	164.179	23.30	157.133	24.30	150.667	25.30	144.711
22.35	163.812	23.35	156.797	24.35	150.357	25.35	144.426
22.40	163.446	23.40	156.462	24.40	150.049	25.40	144.142
22.45	163.082	23.45	156.128	24.45	149.742	25.45	143.859
22.50	162.720	23.50	155.796	24.50	149.437	25.50	143.576
22.55	162.359	23.55	155.465	24.55	149.132	25.55	143.295
22.60	162.000	23.60	155.136	24.60	148.829	25.60	143.016
22.65	161.642	23.65	154.808	24.65	148.527	25.65	142.737
22.70	161.286	23.70	154.481	24.70	148.227	25.70	142.459
22.75	160.932	23.75	154.156	24.75	147.927	25.75	142.183
22.80	160.579	23.80	153.832	24.80	147.629	25.80	141.907
22.85	160.228	23.85	153.509	24.85	147.332	25.85	141.632
22.90	159.878	23.90	153.188	24.90	147.036	25.90	141.359
22.95	159.529	23.95	152.868	24.95	146.741	25.95	141.087

TOP PERFORMERS

	Driver	Starts	Wins	Top Five	Top Ten	Winnings
1	Kyle Petty	29	3	4	11	$829,272
		100%	10.34%	13.79%	37.93%	
2	Dale Earnhardt	32	2	10	21	$640,635
		100%	6.25%	31.25%	65.63%	
3	Darrell Waltrip	44	4	19	29	$578,400
		100%	9.09%	43.18%	65.91%	
4	Bill Elliot	30	3	11	18	$530,285
		100%	10.00%	36.67%	60.00%	
5	Rusty Wallace	22	5	7	10	$496,710
		100%	22.73%	31.82%	45.45%	
6	Terry Labonte	32	2	11	18	$450,220
		100%	6.25%	34.38%	56.25%	
7	Ricky Rudd	34	0	8	12	$386,871
		100%	0.00%	23.53%	35.29%	
8	Geoff Bodine	25	0	5	10	$334,285
		100%	0.00%	20.00%	40.00%	
9	Mark Martin	17	1	6	8	$313,449
		100%	5.88%	35.29%	47.06%	
10	Ken Schrader	20	0	6	10	$298,650
		100%	0.00%	30.00%	50.00%	

Multiple Race Winners

Richard Petty	11
Cale Yarborough	7
David Pearson	5
Rusty Wallace	5
Bobby Allison	4
Darrell Waltrip	4
Donnie Allison	3
Kyle Petty	3
Neil Bonnett	2
Terry Labonte	2
Dale Earnhardt	2

Area	Length	Banking
Total Track	0.625 *mile*	
Front Straight	670 *feet*	3 *degrees*
Turn 1	490 *feet*	14 *degrees*
Turn 2	490 *feet*	14 *degrees*
Back Straight	670 *feet*	3 *degrees*
Turn 3	490 *feet*	14 *degrees*
Turn 4	490 *feet*	14 *degrees*

Pit Road Layout: 36 Pits - All on front
First Winston Cup Race: 1952
Qualifying Record: 119.016 mph (Ernie Irvan 1994)
Fastest Race: 107.360 mph (Geoff Bodine 1992)
Slowest Race: 58.590 mph (Herb Thomas 1952)

SPEED CHART

Sec.	MPH	Sec.	MPH	Sec.	MPH	Sec.	MPH
17.50	128.571	18.50	121.622	19.50	115.385	20.50	109.756
17.55	128.205	18.55	121.294	19.55	115.090	20.55	109.489
17.60	127.841	18.60	120.968	19.60	114.796	20.60	109.223
17.65	127.479	18.65	120.643	19.65	114.504	20.65	108.959
17.70	127.119	18.70	120.321	19.70	114.213	20.70	108.696
17.75	126.761	18.75	120.000	19.75	113.924	20.75	108.434
17.80	126.404	18.80	119.681	19.80	113.636	20.80	108.173
17.85	126.050	18.85	119.363	19.85	113.350	20.85	107.914
17.90	125.698	18.90	119.048	19.90	113.065	20.90	107.656
17.95	125.348	18.95	118.734	19.95	112.782	20.95	107.399
18.00	125.000	19.00	118.421	20.00	112.500	21.00	107.143
18.05	124.654	19.05	118.110	20.05	112.219	21.05	106.888
18.10	124.309	19.10	117.801	20.10	111.940	21.10	106.635
18.15	123.967	19.15	117.493	20.15	111.663	21.15	106.383
18.20	123.626	19.20	117.187	20.20	111.386	21.20	106.132
18.25	123.288	19.25	116.883	20.25	111.111	21.25	105.882
18.30	122.951	19.30	116.580	20.30	110.837	21.30	105.634
18.35	122.616	19.35	116.279	20.35	110.565	21.35	105.386
18.40	122.283	19.40	115.979	20.40	110.294	21.40	105.140
18.45	121.951	19.45	115.681	20.45	110.024	21.45	104.895

TOP PERFORMERS

	Driver	Starts	Wins	Top Five	Top Ten	Winnings	Multiple Race Winners	
1	Dale Earnhardt	32 / 100%	4 / 12.50%	18 / 56.25%	27 / 84.38%	$657,970	Richard Petty	15
2	Darrell Waltrip	41 / 100%	10 / 24.39%	19 / 46.34%	25 / 60.98%	$613,649	Darrell Waltrip	10
3	Terry Labonte	32 / 100%	3 / 9.38%	12 / 37.50%	24 / 75.00%	$490,765	Cale Yarborough	5
4	Geoff Bodine	26 / 100%	3 / 11.54%	12 / 46.15%	16 / 61.54%	$454,920	Dale Earnhardt	4
5	Rusty Wallace	22 / 100%	3 / 13.64%	10 / 45.45%	18 / 81.82%	$386,120	Bobby Allison	4
6	Ricky Rudd	32 / 100%	0 / 0.00%	10 / 31.25%	21 / 65.63%	$315,415	Rusty Wallace	3
7	Bill Elliot	24 / 100%	0 / 0.00%	4 / 16.67%	14 / 58.33%	$297,490	Terry Labonte	3
8	Mark Martin	18 / 100%	1 / 5.56%	6 / 33.33%	9 / 50.00%	$283,666	Geoff Bodine	3
9	Kyle Petty	28 / 100%	0 / 0.00%	7 / 25.00%	13 / 46.43%	$279,115	David Pearson	2
10	Ken Schrader	21 / 100%	0 / 0.00%	3 / 14.29%	7 / 33.33%	$215,375	Junior Johnson	2
							Rex White	2
							Marvin Panch	2

THE TRACK

Short track that has seen a lot of use. Needs to be repaved. It's different, because it goes uphill, down the back chute, and down hill on the front straightaway. So there's an elevation change. The racetrack is worn out. Very hard to get grip. Washboards in Turns Three and Four on the racetrack itself, so the car does not settle down on the springs or shocks very well. You drive down the front straightaway there. You're carrying a lot of speed going into the corner. Then as you get to the bottom, it starts to flatten out. And once it flattens out, the racecar wants to get free and loose. But all of a sudden the banking is back there again. You have to make a very quick transition, and make a very sharp turn back to the left and start going uphill. The racetrack sort of leaves you a little bit coming off that corner; and there's just no grip. You're driving back up hill. Your motor just sort of grunts itself back up that hill. You get ready to go into Turn Three. You have to carry a bit of a wide arc in that corner again, because it's a tight corner and you need to make that great transitional move right in the middle; and get directional again. The washboards are there making the car upset. The car doesn't feel like it's really settled in the racetrack. You're trying to apply throttle, and it's bouncing. It just doesn't give you a lot of good feedback that the car is actually underneath you. You're slipping and sliding; and after five or six laps on the tires, you're starting to lose adhesion coming off the corner. Then you're driving downhill; and the car just slides as it comes off Turn Four. It heads out to the wall and you're going downhill again; and you're getting ready to go back in Turn One. It's a very difficult racetrack.

PHOENIX INTERNATIONAL RACEWAY

Area	Length	Banking
Total Track	1 *mile*	
Front Straight	1179 *feet*	0 *degrees*
Turn 1	637.5 *feet*	11 *degrees*
Turn 2	637.5 *feet*	11 *degrees*
Back Straight	1551 *feet*	0 *degrees*
Turn 3	637.5 *feet*	9 *degrees*
Turn 4	637.5 *feet*	9 *degrees*

Pit Road Layout: 42 Pits - All on front
First Winston Cup Race: 1988
Qualifying Record: 129.833 mph (Sterling Marlin 1994)
Fastest Race: 107.463 mph (Terry Labonte 1994)
Slowest Race: 90.457 mph (Alan Kulwicki 1988)

THE TRACK

Phoenix is a very flat racetrack which has a little banking in Turns One and Two. Two diverse corners. Down the front straightaway, it's very narrow. Not a lot of escape routes. The wall carries all the way down in. A very tough racetrack from the standpoint of the sun late in the day. You can't see the corner. You have to guess going in Turn One late in the day because the windshields are so bad. The sun is in your eyes. You really don't see the corner. You kind of get a feel for it. You drive in just a little on the wide side; let the car settle in, get down on the springs. Then it's almost a deal where you apply the throttle to let the car drift itself out to the wall. You almost leave the bottom of the racetrack and drive for the outer portion of the wall. You get a lot of exit speed there. Then if you get the right turn off of Turn Two, you're almost straight to go through the dogleg without a turn of the wheel. You just come off there, you hardly turn the wheel, and you go through an actual dogleg and it just sends you out to the outer edge of the racetrack again. If you miss that corner and come off low, you have to turn back, and scrub some speed. If you hit it right, it's almost effortless coming off Turn Two from the dogleg. Then you're set up for Turn Three. Drive the car in the corner hard, drive up on the flat apron portion a little bit. Hang the left front tire on the apron and drive straight through and aim as straight as possible for the center portion of the wall. Drive right through the groove. As soon as the car carries all that speed to the point in the middle of the racetrack where you can get the car directional, you get on the brakes a little bit. The car gets a pendulum effect and drives straight back to the bottom again, almost nipping the apron coming off Turn Four. The car drifts and carries you out to the wall and the front straightaway -- the only straight portion of the racetrack.

SPEED CHART

Sec.	MPH	Sec.	MPH	Sec.	MPH	Sec.	MPH
26.00	138.462	27.00	133.333	28.00	128.571	29.00	124.138
26.05	138.196	27.05	133.087	28.05	128.342	29.05	123.924
26.10	137.931	27.10	132.841	28.10	128.114	29.10	123.711
26.15	137.667	27.15	132.597	28.15	127.886	29.15	123.499
26.20	137.405	27.20	132.353	28.20	127.660	29.20	123.288
26.25	137.143	27.25	132.110	28.25	127.434	29.25	123.077
26.30	136.882	27.30	131.868	28.30	127.208	29.30	122.867
26.35	136.622	27.35	131.627	28.35	126.984	29.35	122.658
26.40	136.364	27.40	131.387	28.40	126.761	29.40	122.449
26.45	136.106	27.45	131.148	28.45	126.538	29.45	122.241
26.50	135.849	27.50	130.909	28.50	126.316	29.50	122.034
26.55	135.593	27.55	130.672	28.55	126.095	29.55	121.827
26.60	135.338	27.60	130.435	28.60	125.874	29.60	121.622
26.65	135.084	27.65	130.199	28.65	125.654	29.65	121.417
26.70	134.831	27.70	129.964	28.70	125.436	29.70	121.212
26.75	134.579	27.75	129.730	28.75	125.217	29.75	121.008
26.80	134.328	27.80	129.496	28.80	125.000	29.80	120.805
26.85	134.078	27.85	129.264	28.85	124.783	29.85	120.603
26.90	133.829	27.90	129.032	28.90	124.567	29.90	120.401
26.95	133.581	27.95	128.801	28.95	124.352	29.95	120.200

TOP PERFORMERS

	Driver	Starts	Wins	Top Five	Top Ten	Winnings	Multiple Race Winners	
1	Mark Martin	7	1	4	5	$209,250	Davey Allison	2
		100%	14.29%	57.14%	71.43%			
2	Dale Earnhardt	7	1	2	5	$193,320		
		100%	14.29%	28.57%	71.43%			
3	Terry Labonte	7	1	3	3	$176,075		
		100%	14.29%	42.86%	42.86%			
4	Bill Elliot	7	1	4	4	$171,575		
		100%	14.29%	57.14%	57.14%			
5	Darrell Waltrip	7	0	4	6	$163,285		
		100%	0.00%	57.14%	85.71%			
6	Rusty Wallace	7	0	2	2	$130,245		
		100%	0.00%	28.57%	28.57%			
7	Sterling Marlin	7	0	2	4	$114,665		
		100%	0.00%	28.57%	57.14%			
8	Ken Schrader	7	0	1	2	$110,600		
		100%	0.00%	14.29%	28.57%			
9	Geoff Bodine	7	0	0	4	$101,035		
		100%	0.00%	0.00%	57.14%			
10	Ricky Rudd	7	0	0	2	$100,800		
		100%	0.00%	0.00%	28.57%			

POCONO RACEWAY

Area	Length	Banking
Total Track	2.5 *miles*	
Front Straight	3740 *feet*	0 *degrees*
Turn 1	NA	14 *degrees*
Long Pond Straight	3055 *feet*	8 *degrees*
Turn 2	NA	6 *degrees*
North Straight	1780 *feet*	0 *degrees*

Pit Road Layout: 42 Pits - All on front
First Winston Cup Race: 1974
Qualifying Record: 164.558 mph (Rusty Wallace 1994)
Fastest Race: 142.540 mph (Darrell Waltrip 1978)
Slowest Race: 111.179 mph (David Pearson 1975)

SPEED CHART

Sec.	MPH	Sec.	MPH	Sec.	MPH	Sec.	MPH
53.00	169.811	54.00	166.667	55.00	163.636	56.00	160.714
53.05	169.651	54.05	166.512	55.05	163.488	56.05	160.571
53.10	169.492	54.10	166.359	55.10	163.339	56.10	160.428
53.15	169.332	54.15	166.205	55.15	163.191	56.15	160.285
53.20	169.173	54.20	166.052	55.20	163.043	56.20	160.142
53.25	169.014	54.25	165.899	55.25	162.896	56.25	160.000
53.30	168.856	54.30	165.746	55.30	162.749	56.30	159.858
53.35	168.697	54.35	165.593	55.35	162.602	56.35	159.716
53.40	168.539	54.40	165.441	55.40	162.455	56.40	159.574
53.45	168.382	54.45	165.289	55.45	162.308	56.45	159.433
53.50	168.224	54.50	165.138	55.50	162.162	56.50	159.292
53.55	168.067	54.55	164.986	55.55	162.016	56.55	159.151
53.60	167.910	54.60	164.835	55.60	161.871	56.60	159.011
53.65	167.754	54.65	164.684	55.65	161.725	56.65	158.870
53.70	167.598	54.70	164.534	55.70	161.580	56.70	158.730
53.75	167.442	54.75	164.384	55.75	161.435	56.75	158.590
53.80	167.286	54.80	164.234	55.80	161.290	56.80	158.451
53.85	167.131	54.85	164.084	55.85	161.146	56.85	158.311
53.90	166.976	54.90	163.934	55.90	161.002	56.90	158.172
53.95	166.821	54.95	163.785	55.95	160.858	56.95	158.033

TOP PERFORMERS

	Driver	Starts	Wins	Top Five	Top Ten	Winnings
1	Dale Earnhardt	29	2	9	15	$581,055
		100%	6.90%	31.03%	51.72%	
2	Darrell Waltrip	33	4	12	18	$568,085
		100%	12.12%	36.36%	54.55%	
3	Geoff Bodine	26	3	10	13	$551,520
		100%	11.54%	38.46%	50.00%	
4	Bill Elliot	25	5	11	17	$533,205
		100%	20.00%	44.00%	68.00%	
5	Rusty Wallace	21	2	7	10	$469,477
		100%	9.52%	33.33%	47.62%	
6	Terry Labonte	29	1	5	12	$376,882
		100%	3.45%	17.24%	41.38%	
7	Ken Schrader	20	0	5	10	$356,165
		100%	0.00%	25.00%	50.00%	
8	Ricky Rudd	31	0	4	15	$334,195
		100%	0.00%	12.90%	48.39%	
9	Mark Martin	16	0	6	10	$323,725
		100%	0.00%	37.50%	62.50%	
10	Kyle Petty	25	1	2	11	$317,095
		100%	4.00%	8.00%	44.00%	

Multiple Race Winners

Multiple Race Winners	
Darrell Waltrip	4
Tim Richmond	4
Bill Elliot	4
Bobby Allison	3
Geoff Bodine	3
Richard Petty	2
Harry Gant	2
Dale Earnhardt	2
Cale Yarborough	2
Rusty Wallace	2

THE TRACK

A really different race track, like no other. Long, flat and fast. Some say it's not a circle track but a road course with only left hand turns.

The front straight is long (over seven tenths of a mile) and wide. Cars can easily run five or six abreast with room to spare; however someone has to give up the ghost going into the turns because the groove narrows and it becomes difficult to run even two abreast. The best place to be is on the bottom of the track in the turns. Very hard to pass on the outside. If you are caught on the outside you really have to be careful with the throttle because the track has so little banking it wants to throw the car to the wall. Even though there is still a lot of track on the outside of the turns it's not raceable, especially later in the race as loose rubber and other debris accumulate. If you get high in the turn look out, it may be a very nasty ride.

The speeds are so fast at Pocono a driver has to stay on his toes. Although it is the type of track where you can have a bad lap and recover and really nail the next one. Good visual references going into the turns to time braking. Some drivers set up the car to run the entire track in fourth gear, but most drivers prefer to shift to third for the turns and use fourth down the straights. The track looks really smooth when watching cars race but there are some rough areas where the car really bounces around.

RICHMOND INTERNATIONAL RACEWAY

Area	Length	Banking
Total Track	0.75 *mile*	
Front Straight	*NA*	8 *degrees*
Turn 1	*NA*	14 *degrees*
Turn 2	*NA*	14 *degrees*
Back Straight	860 *feet*	2 *degrees*
Turn 3	*NA*	14 *degrees*
Turn 4	*NA*	14 *degrees*

Pit Road Layout: 42 Pits - All on front
First Winston Cup Race: 1959
Qualifying Record: 124.520 mph (Ted Musgrave 1994)
Fastest Race: 107.709 mph (Davey Allison 1993)
Slowest Race: 51.360 mph (Rex White 1962)

THE TRACK

A very difficult racetrack. Unique. Two different corners. Much like Phoenix. You're always turning there. Except for down the back straightaway. Always in a turn. You're always laying over, running on the right side of the tires. You drive down the front straightaway, and you're turning all the way. It's a big arc. You're banked there. Then you drive into Turn One carrying an enormous amount of speed. The racetrack flattens out, and the car gets exceptionally loose getting in the corner. The corner's so tight. The car has to be free to make the cut. You have to stay wide entering that corner; and then make a late apex there. The car has to be tight enough to do that, but then make the cut and get directional extremely late. You carry a real straight run off Turn Two down the back straightaway. Very short back straightaway. Gives you just enough time to get up some momentum; and you have to stay kind of wide getting in Turn Three again. There's an apron there; and you can drop it on the apron. But if you stay wide just a little bit and the car gets a great turn at that point, it gives you a straighter run off. You have the wall peeking at you coming off Turn Four; and you aim right for the edge of that wall; and you're right on the bottom of the racetrack. Then the racetrack just goes away from you because of the big arc. You're trying to carry so much exit speed that the car just wants to drift out there. To keep it tight, you're applying throttle and turning to the right. The car gets loose coming off that corner; and you just try to use up all the racetrack you can. You use as much power as you can until you run out of room; and there's the wall and you just carry that wall all the way around down past the flag stand. Then you start leaving the wall and start setting up for going back into Turn One. A very difficult racetrack.

SPEED CHART

Sec.	MPH	Sec.	MPH	Sec.	MPH	Sec.	MPH
20.50	131.707	21.50	125.581	22.50	120.000	23.50	114.894
20.55	131.387	21.55	125.290	22.55	119.734	23.55	114.650
20.60	131.068	21.60	125.000	22.60	119.469	23.60	114.407
20.65	130.751	21.65	124.711	22.65	119.205	23.65	114.165
20.70	130.435	21.70	124.424	22.70	118.943	23.70	113.924
20.75	130.120	21.75	124.138	22.75	118.681	23.75	113.684
20.80	129.808	21.80	123.853	22.80	118.421	23.80	113.445
20.85	129.496	21.85	123.570	22.85	118.162	23.85	113.208
20.90	129.187	21.90	123.288	22.90	117.904	23.90	112.971
20.95	128.878	21.95	123.007	22.95	117.647	23.95	112.735
21.00	128.571	22.00	122.727	23.00	117.391	24.00	112.500
21.05	128.266	22.05	122.449	23.05	117.137	24.05	112.266
21.10	127.962	22.10	122.172	23.10	116.883	24.10	112.033
21.15	127.660	22.15	121.896	23.15	116.631	24.15	111.801
21.20	127.358	22.20	121.622	23.20	116.379	24.20	111.570
21.25	127.059	22.25	121.348	23.25	116.129	24.25	111.340
21.30	126.761	22.30	121.076	23.30	115.880	24.30	111.111
21.35	126.464	22.35	120.805	23.35	115.632	24.35	110.883
21.40	126.168	22.40	120.536	23.40	115.385	24.40	110.656
21.45	125.874	22.45	120.267	23.45	115.139	24.45	110.429

TOP PERFORMERS

	Driver	Starts	Wins	Top Five	Top Ten	Winnings
1	Dale Earnhardt	32	5	22	27	$743,620
		100%	15.63%	68.75%	84.38%	
2	Bill Elliot	22	1	8	13	$597,250
		100%	4.55%	36.36%	59.09%	
3	Darrell Waltrip	41	6	22	32	$586,037
		100%	14.63%	53.66%	78.05%	
4	Rusty Wallace	22	4	11	13	$478,375
		100%	18.18%	50.00%	59.09%	
5	Ricky Rudd	32	1	15	18	$443,345
		100%	3.13%	46.88%	56.25%	
6	Terry Labonte	33	1	8	19	$345,325
		100%	3.03%	24.24%	57.58%	
7	Mark Martin	18	1	4	10	$301,035
		100%	5.56%	22.22%	55.56%	
8	Geoff Bodine	24	0	5	10	$277,625
		100%	0.00%	20.83%	41.67%	
9	Kyle Petty	27	1	3	10	$258,115
		100%	3.70%	11.11%	37.04%	
10	Ernie Irvan	12	1	2	3	$194,110
		100%	8.33%	16.67%	25.00%	

Multiple Race Winners

Richard Petty	13
Bobby Allison	7
David Pearson	6
Darrell Waltrip	6
Dale Earnhardt	5
Rusty Wallace	4
Cale Yarborough	3
Joe Weatherly	3
Davey Allison	2
Neil Bonnett	2
Benny Parsons	2
Dave Marcis	2

SEARS POINT RACEWAY (SONOMA)

Total Track: *2.52 miles*
Road Course
11 Turns of various lengths and banking.

Pit Road Layout: 36 on front straight, 6 on back.
First Winston Cup Race: 1989
Qualifying Record: 91.838 mph (Dale Earnhardt 1993)
Fastest Race: 81.42 mph (Ernie Irvan 1992)
Slowest Race: 69.245 mph (Rusty Wallace 1990)

SPEED CHART

Sec.	MPH	Sec.	MPH	Sec.	MPH	Sec.	MPH
91.00	.... 98.901	92.00	.... 97.826	93.00	.... 96.774	94.00	.... 95.745
91.05	.... 98.847	92.05	.... 97.773	93.05	.... 96.722	94.05	.... 95.694
91.10	.... 98.793	92.10	.... 97.720	93.10	.... 96.670	94.10	.... 95.643
91.15	.... 98.738	92.15	.... 97.667	93.15	.... 96.618	94.15	.... 95.592
91.20	.... 98.684	92.20	.... 97.614	93.20	.... 96.567	94.20	.... 95.541
91.25	.... 98.630	92.25	.... 97.561	93.25	.... 96.515	94.25	.... 95.491
91.30	.... 98.576	92.30	.... 97.508	93.30	.... 96.463	94.30	.... 95.440
91.35	.... 98.522	92.35	.... 97.455	93.35	.... 96.411	94.35	.... 95.390
91.40	.... 98.468	92.40	.... 97.403	93.40	.... 96.360	94.40	.... 95.339
91.45	.... 98.414	92.45	.... 97.350	93.45	.... 96.308	94.45	.... 95.289
91.50	.... 98.361	92.50	.... 97.297	93.50	.... 96.257	94.50	.... 95.238
91.55	.... 98.307	92.55	.... 97.245	93.55	.... 96.205	94.55	.... 95.188
91.60	.... 98.253	92.60	.... 97.192	93.60	.... 96.154	94.60	.... 95.137
91.65	.... 98.200	92.65	.... 97.140	93.65	.... 96.103	94.65	.... 95.087
91.70	.... 98.146	92.70	.... 97.087	93.70	.... 96.051	94.70	.... 95.037
91.75	.... 98.093	92.75	.... 97.035	93.75	.... 96.000	94.75	.... 94.987
91.80	.... 98.039	92.80	.... 96.983	93.80	.... 95.949	94.80	.... 94.937
91.85	.... 97.986	92.85	.... 96.931	93.85	.... 95.898	94.85	.... 94.887
91.90	.... 97.933	92.90	.... 96.878	93.90	.... 95.847	94.90	.... 94.837
91.95	.... 97.879	92.95	.... 96.826	93.95	.... 95.796	94.95	.... 94.787

TOP PERFORMERS

	Driver	Starts	Wins	Top Five	Top Ten	Winnings	Multiple Race Winners	
1	Ernie Irvan	6	2	4	5	$218,335	Ernie Irvan	2
		100%	33.33%	66.67%	83.33%			
2	Rusty Wallace	6	1	4	5	$202,995		
		100%	16.67%	66.67%	83.33%			
3	Ricky Rudd	6	1	5	5	$197,445		
		100%	16.67%	83.33%	83.33%			
4	Geoff Bodine	6	1	3	5	$167,485		
		100%	16.67%	50.00%	83.33%			
5	Dale Earnhardt	6	0	2	5	$140,325		
		100%	0.00%	33.33%	83.33%			
6	Mark Martin	6	0	2	4	$125,240		
		100%	0.00%	33.33%	66.67%			
7	Bill Elliot	6	0	2	2	$118,390		
		100%	0.00%	33.33%	33.33%			
8	Terry Labonte	6	0	1	2	$102,390		
		100%	0.00%	16.67%	33.33%			
9	Ken Schrader	6	0	2	4	$95,515		
		100%	0.00%	33.33%	66.67%			
10	Morgan Shepherd	6	0	0	2	$78,215		
		100%	0.00%	0.00%	33.33%			

THE TRACK

Probably one of the most difficult road courses or racetracks that you'll go to, period. Gives you probably the most looks from a driver's standpoint, and probably the most difficult from a compromise in the chassis because of so many different corners. By the time you get to the start/finish line, you're already set up to turn left to a short chute, which is kind of like a dog-leg left, and you take a left turn there and it's got kind of a little bit of a dip and then you start driving up the hill, kind of an incline. You're carrying an enormous amount of speed there. The car wants to lay over on the right rear spring exceptionally hard at that point. You want to drive that car back to the left, but the car is laid over so hard it doesn't really want to make that transition. You've either got to brake there a little bit or shift gears at that point and then drive the car back to the left and drive up over the ribbons or the speed bumps that they've got there. Depends on the driver's style. Some guys like to drive all way up that thing in third gear. Some hit fourth gear down the start/finish line. A lot of guys want to carry all the way up there in fourth gear and drive all the way up that hill and just brake and try to get that car turned and back on the throttle back up the top of that hill. You hit two speed bumps and then all of a sudden it's a sharp right hand turn at the top of that hill. You can drive all the way up in there and use an excessive amount of brake and downshift from fourth to second, with the car laid over to the left. Carrying a lot of speed up in there sometimes is detrimental because you don't get off that corner, and you need to get off that corner exceptionally well. So if you can get in there a little bit easier and have the car set back where you're in second gear, then you're ready to apply throttle. You want to give up getting in that corner a little bit to get off that corner. It falls off to the left there, almost off-cambered at that point, so you need get off there fairly straight. If the car slides off the racetrack you lose a lot of exit speed. And if you get off

Continued on page 4.20

TALLADEGA
SUPERSPEEDWAY

Area	Length	Banking
Total Track	2.66 *miles*	
Front Straight	4300 *feet*	18 *degrees*
Turn 1	1437 *feet*	33 *degrees*
Turn 2	1437 *feet*	33 *degrees*
Back Straight	4000 *feet*	0 *degrees*
Turn 3	1437 *feet*	33 *degrees*
Turn 4	1437 *feet*	33 *degrees*

Pit Road Layout: 42 Pits - All on front
First Winston Cup Race: 1969
Qualifying Record: 212.809 mph (Bill Elliot 1987)
Fastest Race: 186.288 mph (Bill Elliot 1985)
Slowest Race: 130.220 mph (David Pearson 1974)

THE TRACK

It's one of those racetracks that can lull you to sleep. It can reach out and wake you right up. The transition and the banking are very gradual. Relatively smooth. Makes you feel like you're not going as fast as you are. But when you have a problem and things happen, you realize just how fast you are going. Good escape routes from problems. If someone has a problem, you can get out of the way, or you can have time to gather the car up. It's an incredible feeling in the draft here. You're nose to tail. The start/finish line is down past the trioval not like Daytona where it's in the center of the trioval. You're on a flat spot at that point taking the green flag, and you stay up by the wall, and carry the wall going into Turn One. You have a tendency to want to turn the car off in the corner early, but you want to stay up and make a gradual descent to the corner. It feels like a descent, and once you do that it's just a slow progression of the banking taking hold of the car, and when you stay out just a little bit wide it actually turns the car to the bottom of the corner for you. Very little work to turn the car to the corner; the car almost wants to drive itself here. Very smooth down the back straightaway. Same deal; hold your line. Start trying to turn your car in the corner a little bit later than you would like to. Using the banking to help turn the car into the corner keeps your momentum up. Keep the car turning and carry the speed and it almost pushes you around to the bottom of the corner. A few little dips down there. And just a smooth turn-off there onto the front straightaway. Stay up by the wall again; make that later turn again into the trioval. Very smooth. The cars will get loose and free through there when you're traveling at speeds. Drive to the bottom and let the car drive itself, back out of the corner. And at that point you finish the lap. Never, never get out of the throttle. Never lift.

SPEED CHART

Sec.	MPH	Sec.	MPH	Sec.	MPH	Sec.	MPH
47.00	.... 203.745	48.00	.... 199.500	49.00	.... 195.429	50.00	.... 191.520
47.05	.... 203.528	48.05	.... 199.292	49.05	.... 195.229	50.05	.... 191.329
47.10	.... 203.312	48.10	.... 199.085	49.10	.... 195.031	50.10	.... 191.138
47.15	.... 203.097	48.15	.... 198.879	49.15	.... 194.832	50.15	.... 190.947
47.20	.... 202.881	48.20	.... 198.672	49.20	.... 194.634	50.20	.... 190.757
47.25	.... 202.667	48.25	.... 198.466	49.25	.... 194.437	50.25	.... 190.567
47.30	.... 202.452	48.30	.... 198.261	49.30	.... 194.239	50.30	.... 190.378
47.35	.... 202.239	48.35	.... 198.056	49.35	.... 194.043	50.35	.... 190.189
47.40	.... 202.025	48.40	.... 197.851	49.40	.... 193.846	50.40	.... 190.000
47.45	.... 201.812	48.45	.... 197.647	49.45	.... 193.650	50.45	.... 189.812
47.50	.... 201.600	48.50	.... 197.443	49.50	.... 193.455	50.50	.... 189.624
47.55	.... 201.388	48.55	.... 197.240	49.55	.... 193.259	50.55	.... 189.436
47.60	.... 201.176	48.60	.... 197.037	49.60	.... 193.065	50.60	.... 189.249
47.65	.... 200.965	48.65	.... 196.835	49.65	.... 192.870	50.65	.... 189.062
47.70	.... 200.755	48.70	.... 196.632	49.70	.... 192.676	50.70	.... 188.876
47.75	.... 200.545	48.75	.... 196.431	49.75	.... 192.482	50.75	.... 188.690
47.80	.... 200.335	48.80	.... 196.230	49.80	.... 192.289	50.80	.... 188.504
47.85	.... 200.125	48.85	.... 196.029	49.85	.... 192.096	50.85	.... 188.319
47.90	.... 199.916	48.90	.... 195.828	49.90	.... 191.904	50.90	.... 188.134
47.95	.... 199.708	48.95	.... 195.628	49.95	.... 191.712	50.95	.... 187.949

TOP PERFORMERS

	Driver	Starts	Wins	Top Five	Top Ten	Winnings	Multiple Race Winners	
1	Dale Earnhardt	32	7	16	20	$1,183,835	Dale Earnhardt	7
		100%	21.88%	50.00%	62.50%		Darrell Waltrip	4
2	Bill Elliot	36	2	9	19	$744,667	Buddy Baker	4
		100%	5.56%	25.00%	52.78%		Bobby Allison	4
3	Darrell Waltrip	44	4	13	17	$743,850	Davey Allison	3
		100%	9.09%	29.55%	38.64%		David Pearson	3
4	Terry Labonte	32	1	8	15	$565,067	Cale Yarborough	3
		100%	3.13%	25.00%	46.88%		Donnie Allison	2
5	Ernie Irvan	14	2	7	8	$467,705	Pete Hamilton	2
		100%	14.29%	50.00%	57.14%		Richard Petty	2
6	Ricky Rudd	36	0	8	11	$420,041	Bill Elliot	2
		100%	0.00%	22.22%	30.56%		Ernie Irvan	2
7	Kyle Petty	28	0	4	14	$400,805		
		100%	0.00%	14.29%	50.00%			
8	Sterling Marlin	23	0	7	10	$393,410		
		100%	0.00%	30.43%	43.48%			
9	Mark Martin	18	0	5	11	$393,410		
		100%	0.00%	27.78%	61.11%			
10	Geoff Bodine	26	0	2	4	$390,205		
		100%	0.00%	7.69%	15.38%			

WATKINS GLEN
INTERNATIONAL

Total Track: 2.454 *miles*

Road Course

11 Turns of various lengths, and banking from 6 to 10 degrees.

Front Straight: 2150 *feet*
Back Straight: 2600 *feet*

Pit Road Layout: 40 on front straight.
First Winston Cup Race: 1957
Qualifying Record: 119.118 mph (Mark Martin 1993)
Fastest Race: 98.752 mph (Mark Martin 1994)
Slowest Race: 74.096 mph (Ricky Rudd 1988)

SPEED CHART

Sec.	MPH	Sec.	MPH	Sec.	MPH	Sec.	MPH
73.00	120.822	74.00	119.189	75.00	117.600	76.00	116.053
73.05	120.739	74.05	119.109	75.05	117.522	76.05	115.976
73.10	120.657	74.10	119.028	75.10	117.443	76.10	115.900
73.15	120.574	74.15	118.948	75.15	117.365	76.15	115.824
73.20	120.492	74.20	118.868	75.20	117.287	76.20	115.748
73.25	120.410	74.25	118.788	75.25	117.209	76.25	115.672
73.30	120.327	74.30	118.708	75.30	117.131	76.30	115.596
73.35	120.245	74.35	118.628	75.35	117.054	76.35	115.521
73.40	120.163	74.40	118.548	75.40	116.976	76.40	115.445
73.45	120.082	74.45	118.469	75.45	116.899	76.45	115.370
73.50	120.000	74.50	118.389	75.50	116.821	76.50	115.294
73.55	119.918	74.55	118.310	75.55	116.744	76.55	115.219
73.60	119.837	74.60	118.231	75.60	116.667	76.60	115.144
73.65	119.756	74.65	118.151	75.65	116.590	76.65	115.068
73.70	119.674	74.70	118.072	75.70	116.513	76.70	114.993
73.75	119.593	74.75	117.993	75.75	116.436	76.75	114.919
73.80	119.512	74.80	117.914	75.80	116.359	76.80	114.844
73.85	119.431	74.85	117.836	75.85	116.282	76.85	114.769
73.90	119.350	74.90	117.757	75.90	116.206	76.90	114.694
73.95	119.270	74.95	117.678	75.95	116.129	76.95	114.620

TOP PERFORMERS

	Driver	Starts	Wins	Top Five	Top Ten	Winnings	Multiple Race Winners	
1	Mark Martin	7	2	6	6	$367,240	Rusty Wallace	2
		100%	28.57%	85.71%	85.71%		Ricky Rudd	2
2	Rusty Wallace	9	2	4	6	$244,140		
		100%	22.22%	44.44%	66.67%			
3	Ricky Rudd	9	2	5	6	$231,505		
		100%	22.22%	55.56%	66.67%			
4	Dale Earnhardt	9	0	3	7	$213,030		
		100%	0.00%	33.33%	77.78%			
5	Ernie Irvan	7	1	3	3	$170,440		
		100%	14.29%	42.86%	42.86%			
6	Bill Elliot	9	0	3	4	$158,685		
		100%	0.00%	33.33%	44.44%			
7	Morgan Shepherd	9	0	1	4	$144,715		
		100%	0.00%	11.11%	44.44%			
8	Terry Labonte	9	0	1	3	$133,280		
		100%	0.00%	11.11%	33.33%			
9	Kyle Petty	7	1	1	2	$127,665		
		100%	14.29%	14.29%	28.57%			
10	Darrell Waltrip	8	0	1	3	$123,845		
		100%	0.00%	12.50%	37.50%			

THE TRACK

Another very difficult race track, much like Sonoma. Not as many turns but an exceptionally fast racetrack, gives you an enormous sensation of speed. You come take the checkered flag down that front, very narrow racetrack. It narrows up going into turn one, descends downhill going into the first turn. A tendency to have a braking problem there again, because of the weight-load transition. All the weight goes forward in the car and it gets up on its haunches going in the corner. You have to make two shifts from fourth to second gear going downhill, and a very abrupt right-hand turn at that point, then you slide up a little bit of banking in that corner on to some very washboardy fields up on some ribbons again --- these ribbons are not solid but are like washboards and they've got cuts in them, so it's like a washboard effect. And you run up over these ribbons and you're down and you're staying in a straight line and you're driving down this short chute. About that time you get in second gear there and get to the end of that corner there with the stands on your left --- and again you have to make a late corner there, carrying a lot of speed --- you shift to third gear about that point. The car makes a very tight turn to the right; the car is laid over on the right and wants to get loose there. You're driving up a hill at that point and you have to make the transition of the car getting directional and turn back to the left. You have an abrupt left-hand turn at the top of that hill, and you carry the speed bump at the top of that hill. The cars don't want to make that turn as easily as you'd like them to. You're in a drift, and you have a lot of forces against you at that point. You're laid over in the seat, your head is laid over there because you're carrying a lot of speed. You drive up to the top of that hill and the car's laid over, and you just clip that speed bump and it picks the left front tire up, over that speed bump. You'll never ever clip that speed bump if you're getting through there good, because that left front tire actually comes off of the ground and never

Continued on page 4.21

SEARS POINT (CONT.)

there straight, you drive down that little short chute, and if you're in second gear you shift to third gear and then you're getting set up for a sharp left hand turn, almost 90 degrees, back to the left. You have to get off wide to the right, because the car wants to slide on the right side tires a lot. So try to get in there a little bit easy, try to pitch the car a little bit back to the right quickly, let the car set back on the left side springs. The car will actually pick the tire off the ground there and you'll set up for a right hand turn as you going up a hill. Then you carry this hill, and you slide out to the outer portion on the left after you hit that speed bump on the right. You can see nothing. You absolutely do not know where the racetrack is. All you see is a bank and a hill and lots of campers. You go off to the left, you know, where the racetrack is, and all of a sudden it leaves you; it goes down this hill. You come up over this hill and about the time the car starts to settle back down you see the bottom of the corner. You drive down this hill and you're on the left hand portion. You have to watch out for people trying to out-brake you on the inside portion of that turn. You need to be to the left to make the really good turn in that corner. You brake getting in that corner, downshift to second gear, make a turn to the right. You cannot see the apex of the corner. You lose total sight of the speed bumps and the corner. It's a real "feel" corner, and you really have to just over-accentuate the corner and feel the bump and the car drifts back again back to the left. You carry an enormous amount of exit speed there, and you shift to third gear. You have a real fast right-hander coming up. It's tough to get the car directional. You shorten the area but it also helps the car get set and positions you for the next turn. Coming through that corner there you are carrying as much speed as you can and it just throws you to the outer portion of the racetrack. You drive up a hill and it's one of those corners getting ready for the carousel where you get to the top of this hill and if you apply the brakes too soon, it locks them up. You have to wait for the car to come back down going over the top of that carousel to apply brakes. The car is down on the chassis and then you can use the brake. If you use them too hard or if you have too much brake the car gets wheel chatter, wheel hop, and then you spin out and you go right off the end of the tire barriers. So it's a very criti-

cal corner. Again, it is blind. You drive up the hill and you're blind until you actually get the car back on the ground, so not charging that corner is crucial. It is a very slow left-hander all the way round the carousel, where you're running right on the bottom of the race track, in and out of the throttle, to keep the car trying to get turned there. The car wants to push, lay over on the right front spring and not turn. You have to use throttle, manipulate the car on the bottom of the racetrack, in and out of the throttle. When you finally get to the bottom of that hill and you drive off there flat, wide open, hit third gear, and then fourth later as you come underneath the bridge. You're going up toward a short straightaway, part of the cool down of the drag strip that you come back out on to. You kind of aim here there, and there are numbers there for shutdown. You try to carry as much speed as you can there, try to get over to the left to the end of the turn there. But you have to watch for people there driving underneath you trying to out-brake you going into that corner. In the race it's a real varied line getting in there, depending on the competition. Try to get in there wide, shift down from fourth to second, make the turn there on a sharp right hand turn, come up over the speed bump again, get over to the left side. A couple of speed bumps and guard rail all along the right hand side of you, and a drop-off. You've gone up in elevation at that point. You've got a little quick right hand turn, over a speed bump and guard rail right on your right hand side. The car gets pitched right there, and there's another sharp left hand turn, back to the left again and another speed bump on the left. Immediately you pitch the car back, and the car turns and gets directional. You carry the speed bump. You try to carry the left front tire over the entire speed bump so the right side tires almost carry the whole car. The car sets back down, you pitch the car again, another speed bump, you carry the right front tire over that entire speed bump. The car's sliding off that speed bump, and you start to descend off that hill. It's all drop-off on the right, and it's all bank and hill on your left. You come off that corner sliding, you come down the hill, you're carrying a lot of exit speed. You drive down the inner portion of the track then shift to fourth gear. Then you've got a quick, fast, sweeping left-hander. The cars want to get laid over, on the right side springs again. ∎

WATKINS GLEN (CONT.)

touches, you just carry it right over that speed bump. You come out to the edge and it's guard rail on both sides of you, and then you drive off there to the right and the car's drifting again. You exit off there and about that time you have to hit fourth gear, and the car drifts out to the edge portion and it's all grass out there so you can't drop a wheel off. You get out to the edge of that deal there and you run up this back straightaway with a guard rail on the inside away from the racetrack, just grass lining both edges of the asphalt now. You've got a varied line getting into the chicane because of people trying to out-brake you, coming up on the inside. So it's a varied line again to a narrow turn, going exceptionally fast, at the end of that straightaway in fourth gear, downshifting to second gear as you go through a very short, very slow chicane to the right, guarded by speed bumps. You make a jog to the right, hit the speed bump, quick jog back to the left again, almost like an S. Then you make another sharp left and another sharp right again into a big sweeping right-hander with a lot of speed, in second gear. You carry second gear all the way around that corner on the bottom, carrying a lot of speed, running on the bottom of the racetrack. Some guys will drive in that corner, starting wide on that corner and driving to the bottom and run the bottom all the way round. Some guys will drive in a little bit harder, carrying a lot of speed and let the car drive up the middle of the racetrack, diamond it, get a turn, drive straight back for the bottom; and you come off that corner, shift to third gear, it's up in RPM, and the car's drifting exceptionally coming off that corner, off to the edge of the racetrack where there is dirt and grass again. You hit third gear and you get straightened out going off a little bit of a short chute over a little bit of a bridge and you're in third gear there. Some guys shift to fourth at that point and some guys carry third gear and carry a lot of RPM. You come over a little bridge and you're getting ready for a sharp ninety de-

gree left-hand turn. You have to downshift from fourth to third to second. Some guys will just go from third to second, and you wind the motor out really hard there. Then it's a sharp left-hand turn---you almost pitch the car a little bit---carry over that speed bump, again carry the left front tire over that speed bump, never touch it again, and the car just drifts out to the edge portion to the right where they are speed bumps again. You pitch, kind of turn the car back to the left, ride back over the edge of the racetrack where there is grass again. Sharp ninety degree right-hand turn, little bit of a dip down getting in the corner. The car wants to get loose getting in, and then it slides exceptionally hard as you're applying throttle coming off that corner. Then it drifts back out to the edge of the racetrack where it's all grass and speed bumps again. It's sort of banked a little bit on that portion; the car wants to be loose off that corner. You drive off that corner flat out and then you hit third gear and coming down the start/finish line you hit fourth gear and drive back down again, down the short chute, down to Turn One again.

You're going so fast you almost have to envision where everything is and what it typically does to you. And when you get to it you have to be able to manipulate the car to the point that if something gives you a different look or feel you're able to adjust very rapidly to it and take an alternative line or evasive action at that point. It's just a picture that you have in your head of where you're going. You carry so much speed through there it's all by feel. You know where you are, how far you've gone, then you can shift the gear without even looking. You just know where you need to pull the lever. It's a learned behavior, like anything. You've been through it so many times, that hump's always there. And when you know what the hump does to the car you try not to hit that hump. It's kind of a deal that comes with experience. ■

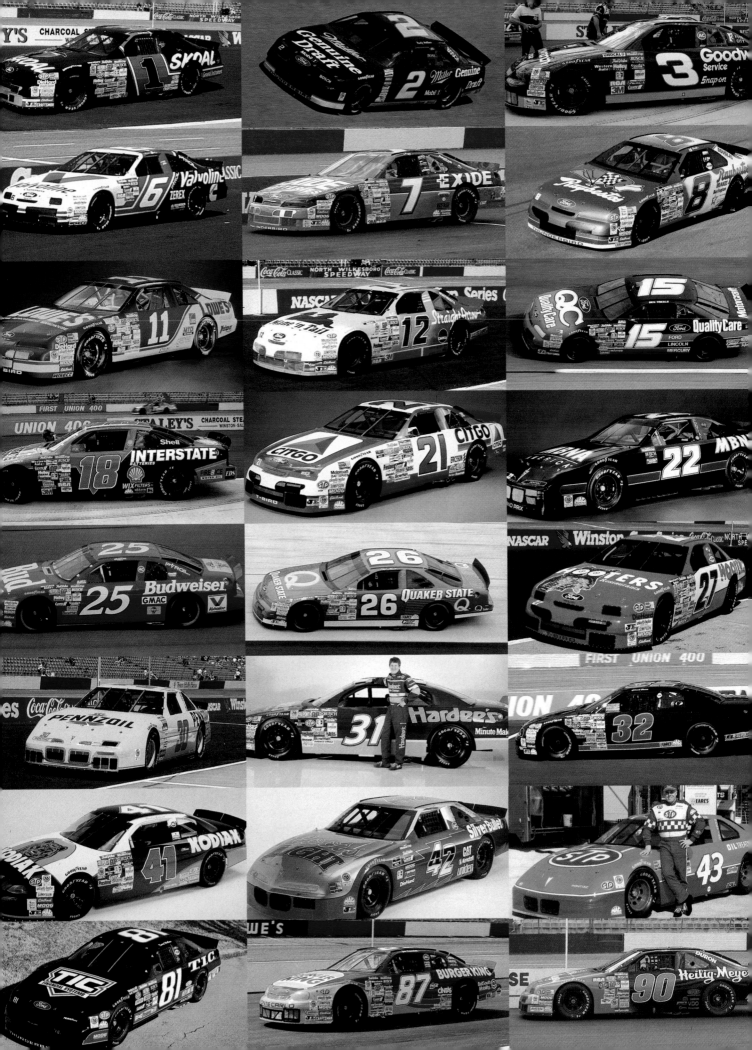

Sponsor: **Skoal Racing**

Team: **Precision Products Racing**
Driver: **Rick Mast**
Owner: **Richard Jackson**
Crew Chief: **Kevin Hamlin**
Car Type: **Ford**

1

DRIVER INFO

Hometown: **Rockbridge Baths, Virginia**
Birthdate: **March 4, 1957**
Height: **6' 1"**   Weight: **215**

Rick Mast's first Winston Cup start was in 1988 at Bristol. In total he has had 154 starts, one pole and $2,235,383 in career winnings. His best career finish is second in the fall of 1994 when he finished behind Dale Earhardt despite driving a car that had hit the wall. His career-best standing also came in 1994 when he finished 18th and won $722,361. One of the high points of his year was winning the pole for the inaugural Brickyard 400.

Rick started driving at the age of 16 in the hobby division at Natural Bridge Speedway and Eastside Speedway. In his rookie year he managed to win, and when he was 17 years old he won a track championship. Later, after moving up to the Busch Grand National circuit in 1984, he scored nine BGN wins.

Family history plays a big part in Rick's career. His father and an uncle were race car owners who also owned and operated a short track. After Rick went to his first race at the age of ten, he had racing in his blood. One of Rick's proudest achievements has to be finishing sixth in the 1989 Daytona 500 — in an unsponsored car.

1994 SEASON RESULTS

Race	Track	Fin	Qlfy	Pts	Winnings
Daytona 500	Daytona	27	30	82	$36,540
Goodwrench 500	Rockingham	3	16	165	36,085
Pontiac Excitement 400	Richmond	7	4	151	9,725
Purolator 500	Atlanta	26	37	85	11,635
TranSouth Financial 400	Darlington	37	10	52	9,530
Food City 500	Bristol	29	28	76	9,950
First Union 400	North Wilkesboro	10	17	134	16,130
Hanes 500	Martinsville	8	11	142	16,875
Winston Select 500	Talladega	20	25	103	17,130
Save Mart 300	Sears Point	34	24	61	13,230
Coca-Cola 600	Charlotte	31	7	75	13,350
Budweiser 500	Dover Downs	30	17	73	14,315
UAW-GM Teamwork 500	Pocono	9	39	143	18,405
Miller Genuine Draft 400	Michigan	13	16	124	18,725
Pepsi 400	Daytona	29	41	76	15,095
Slick 50 300	New Hampshire	9	22	143	20,175
Miller Genuine Draft 500	Pocono	40	24	43	12,060
DieHard 500	Talladega	20	38	103	18,110
Brickyard 400	Indianapolis	2	21	102	103,200
The Bud at the Glen	Watkins Glen	38	39	49	11,465
GM Goodwrench Dealer 400	Michigan	3	9	170	38,320
Goody's 500	Bristol	10	9	134	19,040
Mountain Dew Southern 500	Darlington	20	10	103	14,335
Miller Genuine Draft 400	Richmond	33	11	64	10,775
Splitfire Spark Plug 500	Dover Downs	15	8	118	16,665
Goody's 500	Martinsville	29	35	76	10,425
Tyson Holly Farms 400	North Wilkesboro	3	17	165	32,590
Mello Yello 500	Charlotte	12	19	127	19,700
AC-Delco 500	Rockingham	2	8	175	45,425
Slick 50 500	Phoenix	42	21	37	10,325
Hooters 500	Atlanta	27	24	87	14,055

Career Starts	Wins	Top Five	Top Ten
154	0	6	21
100%	0.00%	3.90%	13.64%

(1992-1994) Starts	Wins	Top Five	Top Ten
90	0	5	16
100%	0.00%	5.56%	17.78%

1994 Starts	Wins	Top Five	Top Ten
31	0	4	10
100%	0.00%	12.90%	32.26%

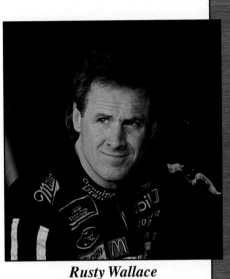

Rusty Wallace

DRIVER INFO

Hometown: **St. Louis, Missouri**
Birthdate: **August 14, 1956**
Height: **6' 0"**   Weight: **175**

In 1984 Rusty Wallace was Winston Cup Rookie of the Year. Earlier, in 1980, he finished second in his debut in Atlanta when he drove for Roger Penske. After 331 Winston Cup starts, he has 39 wins, 15 poles and $11,111,883 in career winnings, making him fourth on the all-time list. His record is spectacular. The 1989 Winston Cup Champion, Rusty was runner-up to Bill Elliott in 1988. In 1993 he was again runner-up, finishing just 80 points behind winner Dale Earnhardt, and in 1994 he finished third and had eight wins.

As his father was a three-time track champion in St. Louis, Rusty came to racing naturally. He was USAC Rookie of the Year in 1979, ASA National Champion in 1983, and NMPA Driver of the Year in 1988 and 1993.

Racing is not Rusty's only interest. In addition to his on-going love of rock and roll, he is infatuated with planes and flying. He has his pilot's license and owns three planes.

Career Starts	Wins	Top Five	Top Ten
331	39	109	172
100%	11.50%	32.15%	50.74%

1992-1994 Starts	Wins	Top Five	Top Ten
90	19	41	53
100%	21.11%	45.56%	58.89%

1994 Starts	Wins	Top Five	Top Ten
31	8	17	20
100%	25.81%	54.84%	64.52%

Sponsor: **Miller Genuine Draft**
Team: **Penske Racing South**
Driver: **Rusty Wallace**
Owner: **Roger Penske**
Crew Chief: **Robin Pemberton**
Car Type: **Ford**

1994 SEASON RESULTS

Race	Track	Fin	Qlfy	Pts	Winnings
Daytona 500	Daytona	41	5	40	$57,865
Goodwrench 500	Rockingham	1	15	185	52,885
Pontiac Excitement 400	Richmond	2	12	175	39,575
Purolator 500	Atlanta	24	12	91	21,495
TranSouth Financial 400	Darlington	33	8	69	17,850
Food City 500	Bristol	7	2	151	23,385
First Union 400	North Wilkesboro	2	16	175	42,215
Hanes 500	Martinsville	1	1	185	173,675
Winston Select 500	Talladega	33	20	64	20,730
Save Mart 300	Sears Point	5	12	155	25,970
Coca-Cola 600	Charlotte	2	21	180	88,075
Budweiser 500	Dover Downs	1	6	180	70,605
UAW-GM Teamwork 500	Pocono	1	1	185	84,525
Miller Genuine Draft 400	Michigan	1	5	185	66,980
Pepsi 400	Daytona	26	13	85	21,655
Slick 50 300	New Hampshire	3	18	165	39,975
Miller Genuine Draft 500	Pocono	9	10	143	24,460
DieHard 500	Talladega	42	26	37	21,425
Brickyard 400	Indianapolis	4	12	165	140,600
The Bud at the Glen	Watkins Glen	17	5	112	19,950
GM Goodwrench Dealer 400	Michigan	4	7	165	34,070
Goody's 500	Bristol	1	4	180	53,015
Mountain Dew Southern 500	Darlington	7	19	151	23,620
Miller Genuine Draft 400	Richmond	4	5	165	30,780
Splitfire Spark Plug 500	Dover Downs	1	10	180	55,055
Goody's 500	Martinsville	1	7	185	69,125
Tyson Holly Farms 400	North Wilkesboro	4	19	160	23,590
Mello Yello 500	Charlotte	37	15	57	16,680
AC-Delco 500	Rockingham	35	14	58	19,200
Slick 50 500	Phoenix	17	2	112	20,420
Hooters 500	Atlanta	32	18	67	17,670

Dale Earnhardt

Sponsor: **GM Goodwrench Service**

Team: **Richard Childress Racing**
Driver: **Dale Earnhardt**
Owner: **Richard Childress**
Crew Chief: **Andy Petree**
Car Type: **Chevrolet**

3

1994 SEASON RESULTS

Race	Track	Fin	Qlfy	Pts	Winnings
Daytona 500	Daytona	7	2	151	$110,340
Goodwrench 500	Rockingham	7	19	151	25,785
Pontiac Excitement 400	Richmond	4	9	165	29,550
Purolator 500	Atlanta	12	16	127	24,550
TranSouth Financial 400	Darlington	1	9	185	70,190
Food City 500	Bristol	1	24	185	72,570
First Union 400	North Wilkesboro	5	19	155	26,740
Hanes 500	Martinsville	11	8	130	21,060
Winston Select 500	Talladega	1	4	180	94,865
Save Mart 300	Sears Point	3	4	170	37,825
Coca-Cola 600	Charlotte	9	24	138	37,950
Budweiser 500	Dover Downs	28	14	79	22,065
UAW-GM Teamwork 500	Pocono	2	19	175	46,425
Miller Genuine Draft 400	Michigan	2	24	175	55,905
Pepsi 400	Daytona	3	1	170	50,050
Slick 50 300	New Hampshire	2	28	175	68,000
Miller Genuine Draft 500	Pocono	7	20	146	26,210
DieHard 500	Talladega	34	1	66	30,725
Brickyard 400	Indianapolis	5	2	160	121,625
The Bud at the Glen	Watkins Glen	3	6	170	39,605
GM Goodwrench Dealer 400	Michigan	37	11	52	22,915
Goody's 500	Bristol	3	14	170	33,265
Mountain Dew Southern 500	Darlington	2	27	175	45,030
Miller Genuine Draft 400	Richmond	3	12	170	38,830
Splitfire Spark Plug 500	Dover Downs	2	37	175	47,980
Goody's 500	Martinsville	2	20	175	42,400
Tyson Holly Farms 400	North Wilkesboro	7	3	151	21,315
Mello Yello 500	Charlotte	3	38	170	66,000
AC-Delco 500	Rockingham	1	20	185	60,600
Slick 50 500	Phoenix	40	8	43	19,575
Hooters 500	Atlanta	2	30	175	55,950

DRIVER INFO

Hometown: **Kannapolis, North Carolina**
Birthdate: **April 29, 1952**
Height: **6' 1"**   *Weight:* **185**

Dale Earnhardt was Winston Cup Rookie of the Year in 1979, and the following season he won the Winston Cup championship, becoming the first driver to win those honors in successive seasons. His first win came in his 16th start at the Southeastern 500 in 1979. Now, after 480 career starts, he has 63 wins, making him sixth on the all-time list. He has 17 poles and a record $22,794,304 in career winnings. He is a seven-time NASCAR Winston Cup Champion, and is tied with Richard Petty. In 1994 he was named Motorsports National Driver of the Year for the second time; he also won the Winston Cup championship, four races and $3,300,733.

Dale does have a life beyond racing, as he loves hunting and fishing. He also owns a farm, a 76-foot Hatteras boat, and a Lear Jet 31A. Other sports interest Dale, including tennis and professional football.

Dale is truly one of Winston Cup's most talented and consistent drivers.

Career Starts	Wins	Top Five	Top Ten
480	63	217	314
100%	13.13%	45.21%	65.42%

(1992-1994) Starts	Wins	Top Five	Top Ten
90	11	43	61
100%	12.22%	47.78%	67.78%

1994 Starts	Wins	Top Five	Top Ten
31	4	20	25
100%	12.90%	64.52%	80.65%

Sterling Marlin

DRIVER INFO

Hometown: **Columbia, Tennessee**
Birthdate: **June 30, 1957**
Height: **6' 0"**   Weight: **175**

Sterling Marlin made his Winston Cup debut in 1976 when he replaced his father, Coo Coo Marlin, after a crash broke Coo Coo's shoulder. Sterling did not regularly participate in Winston Cup racing until 1983, when he was Rookie of the Year. In 309 starts he has eight poles, one win, and $5,098,730 in career winnings. His career-best in the Winston Cup standings was seventh in 1991. In 1994 he finished 14th and won at Daytona after he had posted nine runner-up finishes.

Sterling was racing long before Winston Cup. He was a Tennessee short-track and ARCA driver, and in the early eighties he was a Nashville Raceway champion.

There is more to Sterling's life than racing. In high school he was an outstanding football player who was captain of the team his senior year. He also played high school basketball. One of his hobbies is collecting civil war relics around Tennessee.

Career Starts	Wins	Top Five	Top Ten
309	1	40	102
100%	0.32%	12.94%	33.01%

(1992-1994) Starts	Wins	Top Five	Top Ten
90	1	12	32
100%	1.11%	13.33%	35.56%

1994 Starts	Wins	Top Five	Top Ten
31	1	5	11
100%	3.23%	16.13%	35.48%

Sponsor: **Kodak Film**
Team: **Morgan-McClure Motorsports, Inc.**
Driver: **Sterling Marlin**
Owner: **Larry McClure**
Crew Chief: **Tony Glover**
Car Type: **Chevrolet**

4

1994 SEASON RESULTS

Race	Track	Fin	Qlfy	Pts	Winnings
Daytona 500	Daytona	1	4	180	$253,275
Goodwrench 500	Rockingham	2	21	175	48,935
Pontiac Excitement 400	Richmond	19	6	106	17,225
Purolator 500	Atlanta	25	23	88	19,190
TranSouth Financial 400	Darlington	34	2	66	16,765
Food City 500	Bristol	8	18	142	20,285
First Union 400	North Wilkesboro	17	7	112	15,425
Hanes 500	Martinsville	27	2	82	16,625
Winston Select 500	Talladega	8	10	147	26,850
Save Mart 300	Sears Point	29	13	76	17,470
Coca-Cola 600	Charlotte	15	32	118	23,850
Budweiser 500	Dover Downs	8	30	142	22,415
UAW-GM Teamwork 500	Pocono	38	18	49	17,260
Miller Genuine Draft 400	Michigan	34	20	61	18,140
Pepsi 400	Daytona	28	4	84	20,190
Slick 50 300	New Hampshire	10	7	139	25,125
Miller Genuine Draft 500	Pocono	12	18	127	20,160
DieHard 500	Talladega	5	8	160	32,675
Brickyard 400	Indianapolis	14	9	121	49,000
The Bud at the Glen	Watkins Glen	26	22	85	16,785
GM Goodwrench Dealer 400	Michigan	34	12	61	18,265
Goody's 500	Bristol	6	24	150	21,265
Mountain Dew Southern 500	Darlington	5	24	160	26,870
Miller Genuine Draft 400	Richmond	13	21	124	17,705
Splitfire Spark Plug 500	Dover Downs	30	18	73	18,215
Goody's 500	Martinsville	7	9	146	20,075
Tyson Holly Farms 400	North Wilkesboro	31	24	70	14,300
Mello Yello 500	Charlotte	36	23	60	14,490
AC-Delco 500	Rockingham	14	37	126	20,050
Slick 50 500	Phoenix	3	1	170	40,330
Hooters 500	Atlanta	40	13	43	16,100

Terry Labonte

Sponsor: # Kellogg's Corn Flakes

Team: **Hendrick Motorsports**
Driver: **Terry Labonte**
Owner: **Rick Hendrick**
Crew Chief: **Gary DeHart**
Car Type: **Chevrolet**

5

1994 SEASON RESULTS

Race	Track	Fin	Qlfy	Pts	Winnings
Daytona 500	Daytona	3	9	170	$138,475
Goodwrench 500	Rockingham	17	27	112	19,435
Pontiac Excitement 400	Richmond	9	37	143	20,825
Purolator 500	Atlanta	14	3	126	21,360
TranSouth Financial 400	Darlington	35	24	58	15,580
Food City 500	Bristol	24	12	91	18,130
First Union 400	North Wilkesboro	1	10	180	61,640
Hanes 500	Martinsville	15	30	118	16,675
Winston Select 500	Talladega	32	21	67	19,060
Save Mart 300	Sears Point	28	5	79	17,680
Coca-Cola 600	Charlotte	35	10	58	16,750
Budweiser 500	Dover Downs	26	22	85	18,415
UAW-GM Teamwork 500	Pocono	18	15	109	18,905
Miller Genuine Draft 400	Michigan	20	4	108	20,610
Pepsi 400	Daytona	15	9	118	21,850
Slick 50 300	New Hampshire	11	11	130	22,675
Miller Genuine Draft 500	Pocono	15	28	118	19,910
DieHard 500	Talladega	10	12	134	25,250
Brickyard 400	Indianapolis	12	21	127	57,500
The Bud at the Glen	Watkins Glen	6	10	150	22,810
GM Goodwrench Dealer 400	Michigan	8	17	142	24,640
Goody's 500	Bristol	33	3	64	18,035
Mountain Dew Southern 500	Darlington	10	22	134	21,930
Miller Genuine Draft 400	Richmond	1	3	185	67,765
Splitfire Spark Plug 500	Dover Downs	7	29	146	23,015
Goody's 500	Martinsville	14	17	121	16,525
Tyson Holly Farms 400	North Wilkesboro	2	10	170	39,365
Mello Yello 500	Charlotte	7	9	146	32,850
AC-Delco 500	Rockingham	5	2	160	28,750
Slick 50 500	Phoenix	1	19	185	67,885
Hooters 500	Atlanta	8	10	142	22,550

DRIVER INFO

Hometown: **Corpus Cristi, Texas**
Birthdate: **November 16, 1956**
Height: **5' 10"**   Weight: **165**

In Terry Labonte's first Winston Cup Race, the 1978 Southern 500, he finished fourth. His first win came in his 59th start at the 1980 Southern 500. Now, after 480 Winston Cup starts, he has 13 wins and $8,896,096 in career winnings. He was the 1984 Winston Cup Champion with two wins, six second places, and six third-place finishes. In 1994 he finished seventh in the point standings and crossed the $1 million mark in earnings for the first time in his career with $1,125,921. He had six top-fives and fourteen top-tens. The last third of the season was particularly good for him, as he was second only to Dale Earnhardt in consistently producing points.

Terry began racing with quarter midgets in Texas in 1964. He was Corpus Christi, Texas, Sportsman of the Year in 1979 and 1984. As he was competing for Winston Cup honors, he also won the 1985 Busch Clash, the 1988 The Winston Select at Charlotte, and the 1989 IROC championship, as well as the1990 Christmas 400K in Melbourne, Australia.

Career Starts	Wins	Top Five	Top Ten
480	13	123	248
100%	2.71%	25.63%	51.67%

(1992-1994) Starts	Wins	Top Five	Top Ten
90	3	10	40
100%	3.33%	11.11%	44.44%

1994 Starts	Wins	Top Five	Top Ten
31	3	6	14
100%	9.68%	19.35%	45.16%

Sponsor: *Valvoline*

Team: **Roush Racing**
Driver: **Mark Martin**
Owner: **Jack Roush**
Crew Chief: **Steve Hmiel**
Car Type: **Ford**

6

DRIVER INFO

Hometown: **Batesville, Arkansas**
Birthdate: **January 9, 1959**
Height: **5' 6"**   *Weight:* **150**

Mark Martin started Winston Cup racing in 1981 when he won two poles in five races. He went on to finish second as 1982 Rookie of the Year. He did not have another full season until 1988, when he posted one runner-up finish. His first win came in his 113th start in the 1989 AC Delco 500 at Rockingham. Now, after 263 starts, 14 wins, and 24 poles, he has amassed $8,137,293 in winnings. For six consecutive years he won $1 million or more. In 1989 he won NMPA Driver of the Year honors, and in 1990 he lost the Winston Cup title to Dale Earnhardt by only a few points. In 1994 he once more placed second behind Earnhardt in the race for the title. He led late in several races but was plagued with a variety of troubles, from cut tires to engine failure. Neverthe-less, he had a total of fifteen top-five finishes for the year. His second win of 1994 came in the last race at Atlanta. As in 1993 he went over the $1.6 million mark in earnings.

Career Starts	Wins	Top Five	Top Ten
263	14	88	137
100%	5.32%	33.46%	52.09%

(1992-1994) Starts	Wins	Top Five	Top Ten
90	9	37	56
100%	10.00%	41.11%	62.22%

1994 Starts	Wins	Top Five	Top Ten
31	2	15	20
100%	6.45%	48.39%	64.52%

1994 SEASON RESULTS

Race	Track	Fin	Qlfy	Pts	Winnings
Daytona 500	Daytona	13	7	129	$65,670
Goodwrench 500	Rockingham	4	2	165	28,986
Pontiac Excitement 400	Richmond	6	2	155	23,150
Purolator 500	Atlanta	5	4	155	30,300
TranSouth Financial 400	Darlington	2	3	175	42,835
Food City 500	Bristol	21	3	105	20,405
First Union 400	North Wilkesboro	13	13	124	17,650
Hanes 500	Martinsville	3	6	170	33,425
Winston Select 500	Talladega	38	15	49	20,106
Save Mart 300	Sears Point	8	2	142	24,120
Coca-Cola 600	Charlotte	32	11	67	18,450
Budweiser 500	Dover Downs	4	32	165	29,765
UAW-GM Teamwork 500	Pocono	5	3	160	30,400
Miller Genuine Draft 400	Michigan	3	8	170	42,330
Pepsi 400	Daytona	4	4	165	36,575
Slick 50 300	New Hampshire	4	10	160	33,625
Miller Genuine Draft 500	Pocono	31	12	75	21,460
DieHard 500	Talladega	6	6	150	29,550
Brickyard 400	Indianapolis	35	10	58	34,300
The Bud at the Glen	Watkins Glen	1	1	185	85,100
GM Goodwrench Dealer 400	Michigan	2	13	175	50,320
Goody's 500	Bristol	2	8	175	35,915
Mountain Dew Southern 500	Darlington	25	6	93	20,975
Miller Genuine Draft 400	Richmond	6	14	150	22,780
Splitfire Spark Plug 500	Dover Downs	19	4	111	23,065
Goody's 500	Martinsville	16	5	115	18,425
Tyson Holly Farms 400	North Wilkesboro	5	4	155	24,090
Mello Yello 500	Charlotte	39	12	46	16,260
AC-Delco 500	Rockingham	7	10	146	23,850
Slick 50 500	Phoenix	2	6	175	46,155
Hooters 500	Atlanta	1	5	185	104,200

Geoff Bodine

Sponsor: **Exide Corporation**
Team: **Geoff Bodine Racing, Inc.**
Driver: **Geoff Bodine**
Owner: **Geoff Bodine**
Crew Chief: **Paul Andrews**
Car Type: **Ford**

DRIVER INFO

Hometown: **Chemung, New York**
Birthdate: **April 18, 1949**
Height: **5' 8"**   Weight: **160**

Geoff Bodine was Winston Cup Rookie of the Year in 1982. In 1984 he claimed his first Winston Cup win at Martinsville in his 69th start. In 1994, his first full season as owner-driver, he finished 17th in points, chalked up three victories, and won five poles. He also won $1,276,126, the highest total of his career. After 381 career starts, 17 wins, and 35 poles, he has $8,401,701 in winnings, making him 8th on the money-earned list. His career-best finish in the Winston Cup standings was a third in 1990.

The oldest of the racing Bodine brothers, Geoff started driving micro-midgets in New York in 1955. By 1977 he finished second in the national modified standings. On the Busch Grand National circuit he has claimed six victories.

In addition to being a talented driver, Geoff is an innovator. He introduced modern-day power steering to Winston Cup. He also assisted in the engineering for a bobsled for the 1994 USA Bobsled team.

1994 SEASON RESULTS

Race	Track	Fin	Qlfy	Pts	Winnings
Daytona 500	Daytona	11	39	135	$52,065
Goodwrench 500	Rockingham	15	1	123	22,685
Pontiac Excitement 400	Richmond	32	17	67	12,800
Purolator 500	Atlanta	38	2	54	14,150
TranSouth Financial 400	Darlington	40	7	43	9,357
Food City 500	Bristol	4	27	165	24,365
First Union 400	North Wilkesboro	7	5	146	16,565
Hanes 500	Martinsville	34	3	66	12,375
Winston Select 500	Talladega	41	23	40	12,220
Save Mart 300	Sears Point	2	26	170	45,640
Coca-Cola 600	Charlotte	3	3	170	75,500
Budweiser 500	Dover Downs	41	2	45	12,180
UAW-GM Teamwork 500	Pocono	19	30	106	15,355
Miller Genuine Draft 400	Michigan	28	27	9	15,965
Pepsi 400	Daytona	6	7	155	25,875
Slick 50 300	New Hampshire	31	16	75	16,700
Miller Genuine Draft 500	Pocono	1	1	185	103,270
DieHard 500	Talladega	33	20	64	13,520
Brickyard 400	Indianapolis	39	4	51	45,600
The Bud at the Glen	Watkins Glen	29	15	76	12,755
GM Goodwrench Dealer 400	Michigan	1	1	185	89,595
Goody's 500	Bristol	23	2	104	17,235
Mountain Dew Southern 500	Darlington	27	1	87	17,805
Miller Genuine Draft 400	Richmond	18	9	109	13,980
Splitfire Spark Plug 500	Dover Downs	5	1	165	31,520
Goody's 500	Martinsville	18	2	114	14,630
Tyson Holly Farms 400	North Wilkesboro	1	18	185	61,440
Mello Yello 500	Charlotte	32	6	77	31,340
AC-Delco 500	Rockingham	40	3	48	12,500
Slick 50 500	Phoenix	8	37	142	20,520
Hooters 500	Atlanta	34	4	66	16,740

Career Starts	Wins	Top Five	Top Ten
381	17	83	158
100%	4.46%	21.78%	41.47%

(1992-1994) Starts	Wins	Top Five	Top Ten
90	6	16	30
100%	6.67%	17.78%	33.33%

1994 Starts	Wins	Top Five	Top Ten
31	3	7	10
100%	9.68%	22.58%	32.26%

Jeff Burton

DRIVER INFO

Hometown: **South Boston, Virginia**
Birthdate: **June 29, 1967**
Height: **5' 7"**   Weight: **160**

Jeff Burton is new to the Winston Cup circuit. He made his debut in 1993 in Loudon, New Hampshire, where he qualified sixth and finished 37th. In 1994 he made 30 of 31 races and earned two top-fives. He was also 1994 MAXX Race Cards Rookie of the Year. In 31 Winston Cup starts, he has $604,250 in winnings.

From the age of five, Jeff was interested in racing, as he watched his brother Ward race go-karts. He drove go-karts himself when he was older, then moved to Pure Stock and Late Model divisions on short tracks in the area of South Boston, Virginia. He was the 1987 Orange County Speedway Champion and the 1988 South Boston Most Popular Driver. He moved to the Busch Grand National Series in 1988 and in 153 starts chalked up four wins.

At Halifax County High School Jeff participated in basketball and soccer. He still enjoys basketball but also finds time for fishing. When he is not being active he likes watching the Duke Blue Devils and an occasional movie.

Career Starts	Wins	Top Five	Top Ten
31	0	2	3
100%	0.00%	6.45%	9.68%

1992-1994* Starts	Wins	Top Five	Top Ten
31	0	2	3
100%	0.00%	6.45%	9.68%

1994 Starts	Wins	Top Five	Top Ten
30	0	2	3
100%	0.00%	6.67%	10.00%

*2 years (1993 & 1994)

Sponsor: **Raybestos Brakes**
Team: **Stavola Brothers Racing**
Driver: **Jeff Burton**
Owner: **William Stavola**
Crew Chief: **Donnie Richeson**
Car Type: **Ford**

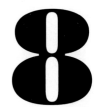

1994 SEASON RESULTS

Race	Track	Fin	Qlfy	Pts	Winnings
Daytona 500	Daytona	26	35	85	$37,145
Goodwrench 500	Rockingham	20	39	103	17,285
Pontiac Excitement 400	Richmond	20	25	103	15,350
Purolator 500	Atlanta	4	13	165	32,600
TranSouth Financial 400	Darlington	20	22	103	14,040
Food City 500	Bristol	31	35	70	12,625
First Union 400	North Wilkesboro	33	35	64	9,700
Hanes 500	Martinsville	36	21	55	10,875
Winston Select 500	Talladega	39	34	46	12,250
Save Mart 300	Sears Point	15	21	118	16,705
Coca-Cola 600	Charlotte	29	15	76	13,080
Budweiser 500	Dover Downs	33	26	64	13,555
UAW-GM Teamwork 500	Pocono	22	35	97	16,650
Miller Genuine Draft 400	Michigan	21	32	100	16,590
Pepsi 400	Daytona	18	27	109	18,080
Slick 50 300	New Hampshire	38	39	49	13,700
Miller Genuine Draft 500	Pocono	4	4	165	29,640
DieHard 500	Talladega	26	39	85	16,035
Brickyard 400	Indianapolis	19	38	106	41,600
The Bud at the Glen	Watkins Glen	25	36	88	13,145
GM Goodwrench Dealer 400	Michigan	33	28	64	12,315
Goody's 500	Bristol	20	20	103	16,285
Mountain Dew Southern 500	Darlington	8	14	142	19,500
Splitfire Spark Plug 500	Dover Downs	37	6	57	13,280
Goody's 500	Martinsville	36	3	55	10,375
Tyson Holly Farms 400	North Wilkesboro	28	14	84	10,210
Mello Yello 500	Charlotte	25	31	88	11,390
AC-Delco 500	Rockingham	11	30	130	18,450
Slick 50 500	Phoenix	27	36	82	13,110
Hooters 500	Atlanta	31	19	70	12,635

Lake Speed

9

Sponsor: **Spam**
Team: **Melling Racing**
Driver: **Lake Speed**
Owner: **Harry Melling**
Crew Chief: **Peter Sospenzo**
Car Type: **Ford**

DRIVER INFO

Hometown: *Jackson, Mississippi*
Birthdate: *January 17, 1948*
Height: *5' 6"*   Weight: *145*

Lake Speed drove his first Winston Cup race in 1980. In 1985 he achieved his career-best standing in Winston Cup points with a tenth. Now, after 299 Winston Cup starts, he has one win, in the 1988 TranSouth 500 at Darlington on his 164th start. He also has $2,837,982 in career winnings and 16 top-five finishes. He finished eleventh in the 1994 Winston Cup standings and won $832,463.

Lake's racing career began with go-karts. In fact, he won the 1978 World Karting Championship in LeMans, France.

1994 SEASON RESULTS

Race	Track	Fin	Qlfy	Pts	Winnings
Daytona 500	Daytona	14	22	121	$50,530
Goodwrench 500	Rockingham	21	37	100	18,610
Pontiac Excitement 400	Richmond	14	30	121	17,575
Purolator 500	Atlanta	6	34	150	24,850
TranSouth Financial 400	Darlington	5	35	155	26,300
Food City 500	Bristol	3	13	165	35,020
First Union 400	North Wilkesboro	12	29	127	15,975
Hanes 500	Martinsville	30	25	73	14,375
Winston Select 500	Talladega	7	18	146	28,300
Save Mart 300	Sears Point	32	29	67	17,305
Coca-Cola 600	Charlotte	14	39	121	24,500
Budweiser 500	Dover Downs	12	40	127	20,115
UAW-GM Teamwork 500	Pocono	23	33	94	18,185
Miller Genuine Draft 400	Michigan	40	28	43	17,880
Pepsi 400	Daytona	10	33	134	25,825
Slick 50 300	New Hampshire	15	34	118	22,625
Miller Genuine Draft 500	Pocono	20	40	103	19,365
DieHard 500	Talladega	14	18	126	21,960
Brickyard 400	Indianapolis	15	41	123	52,350
The Bud at the Glen	Watkins Glen	13	21	129	18,420
GM Goodwrench Dealer 400	Michigan	13	29	124	21,790
Goody's 500	Bristol	25	35	88	17,915
Mountain Dew Southern 500	Darlington	40	40	43	15,330
Miller Genuine Draft 400	Richmond	21	36	100	17,180
Splitfire Spark Plug 500	Dover Downs	9	22	138	21,765
Goody's 500	Martinsville	34	15	66	14,375
Tyson Holly Farms 400	North Wilkesboro	25	36	88	14,925
Mello Yello 500	Charlotte	5	24	155	42,925
AC-Delco 500	Rockingham	10	41	134	25,650
Slick 50 500	Phoenix	14	10	121	18,520
Hooters 500	Atlanta	4	20	165	32,000

Career Starts	Wins	Top Five	Top Ten
299	1	16	71
100%	0.33%	5.35%	23.75%

1992-1994 Starts	Wins	Top Five	Top Ten
61	0	4	10
100%	0.00%	6.56%	16.39%

1994 Starts	Wins	Top Five	Top Ten
31	0	4	9
100%	0.00%	12.90%	29.03%

Ricky Rudd

Team: **Rudd Performance Motorsports, Inc.**
Driver: **Ricky Rudd**
Owner: **Ricky Rudd**
Crew Chief: **Bill Ingle**
Car Type: **Ford**

10

DRIVER INFO

Hometown: **Chesapeake, Virginia**
Birthdate: **September 12, 1956**
Height: **5' 8"**   Weight: **160**

In 1975 Ricky was in his first Winston Cup race; in 1977 he was Rookie of the Year; and in 1983, on his 161st start, he got his first win in the Budweiser 400 at Riverside. His first pole came in his 96th attempt, in 1981 in the Virginia 500 at Martinsville. He has to his credit 500 starts, 15 wins, 21 poles, and $8,685,611 in career winnings. In 1991 he was runner-up to Dale Earnhardt for the Winston Cup title. In 1994 he won $1,044,441 and finished fifth in the Winston Cup standings. His win at Loudon, New Hampshire, was his 15th career victory. Currently he ranks sixth on the all-time money-won list.

Not only is Ricky a driver; now he is also the owner of the RPM Racing Team and drives his own Ford Thunderbirds.

Believe it or not, Ricky does have spare time and enjoys other outdoor activities, especially any type of water sport.

Career Starts	Wins	Top Five	Top Ten
500	15	128	250
100%	3.00%	25.60%	50.00%

(1992-1994) Starts	Wins	Top Five	Top Ten
90	3	24	47
100%	3.33%	26.67%	52.22%

1994 Starts	Wins	Top Five	Top Ten
31	1	6	15
100%	3.23%	19.35%	48.39%

1994 SEASON RESULTS

Race	Track	Fin	Qlfy	Pts	Winnings
Daytona 500	Daytona	8	20	142	$56,465
Goodwrench 500	Rockingham	11	34	130	12,885
Pontiac Excitement 400	Richmond	18	34	109	7,250
Purolator 500	Atlanta	9	22	138	12,350
TranSouth Financial 400	Darlington	9	25	138	9,260
Food City 500	Bristol	32	11	67	6,625
First Union 400	North Wilkesboro	6	25	155	8,390
Hanes 500	Martinsville	12	19	127	6,825
Winston Select 500	Talladega	25	33	88	9,045
Save Mart 300	Sears Point	14	3	121	9,155
Coca-Cola 600	Charlotte	6	13	155	28,700
Budweiser 500	Dover Downs	19	18	106	11,465
UAW-GM Teamwork 500	Pocono	21	2	105	10,850
Miller Genuine Draft 400	Michigan	4	6	160	31,430
Pepsi 400	Daytona	17	31	117	13,985
Slick 50 300	New Hampshire	1	3	180	91,875
Miller Genuine Draft 500	Pocono	6	6	150	17,260
DieHard 500	Talladega	7	28	151	19,350
Brickyard 400	Indianapolis	11	8	130	57,100
The Bud at the Glen	Watkins Glen	5	7	160	20,875
GM Goodwrench Dealer 400	Michigan	10	15	134	17,940
Goody's 500	Bristol	12	33	127	16,540
Mountain Dew Southern 500	Darlington	4	18	165	24,715
Miller Genuine Draft 400	Richmond	5	32	155	26,705
Splitfire Spark Plug 500	Dover Downs	18	16	109	15,450
Goody's 500	Martinsville	25	13	88	10,975
Tyson Holly Farms 400	North Wilkesboro	11	26	130	13,550
Mello Yello 500	Charlotte	29	16	76	10,420
AC-Delco 500	Rockingham	4	1	165	28,076
Slick 50 500	Phoenix	7	4	151	20,220
Hooters 500	Atlanta	14	8	121	17,200

Brett Bodine

11

Sponsor: **Lowe's**
Home Improvement Warehouse
Team: **Junior Johnson**
& Associates
Driver: **Brett Bodine**
Owner: **Junior Johnson**
Car Type: **Ford**

1994 SEASON RESULTS

Race	Track	Fin	Qlfy	Pts	Winnings
Daytona 500	Daytona	32	10	67	$39,865
Goodwrench 500	Rockingham	6	4	155	20,535
Pontiac Excitement 400	Richmond	8	13	142	16,525
Purolator 500	Atlanta	31	15	70	14,745
TranSouth Financial 400	Darlington	36	5	55	11,045
Food City 500	Bristol	13	19	124	16,155
First Union 400	North Wilkesboro	23	2	94	11,525
Hanes 500	Martinsville	24	35	91	11,275
Winston Select 500	Talladega	17	28	112	17,420
Save Mart 300	Sears Point	13	23	124	6,355
Coca-Cola 600	Charlotte	42	5	42	8,975
Budweiser 500	Dover Downs	32	21	72	14,605
UAW-GM Teamwork 500	Pocono	8	6	142	19,405
Miller Genuine Draft 400	Michigan	32	10	67	14,390
Pepsi 400	Daytona	16	22	115	18,310
Slick 50 300	New Hampshire	12	23	127	19,775
Miller Genuine Draft 500	Pocono	35	14	58	11,860
DieHard 500	Talladega	17	19	112	18,185
Brickyard 400	Indianapolis	2	7	175	203,575
The Bud at the Glen	Watkins Glen	28	16	79	12,915
GM Goodwrench Dealer 400	Michigan	12	21	127	17,190
Goody's 500	Bristol	14	22	121	15,540
Mountain Dew Southern 500	Darlington	29	5	76	12,385
Miller Genuine Draft 400	Richmond	8	27	142	16,580
Splitfire Spark Plug 500	Dover Downs	26	5	85	14,615
Goody's 500	Martinsville	30	25	73	9,875
Tyson Holly Farms 400	North Wilkesboro	33	15	64	8,225
Mello Yello 500	Charlotte	6	8	155	37,450
AC-Delco 500	Rockingham	18	5	109	20,150
Slick 50 500	Phoenix	13	9	124	15,920
Hooters 500	Atlanta	36	14	60	12,510

DRIVER INFO

Hometown: **Chemung, New York**
Birthdate: **January 11, 1959**
Height: **5' 7"**   Weight: **160**

Brett Bodine made his debut on the Winston Cup circuit in 1986 at the World 600, where he finished 17th and was named Rookie of the Race. After 220 starts and one win, he has $3,463,760 in career winnings. His first victory was claimed in his 80th start, at North Wilkesboro during the 1990 season, and his first pole was later that year at the Mello Yello 500 at Charlotte. His career-best in the standings was a 12th in 1990. In 1994 he earned $791,444 and finished nineteenth.

Like many drivers, Brett started his racing career in hobby cars. Later he moved to modifieds, then the Busch Grand National in 1985. The next year he was runner-up for the Busch Grand National championship.

Racing has not been Brett's only interest. He attended State University of New York at Alfred and majored in Mechanical Engineering. He enjoys working with young people and regularly speaks in high schools around the country on the benefits of education. He is also an avid golfer.

Career Starts	Wins	Top Five	Top Ten
220	1	16	54
100%	0.45%	7.27%	24.55%

(1992-1994) Starts	Wins	Top Five	Top Ten
89	0	6	28
100%	0.00%	6.74%	31.46%

1994 Starts	Wins	Top Five	Top Ten
31	0	1	6
100%	0.00%	3.23%	19.35%

Derrike Cope

DRIVER INFO

Hometown: **San Diego, California**
Birthdate: **November 3, 1958**
Height: **5' 9"**   Weight: **190**

Derrike Cope joined Winston Cup racing in 1986. His first win was the 1990 Daytona 500, in his 71st start. Derrike also won at Dover a few weeks later. In 217 Winston Cup starts, he has two wins and $2,381,462 in career earnings. His career-best finish in the standings was 18th in 1990. In 1994 he had six top-twenties in the final eight races, including a seventh in the last race at Atlanta. He finished 30th in the standings and won $398,436.

Derrike was the 1980 NASCAR Late Model Sportsman Rookie of the Year and in 1983 he was that series' champion. He won the Yakima Speedway championship two times. He was the 1984 Winston West Rookie of the Year and almost won the championship. He was only four points behind the winner. Not surprisingly, he says his most memorable race was the win at Daytona.

In high school Derrike was a good baseball player, qualifying as a professional prospect before a knee injury. When he is not racing, he enjoys country music and an occasional movie.

Career Starts	Wins	Top Five	Top Ten
217	2	3	19
100%	0.92%	1.38%	8.76%

(1992-1994) Starts	Wins	Top Five	Top Ten
89	0	0	6
100%	0.00%	0.00%	6.74%

1994 Starts	Wins	Top Five	Top Ten
30	0	0	2
100%	0.00%	0.00%	6.67%

Sponsor: **Straight Arrow / Mane 'n Tail**
Team: **Bobby Allison Motorsports Team, Inc.**
Driver: **Derrike Cope**
Owner: **Bobby Allison**
Crew Chief: **Jimmy Fennig**
Car Type: **Ford**

12

1994 SEASON RESULTS

Race	Track	Fin	Qlfy	Pts	Winnings
Daytona 500	Daytona	21	16	105	$36,220
Goodwrench 500	Rockingham	29	32	76	9,900
Pontiac Excitement 400	Richmond	29	33	76	9,075
Purolator 500	Atlanta	34	29	61	9,955
TranSouth Financial 400	Darlington	16	12	115	10,405
Food City 500	Bristol	27	17	82	10,231
First Union 400	North Wilkesboro	27	22	82	7,050
Hanes 500	Martinsville	28	14	79	6,825
Winston Select 500	Talladega	31	31	70	10,115
Save Mart 300	Sears Point	43	17	34	8,600
Coca-Cola 600	Charlotte	18	22	109	13,040
Budweiser 500	Dover Downs	23	24	94	10,965
UAW-GM Teamwork 500	Pocono	40	36	43	7,150
Miller Genuine Draft 400	Michigan	37	14	52	9,490
Pepsi 400	Daytona	23	39	94	12,165
Slick 50 300	New Hampshire	35	8	58	12,000
Miller Genuine Draft 500	Pocono	19	27	106	9,110
Brickyard 400	Indianapolis	27	39	82	26,000
The Bud at the Glen	Watkins Glen	40	17	43	9,965
GM Goodwrench Dealer 400	Michigan	18	24	109	16,590
Goody's 500	Bristol	16	19	115	15,085
Mountain Dew Southern 500	Darlington	35	20	58	11,140
Miller Genuine Draft 400	Richmond	18	19	106	13,855
Splitfire Spark Plug 500	Dover Downs	12	17	127	13,415
Goody's 500	Martinsville	17	19	112	13,225
Tyson Holly Farms 400	North Wilkesboro	19	16	106	11,850
Mello Yello 500	Charlotte	8	7	142	28,100
AC-Delco 500	Rockingham	37	4	52	10,950
Slick 50 500	Phoenix	30	22	73	12,935
Hooters 500	Atlanta	7	3	151	21,030

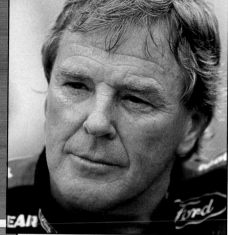

Dick Trickle

Sponsor: **Ford Quality Care**
Team: **Bud Moore Engineering**
Driver: **Dick Trickle**
Owner: **Bud Moore**
Crew Chief: **Donnie Wingo**
Car Type: **Ford**

15

1994 SEASON RESULTS

Race	Track	Fin	Qlfy	Pts	Winnings
Daytona 500	Daytona	20	29	103	$33,475
Goodwrench 500	Rockingham	14	29	121	10,035
Pontiac Excitement 400	Richmond	37	20	52	6,775
Purolator 500	Atlanta	28	20	79	8,955
TranSouth Financial 400	Darlington	29	39	76	5,865
Food City 500	Bristol	34	32	61	6,625
First Union 400	North Wilkesboro	24	34	91	5,000
Hanes 500	Martinsville	32	34	67	4,375
Winston Select 500	Talladega	36	38	55	8,440
Coca-Cola 600	Charlotte	38	36	49	6,325
Budweiser 500	Dover Downs	38	19	49	7,780
UAW-GM Teamwork 500	Pocono	34	8	61	7,525
Pepsi 400	Daytona	21	25	100	12,655
Slick 50 300	New Hampshire	34	29	61	12,100
The Bud at the Glen	Watkins Glen	32	33	67	8,265
GM Goodwrench Dealer 400	Michigan	41	34	40	8,565
Goody's 500	Bristol	17	6	112	10,935
Mountain Dew Southern 500	Darlington	38	17	49	5,476
Miller Genuine Draft 400	Richmond	12	30	127	10,855
Splitfire Spark Plug 500	Dover Downs	21	2	100	11,165
Goody's 500	Martinsville	32	27	67	4,375
Tyson Holly Farms 400	North Wilkesboro	16	31	115	8,225
Mello Yello 500	Charlotte	13	10	124	14,500
AC-Delco 500	Rockingham	8	21	147	15,625
Slick 50 500	Phoenix	39	35	46	6,490

DRIVER INFO

Hometown: **Wisconsin Rapids, Wisconsin**
Birthdate: **October 27, 1941**
Height: **5' 10"**   Weight: **185**

Though Dick Trickle's first Winston Cup race had been in 1970 at the Daytona 500, it was in 1989, at the age of 48, that he won Rookie of the Year honors. He has to his credit 167 Winston Cup starts, one pole, and $1,797,448 in career winnings. He has finished third four times and won the 1990 Winston Open. In 1989 he finished 15th in Winston Cup standings, and in 1994 he was 34th.

Racing has long been a part of Dick's life. He began competing in the fifties and was to become a legend in the short-track circuit. He has more than 1200 feature race wins and two ASA championships. He was runner-up nine times. He was a nine-time ARCA champion in the Mid-West Series.

Career Starts	Wins	Top Five	Top Ten
167	0	13	31
100%	0.00%	7.78%	18.56%

1992-1994 Starts	Wins	Top Five	Top Ten
80	0	4	12
100%	0.00%	5.00%	15.00%

1994 Starts	Wins	Top Five	Top Ten
25	0	0	1
100%	0.00%	0.00%	4.00%

Ted Musgrave

Sponsor: **The Family Channel**
Team: **Roush Racing**
Driver: **Ted Musgrave**
Owner: **Jack Roush**
Crew Chief: **Howard Comstock**
Car Type: **Ford**

16

DRIVER INFO

Hometown: **Franklin, Wisconsin**
Birthdate: **December 18, 1955**
Height: **6' 1"**   Weight: **185**

Ted Musgrave's first Winston Cup race was in 1990, and in 1991, his first full season, he was runner-up for Winston Cup Rookie of the Year. He finished a career-best 13th in the 1994 point standings and in a total of 122 Winston Cup starts has won $1,782,023. He has a total of four top-five finishes, one of which came in 1994. He took three poles in 1994.

Ted's early racing experiences include Wisconsin short tracks, ARTGO, All-Pro and ASA. He was 1987 ASA Rookie of the Year. In 1990 he was called to drive for Rich Vogler, who was killed in an accident at Salem Speedway.

After his driving career, Ted aspires to be a Winston Cup crew chief.

When he is not racing, Ted finds time for movies and music, always enjoying his leisure hours.

Career Starts	Wins	Top Five	Top Ten
122	0	4	20
100%	0.00%	0.00%	0.00%

(1992-1994) Starts	Wins	Top Five	Top Ten
89	0	4	20
100%	0.00%	4.49%	22.47%

1994 Starts	Wins	Top Five	Top Ten
31	0	1	8
100%	0.00%	3.23%	25.81%

1994 SEASON RESULTS

Race	Track	Fin	Qlfy	Pts	Winnings
Daytona 500	Daytona	38	24	49	$32,360
Goodwrench 500	Rockingham	13	5	124	17,435
Pontiac Excitement 400	Richmond	13	1	129	19,375
Purolator 500	Atlanta	11	35	130	18,520
TranSouth Financial 400	Darlington	10	20	134	18,405
Food City 500	Bristol	19	5	106	15,170
First Union 400	North Wilkesboro	21	3	100	11,800
Hanes 500	Martinsville	10	28	134	17,725
Winston Select 500	Talladega	11	17	130	20,495
Save Mart 300	Sears Point	6	15	150	20,370
Coca-Cola 600	Charlotte	16	42	115	18,950
Budweiser 500	Dover Downs	35	7	58	11,805
UAW-GM Teamwork 500	Pocono	15	9	118	16,555
Miller Genuine Draft 400	Michigan	9	40	138	23,400
Pepsi 400	Daytona	14	16	121	18,840
Slick 50 300	New Hampshire	7	6	151	20,475
Miller Genuine Draft 500	Pocono	32	32	67	14,110
DieHard 500	Talladega	41	17	40	13,228
Brickyard 400	Indianapolis	13	37	129	52,800
The Bud at the Glen	Watkins Glen	19	29	106	14,175
GM Goodwrench Dealer 400	Michigan	24	38	91	15,165
Goody's 500	Bristol	11	18	130	16,340
Mountain Dew Southern 500	Darlington	39	31	46	9,390
Miller Genuine Draft 400	Richmond	17	1	117	18,630
Splitfire Spark Plug 500	Dover Downs	14	26	121	16,615
Goody's 500	Martinsville	9	1	138	21,275
Tyson Holly Farms 400	North Wilkesboro	9	29	138	15,950
Mello Yello 500	Charlotte	18	29	109	13,500
AC-Delco 500	Rockingham	13	26	124	17,450
Slick 50 500	Phoenix	5	12	155	25,405
Hooters 500	Atlanta	28	21	79	14,940

Darrell Waltrip

Sponsor: **Western Auto**

Team: **DarWal, Inc.**

Driver: **Darrell Waltrip**

Owner: **Darrell Waltrip**

Crew Chief: **Pete Peterson**

Car Type: **Chevrolet**

17

1994 SEASON RESULTS

Race	Track	Fin	Qlfy	Pts	Winnings
Daytona 500	Daytona	28	32	79	$35,435
Goodwrench 500	Rockingham	23	9	94	14,935
Pontiac Excitement 400	Richmond	16	27	115	14,500
Purolator 500	Atlanta	3	40	170	44,450
TranSouth Financial 400	Darlington	26	36	85	12,275
Food City 500	Bristol	15	37	118	15,755
First Union 400	North Wilkesboro	28	33	79	10,985
Hanes 500	Martinsville	4	16	165	23,050
Winston Select 500	Talladega	14	16	121	19,005
Save Mart 300	Sears Point	18	33	109	14,580
Coca-Cola 600	Charlotte	30	29	73	12,850
Budweiser 500	Dover Downs	6	16	150	22,365
UAW-GM Teamwork 500	Pocono	30	12	73	13,800
Miller Genuine Draft 400	Michigan	10	34	134	22,750
Pepsi 400	Daytona	25	37	88	15,725
Slick 50 300	New Hampshire	23	14	94	17,800
Miller Genuine Draft 500	Pocono	28	26	79	14,810
DieHard 500	Talladega	24	22	91	16,640
Brickyard 400	Indianapolis	6	27	150	82,600
The Bud at the Glen	Watkins Glen	7	13	151	18,890
GM Goodwrench Dealer 400	Michigan	9	30	143	21,190
Goody's 500	Bristol	4	16	160	28,730
Mountain Dew Southern 500	Darlington	13	21	129	16,180
Miller Genuine Draft 400	Richmond	10	29	139	18,280
Splitfire Spark Plug 500	Dover Downs	3	35	170	36,705
Goody's 500	Martinsville	10	11	134	17,825
Tyson Holly Farms 400	North Wilkesboro	13	7	124	12,950
Mello Yello 500	Charlotte	9	35	143	29,200
AC-Delco 500	Rockingham	23	22	94	16,900
Slick 50 500	Phoenix	10	18	134	19,770
Hooters 500	Atlanta	21	16	100	10,745

DRIVER INFO

Hometown: **Franklin, Tennessee**

Birthdate: **February 5, 1947**

Height: **6' 1"**   Weight: **190**

Darrell Waltrip loves racing. At age twelve it was go-karts, then on to the Late Model Sportsman division at Tennessee short tracks, finally to the Winston Cup circuit. In 627 starts he has accumulated $13,591,234 in career winnings, making him third on the all-time list. His first Winston Cup race was in 1972, and three years later, on his fiftieth start, he claimed his first win. In 1981, 1982, and 1985 he was Winston Cup Champion. Now, 84 Winston Cup wins later, he ranks third on the all-time win list and is tops in the modern era.

Beginning with basketball and track in high school, Darrell has maintained other non-racing interests. He plays golf, watches football and basketball, and looks after his pets.

Darrell Waltrip is truly one of NASCAR's legendary drivers.

Career Starts	Wins	Top Five	Top Ten
627	84	270	374
100%	13.40%	43.06%	59.65%

1992-1994 Starts	Wins	Top Five	Top Ten
90	3	18	36
100%	3.33%	20.00%	40.00%

1994 Starts	Wins	Top Five	Top Ten
31	0	4	13
100%	0.00%	12.90%	41.94%

Bobby Labonte

DRIVER INFO

Hometown: *Corpus Cristi, Texas*
Birthdate: *May 8, 1964*
Height: *5' 8"*　　　**Weight:** *165*

Bobby Labonte's first Winston Cup race was in the 1991 Peak 500 at Dover. After 63 starts, he has $954,315 in career winnings. His first pole came in the fall of 1993 at Richmond, and his best finish is a fifth at the 1994 Watkins Glen. In 1994 he finished 21st in the standings, won $550,305, and had eight top-tens.

The younger brother of Terry Labonte, Bobby began racing early — quarter midgets in Texas in 1969, go-karts in 1978, and Late Model Stock Cars in 1986. He moved to Late Model Sportsman division in 1988 and Busch Grand National in 1990 and was the BGN Most Popular Driver that year with five wins and four poles. In 1991 he was the NASCAR BGN champion, and the next year he was runner-up for the title, finishing just three points behind Joe Nemechek.

Bobby owns a Busch Grand National car, and one of his thrills of 1994 was having driver David Green win the championship in it.

In his time away from racing, Bobby enjoys movies and several other hobbies.

Career Starts	Wins	Top Five	Top Ten
63	0	1	8
100%	0.00%	1.59%	12.70%

(1992-1994) Starts	Wins	Top Five	Top Ten
63	0	1	8
100%	0.00%	1.59%	12.70%

1994 Starts	Wins	Top Five	Top Ten
31	0	1	2
100%	0.00%	3.23%	6.45%

Sponsor: *Interstate Batteries*
Team: *Joe Gibbs Racing*
Driver: *Bobby Labonte*
Owner: *Joe Gibbs*
Crew Chief: *Jimmy Makar*
Car Type: *Chevrolet*

18

1994 SEASON RESULTS

Race	Track	Fin	Qlfy	Pts	Winnings
Daytona 500	Daytona	16	42	115	$43,195
Goodwrench 500	Rockingham	19	20	106	15,985
Pontiac Excitement 400	Richmond	24	31	91	13,525
Purolator 500	Atlanta	15	30	118	17,880
TranSouth Financial 400	Darlington	39	16	46	9,480
Food City 500	Bristol	6	9	150	18,785
First Union 400	North Wilkesboro	26	36	85	11,225
Hanes 500	Martinsville	19	22	106	11,975
Winston Select 500	Talladega	22	41	97	15,940
Save Mart 300	Sears Point	17	22	112	14,730
Coca-Cola 600	Charlotte	40	25	43	10,275
Budweiser 500	Dover Downs	20	4	103	15,965
UAW-GM Teamwork 500	Pocono	25	27	88	14,250
Miller Genuine Draft 400	Michigan	15	30	118	18,025
Pepsi 400	Daytona	22	14	97	16,435
Slick 50 300	New Hampshire	13	4	129	19,575
Miller Genuine Draft 500	Pocono	13	13	124	17,160
DieHard 500	Talladega	12	35	127	21,450
Brickyard 400	Indianapolis	16	5	115	43,800
The Bud at the Glen	Watkins Glen	18	12	109	14,430
GM Goodwrench Dealer 400	Michigan	5	5	155	28,415
Goody's 500	Bristol	31	10	70	11,735
Mountain Dew Southern 500	Darlington	36	8	55	10,080
Miller Genuine Draft 400	Richmond	24	4	91	13,355
Splitfire Spark Plug 500	Dover Downs	17	31	112	15,665
Goody's 500	Martinsville	31	22	70	8,375
Tyson Holly Farms 400	North Wilkesboro	15	20	118	12,950
Mello Yello 500	Charlotte	42	20	37	8,455
AC-Delco 500	Rockingham	28	19	79	13,900
Slick 50 500	Phoenix	16	28	120	14,820
Hooters 500	Atlanta	37	11	52	10,170

Sponsor: *Fina*
Team: *Moroso Racing, Inc.*
Driver: *To Be Announced*
Owner: *Dick Moroso*
Crew Chief: *Dennis Connor*
Car Type: *Ford*

20

DRIVER INFO

DRIVER
TO BE
ANNOUNCED

1994 SEASON RESULTS

DRIVER
TO BE
ANNOUNCED

Morgan Shepherd

Hometown: **Conover, North Carolina**
Birthdate: **October 12, 1941**
Height: **5' 9"**   *Weight:* **170**

In 1981 Morgan Shepherd became the fourth Winston Cup rookie to win a race in his first full season. In 383 starts, he has four wins, seven poles, and $5,715,816 in earnings. In 1994 he passed the $1 million mark with $1,089,038, finished sixth in the standings, and chalked up nine top-5 finishes. Morgan's career-best in the Winston Cup standings was fifth in 1990.

Though his first Winston Cup race was in 1970, Morgan only drove occasionally, never more than in three races, until 1981. He was, however, the 1980 NASCAR National Sportsman (now Busch series) champion.

A devout Christian, Morgan has for years given time and encouragement to those who are mentally and physically handicapped. He also enjoys spending time with his kids.

His expertise with cars goes back a long way, as he learned at an early age how to take an automobile engine apart and re-assemble it.

Career Starts	Wins	Top Five	Top Ten
383	4	57	150
100%	1.04%	14.88%	39.16%

1992-1994 Starts	Wins	Top Five	Top Ten
90	1	15	42
100%	1.11%	16.67%	46.67%

1994 Starts	Wins	Top Five	Top Ten
31	0	9	16
100%	0.00%	29.03%	51.61%

Sponsor: # Citgo Petroleum Corp.
Team: **Wood Brothers Racing Team**
Driver: **Morgan Shepherd**
Owner: **Glen Wood**
Crew Chief: **Leonard Wood**
Car Type: **Ford**

21

1994 SEASON RESULTS

Race	Track	Fin	Qlfy	Pts	Winnings
Daytona 500	Daytona	5	12	160	$92,805
Goodwrench 500	Rockingham	16	11	120	19,635
Pontiac Excitement 400	Richmond	15	32	118	17,835
Purolator 500	Atlanta	2	14	175	48,300
TranSouth Financial 400	Darlington	32	17	67	15,710
Food City 500	Bristol	18	10	109	18,580
First Union 400	North Wilkesboro	22	15	97	15,150
Hanes 500	Martinsville	5	32	155	23,875
Winston Select 500	Talladega	9	12	143	25,550
Save Mart 300	Sears Point	7	19	151	22,020
Coca-Cola 600	Charlotte	28	17	79	17,110
Budweiser 500	Dover Downs	25	9	88	19,465
UAW-GM Teamwork 500	Pocono	4	26	165	24,900
Miller Genuine Draft 400	Michigan	5	12	155	31,025
Pepsi 400	Daytona	9	24	138	24,275
Slick 50 300	New Hampshire	6	9	150	21,275
Miller Genuine Draft 500	Pocono	5	33	155	30,635
DieHard 500	Talladega	15	31	123	22,135
Brickyard 400	Indianapolis	10	11	134	67,350
The Bud at the Glen	Watkins Glen	16	11	115	17,870
GM Goodwrench Dealer 400	Michigan	26	36	85	18,815
Goody's 500	Bristol	18	21	109	18,285
Mountain Dew Southern 500	Darlington	3	13	165	32,730
Miller Genuine Draft 400	Richmond	14	28	121	17,605
Splitfire Spark Plug 500	Dover Downs	10	20	134	23,565
Goody's 500	Martinsville	15	23	123	16,775
Tyson Holly Farms 400	North Wilkesboro	30	35	73	14,350
Mello Yello 500	Charlotte	2	27	175	71,900
AC-Delco 500	Rockingham	3	6	170	32,100
Slick 50 500	Phoenix	12	13	127	19,020
Hooters 500	Atlanta	6	33	150	24,100

Randy LaJoie

Sponsor: **MBNA America Bank**

Team: **Bill Davis Racing, Inc.**
Driver: **Randy LaJoie**
Owner: **Bill Davis**
Crew Chief: **Chris Hussey**
Car Type: **Pontiac**

22

1994 SEASON RESULTS

Race	Track	Fin	Qlfy	Pts	Winnings
Coca-Cola 600	Charlotte	20	27	103	$ 9,815
Slick 50 300	New Hampshire	20	19	103	12,175

DRIVER INFO

Hometown: Norwalk, Connecticut
Birthdate: August 18, 1961
Height: 6' 1"   Weight: 205

Randy LaJoie drove in his first Winston Cup race in 1985, but 1995 is his first full season. In 1994 he finished 16th in the Busch Grand National standings. He posted seven top-ten finishes and won $129,438. Since 1985 he has started 13 Winston Cup events, including three in 1994. His career Winston Cup earnings are $75,890, and he is still looking for his first top-ten finish.

Randy's racing career began in 1980 at the Danbury Race Arena in Connecticut. He won the Danbury points title in 1981, winning fourteen of twenty-two Modified Sportsman events. Then in 1983 he won the Busch Grand National North Series Rookie of the Year, with two wins and a fourth in the overall point standings. In 1985 he took the Busch North title.

Career Starts	Wins	Top Five	Top Ten
13	0	0	0
100%	0.00%	0.00%	0.00%

(1992-1994) Starts	Wins	Top Five	Top Ten
3	0	0	0
100%	0.00%	0.00%	0.00%

1994 Starts	Wins	Top Five	Top Ten
3	0	0	0
100%	0.00%	0.00%	0.00%

Jimmy Spencer

DRIVER INFO

Hometown: **Berwick, Pennsylvania**
Birthdate: **February 15, 1957**
Height: **6' 1"**   Weight: **220**

Jimmy Spencer came to Winston Cup racing in 1989. In 1994, his fourth full season on the circuit, he earned his first two Winston Cup victories at the summer races at Daytona and Talladega. He also won his first career pole at North Wilkesboro and finished 29th in the standings. In 143 Winston Cup starts, he has $1,975,806 in winnings.

In 1992 Jimmy posted three top-five finishes in the final four races of 1992. In 1993 he had five top-five finishes, including a second in the Winston 500.

Jimmy started his racing career at Port Royal Speedway, and he won Rookie of the Year honors in the Late Model division. Then, at Shangri-La Speedway, he again won the Rookie title in the Modified Division. In 1986 and 1987 he was NASCAR Winston Modified national champion, and it was here that he was dubbed with the nickname "Mr. Excitement." He was a Busch Grand National regular in 1988 and 1992.

In his spare time Jimmy enjoys playing golf.

Career Starts	Wins	Top Five	Top Ten
143	2	12	28
100%	1.40%	8.39%	19.58%

1992-1994 Starts	Wins	Top Five	Top Ten
71	2	11	17
100%	2.82%	15.49%	23.94%

1994 Starts	Wins	Top Five	Top Ten
29	2	3	4
100%	6.90%	10.34%	13.79%

Sponsor: **Camel Cigarettes**
Team: **Smokin' Joe's Racing**
Driver: **Jimmy Spencer**
Owner: **Travis Carter**
Crew Chief: **Cecil Gordon**
Car Type: **Ford**

23

1994 SEASON RESULTS

Race	Track	Fin	Qlfy	Pts	Winnings
Daytona 500	Daytona	37	21	52	$28,790
Goodwrench 500	Rockingham	12	26	127	13,735
Pontiac Excitement 400	Richmond	22	10	97	9,725
Purolator 500	Atlanta	10	25	134	17,500
TranSouth Financial 400	Darlington	27	27	82	8,110
Food City 500	Bristol	35	16	58	6,625
First Union 400	North Wilkesboro	32	8	67	6,225
Hanes 500	Martinsville	18	4	109	8,630
Winston Select 500	Talladega	4	5	165	32,570
Save Mart 300	Sears Point	26	25	85	9,780
Coca-Cola 600	Charlotte	19	33	106	12,300
Budweiser 500	Dover Downs	39	28	46	7,780
UAW-GM Teamwork 500	Pocono	37	29	52	7,300
Miller Genuine Draft 400	Michigan	23	21	94	12,165
Pepsi 400	Daytona	1	3	185	75,880
Slick 50 300	New Hampshire	32	13	67	12,500
Miller Genuine Draft 500	Pocono	24	42	91	10,910
DieHard 500	Talladega	1	2	180	81,450
Brickyard 400	Indianapolis	43	34	34	21,825
GM Goodwrench Dealer 400	Michigan	20	41	108	12,640
Mountain Dew Southern 500	Darlington	37	30	52	5,570
Miller Genuine Draft 400	Richmond	35	23	58	6,755
Splitfire Spark Plug 500	Dover Downs	39	27	46	7,780
Goody's 500	Martinsville	20	28	108	8,425
Tyson Holly Farms 400	North Wilkesboro	23	1	99	13,425
Mello Yello 500	Charlotte	16	25	115	10,800
AC-Delco 500	Rockingham	38	32	49	6,925
Slick 50 500	Phoenix	38	20	49	6,505
Hooters 500	Atlanta	20	25	103	11,710

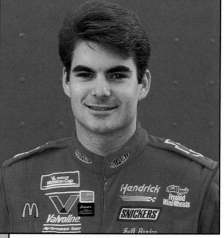

Jeff Gordon

Sponsor: **Dupont Automotive Finishes**
Team: **Hendrick Motorsports**
Driver: **Jeff Gordon**
Owner: **Rick Hendrick**
Crew Chief: **Ray Evernham**
Car Type: **Chevrolet**

24

1994 SEASON RESULTS

Race	Track	Fin	Qlfy	Pts	Winnings
Daytona 500	Daytona	4	6	165	$112,525
Goodwrench 500	Rockingham	32	3	67	13,500
Pontiac Excitement 400	Richmond	3	8	170	34,000
Purolator 500	Atlanta	8	17	142	21,550
TranSouth Financial 400	Darlington	31	13	70	11,745
Food City 500	Bristol	22	4	102	14,855
First Union 400	North Wilkesboro	15	12	118	13,100
Hanes 500	Martinsville	33	13	64	10,475
Winston Select 500	Talladega	24	40	96	15,525
Save Mart 300	Sears Point	37	6	52	12,675
Coca-Cola 600	Charlotte	1	1	180	196,500
Budweiser 500	Dover Downs	5	23	155	33,570
UAW-GM Teamwork 500	Pocono	6	4	155	23,505
Miller Genuine Draft 400	Michigan	12	7	132	22,175
Pepsi 400	Daytona	8	12	147	25,175
Slick 50 300	New Hampshire	39	2	51	22,100
Miller Genuine Draft 500	Pocono	8	7	142	21,760
DieHard 500	Talladega	31	15	70	19,660
Brickyard 400	Indianapolis	1	3	185	613,000
The Bud at the Glen	Watkins Glen	9	3	138	19,950
GM Goodwrench Dealer 400	Michigan	15	3	123	21,565
Goody's 500	Bristol	32	12	72	17,735
Mountain Dew Southern 500	Darlington	6	7	150	22,765
Miller Genuine Draft 400	Richmond	2	13	175	40,365
Splitfire Spark Plug 500	Dover Downs	11	12	130	20,615
Goody's 500	Martinsville	11	6	135	19,810
Tyson Holly Farms 400	North Wilkesboro	8	12	142	16,875
Mello Yello 500	Charlotte	28	5	84	16,730
AC-Delco 500	Rockingham	29	15	81	26,300
Slick 50 500	Phoenix	4	14	165	26,780
Hooters 500	Atlanta	15	6	118	20,125

DRIVER INFO

Hometown: **Pittsboro, Indiana**
Birthdate: **August 4, 1971**
Height: **5' 7"**   Weight: **150**

Jeff Gordon's Winston Cup career began in 1992 at the Hooter's 500 at Atlanta, and since then he has had spectacular success. He was the 1993 Winston Cup Rookie of the Year and became the youngest driver ever to win the 145 mile qualifying race for the Daytona 500. Then in 1994 he won two Winston Cup races, including the Inaugural Brickyard 400 at Indianapolis. The other victory was the Coca-Cola 600 at Charlotte. During last year's 31 races he won $1,779,523 and finished eighth in points. In 62 Winston Cup starts, he has $2,550,976 in winnings.

Jeff's racing began with go-karts and quarter midgets. He has a string of accomplishments in succeeding years: 1979 and 1981 Quarter Midget National Champion, 1990 USAC Midget champion, 1991 Busch Grand National Rookie of the Year and posted more than 500 short-track wins. That same year he had over 500 wins on short tracks. He also won the national championship of the United States Auto Club Silver Crown Division.

In his spare time Jeff enjoys several leisure activities, including golf and racquetball.

Career Starts	Wins	Top Five	Top Ten
62	2	14	25
100%	3.23%	22.58%	40.32%

(1992-1994) Starts	Wins	Top Five	Top Ten
62	2	14	25
100%	3.23%	22.58%	40.32%

1994 Starts	Wins	Top Five	Top Ten
31	2	7	14
100%	6.45%	22.58%	45.16%

Ken Schrader

Hometown: **Fenton, Missouri**
Birthdate: **May 29, 1955**
Height: **5' 10"**   Weight: **190**

Ken Schrader's first Winston Cup race was in 1984 at Nashville, Tennessee, when he finished 18th. He was the 1985 Winston Cup Rookie of the Year. His first win was in his 108th start, in the July, 1988 Diehard 500. He has a total of 297 starts, four wins, 17 poles and an impressive $6,816,617 in winnings. In 1994 he finished a career-best fourth in Winston Cup standings and won $1,171,062 with nine top-five finishes.

Ken started racing in 1971 and claimed the Lakehill Speedway track championship. He moved on to USAC, where he has 33 wins and is 24th on the all-time win list. In Sprint he was 1983 national champion.

All types of vehicles interest Ken. He owns two planes and a variety of old pickup trucks and cars, as well as a Winnebago and two motorcycles. As he races more than one hundred times a year, fans might wonder how he has time to spend on his hobbies!

Career Starts	Wins	Top Five	Top Ten
297	4	54	124
100%	1.35%	18.18%	41.75%

1992-1994 Starts	Wins	Top Five	Top Ten
90	0	22	44
100%	0.00%	24.44%	48.89%

1994 Starts	Wins	Top Five	Top Ten
31	0	9	18
100%	0.00%	29.03%	58.06%

Sponsor: **Budweiser**
Team: **Hendrick Motorsports**
Driver: **Ken Schrader**
Owner: **Joseph R. Hendrick Jr.**
Crew Chief: **Ken Howes**
Car Type: **Chevrolet**

1994 SEASON RESULTS

Race	Track	Fin	Qlfy	Pts	Winnings
Daytona 500	Daytona	10	13	134	$59,565
Goodwrench 500	Rockingham	9	13	138	18,935
Pontiac Excitement 400	Richmond	11	16	130	15,325
Purolator 500	Atlanta	16	24	115	17,270
TranSouth Financial 400	Darlington	7	6	146	18,395
Food City 500	Bristol	2	22	170	43,445
First Union 400	North Wilkesboro	9	9	143	15,025
Hanes 500	Martinsville	31	17	70	10,575
Winston Select 500	Talladega	5	7	160	33,540
Save Mart 300	Sears Point	9	8	138	18,170
Coca-Cola 600	Charlotte	24	4	91	16,620
Budweiser 500	Dover Downs	3	20	165	35,605
UAW-GM Teamwork 500	Pocono	3	5	170	33,400
Miller Genuine Draft 400	Michigan	6	31	150	25,300
Pepsi 400	Daytona	5	6	155	30,150
Slick 50 300	New Hampshire	24	5	91	17,700
Miller Genuine Draft 500	Pocono	39	19	46	11,635
DieHard 500	Talladega	4	4	165	33,530
Brickyard 400	Indianapolis	7	23	146	77,400
The Bud at the Glen	Watkins Glen	4	2	160	26,245
GM Goodwrench Dealer 400	Michigan	11	19	130	17,690
Goody's 500	Bristol	19	31	106	14,775
Mountain Dew Southern 500	Darlington	32	2	77	13,350
Miller Genuine Draft 400	Richmond	9	10	138	16,280
Splitfire Spark Plug 500	Dover Downs	4	14	165	32,965
Goody's 500	Martinsville	6	14	150	18,775
Tyson Holly Farms 400	North Wilkesboro	14	27	121	12,725
Mello Yello 500	Charlotte	4	11	165	47,800
AC-Delco 500	Rockingham	32	24	72	13,300
Slick 50 500	Phoenix	15	7	118	15,470
Hooters 500	Atlanta	11	38	130	18,375

Hut Stricklin

Sponsor: **Quaker State**

Team: **King Racing, Inc.**
Driver: **Hut Stricklin**
Owner: **Kenny Bernstein**
Crew Chief: **Richard Broome**
Car Type: **Ford**

26

DRIVER INFO

Hometown: **Calera, Alabama**
Birthdate: **June 24, 1961**
Height: **6' 1"**   *Weight:* **185**

In 1987 Wayman "Hut" Stricklin, the 1986 NASCAR Dash Series champion, made his Winston Cup debut at North Wilkesboro in the Holly Farms 400. In 1989, his first full NASCAR Winston Cup season, he was runner-up for Rookie of the Year. In 170 starts, he has earned $1,918,372. His career-best finish was a second at Michigan in 1990, and his best standing was in 1991 with a 16th. He finished 26th in 1994.

Hut's association with racing goes back to his childhood, when he accompanied his father to local Alabama tracks. In 1986 he was Goody's Dash Series Champion. He won nine of 17 races and ten poles during his run for the title. His own career is not his only tie to the sport, as his wife Pam is the daughter of Donnie Allison.

In his spare time Hut enjoys country music, movies, and spending time restoring his two classic Chevy Novas.

1994 SEASON RESULTS

Race	Track	Fin	Qlfy	Pts	Winnings
Daytona 500	Daytona	33	38	64	$28,235
Goodwrench 500	Rockingham	26	24	85	8,025
Purolator 500	Atlanta	17	39	112	10,060
TranSouth Financial 400	Darlington	17	15	112	7,250
Food City 500	Bristol	14	26	121	8,905
First Union 400	North Wilkesboro	20	14	103	5,950
Hanes 500	Martinsville	20	26	103	5,825
Winston Select 500	Talladega	18	26	109	10,180
Save Mart 300	Sears Point	20	37	103	8,480
Coca-Cola 600	Charlotte	12	40	127	18,700
Budweiser 500	Dover Downs	9	38	138	17,165
UAW-GM Teamwork 500	Pocono	13	23	124	12,805
Miller Genuine Draft 400	Michigan	22	39	97	11,875
Pepsi 400	Daytona	42	20	37	8,705
Slick 50 300	New Hampshire	36	30	55	11,400
Miller Genuine Draft 500	Pocono	22	35	97	11,260
DieHard 500	Talladega	25	37	88	12,210
Brickyard 400	Indianapolis	36	20	55	24,000
The Bud at the Glen	Watkins Glen	30	18	73	8,595
Goody's 500	Bristol	35	26	58	7,735
Mountain Dew Southern 500	Darlington	14	36	121	11,890
Miller Genuine Draft 400	Richmond	30	2	78	8,355
Splitfire Spark Plug 500	Dover Downs	32	32	67	9,605
Goody's 500	Martinsville	23	21	99	7,225
Tyson Holly Farms 400	North Wilkesboro	22	25	97	7,375
Mello Yello 500	Charlotte	21	33	100	8,350
AC-Delco 500	Rockingham	27	34	82	13,200
Slick 50 500	Phoenix	24	31	91	9,485
Hooters 500	Atlanta	16	39	115	12,450

Career Starts	Wins	Top Five	Top Ten
170	0	5	20
100%	0.00%	2.94%	11.76%

1992-1994 Starts	Wins	Top Five	Top Ten
87	0	1	7
100%	0.00%	1.15%	8.05%

1994 Starts	Wins	Top Five	Top Ten
29	0	0	1
100%	0.00%	0.00%	3.45%

Hometown: **Raleigh, North Carolina**
Birthdate: **April 7, 1966**
Height: **5' 8"**   Weight: **160**

Loy Allen is relatively new to Winston Cup racing, and he is off to an impressive beginning. In 1993 he had five Winston Cup starts. Then in 1994, his first full season, he became the first NASCAR rookie to win the pole for the Daytona 500. In that race he finished 22nd, the highest position of any rookie. Later in the season he took poles at Michigan and Atlanta. He finished the year 39th in points.

Before the 1992 Winston Cup race at Talladega, Loy had not raced on a track larger than 5/8 of a mile. But he really got a big break that year when he won his first stock car competition, ARCA's Motorcraft 500K at Atlanta, in front of Hooters executives.

Early in his racing career Loy participated in the World Karting Association, becoming the WKA North Carolina champion. He was also the 1983 NDRA Super Late Model Rookie of the Year.

In high school Loy was another sort of champion — in wrestling. Currently he finds time for other interests, including golf, skiing, and movies.

Career Starts	Wins	Top Five	Top Ten
24	0	0	0
100%	0.00%	0.00%	0.00%

(1992-1994)* Starts	Wins	Top Five	Top Ten
24	0	0	0
100%	0.00%	0.00%	0.00%

1994 Starts	Wins	Top Five	Top Ten
19	0	0	0
100%	0.00%	0.00%	0.00%

*2 years (1993 & 1994)

Sponsor: **Hooters**
Team: **Junior Johnson & Associates**
Driver: **Loy Allen**
Owner: **Junior Johnson**
Crew Chief: **Mike Hill**
Car Type: **Ford**

1994 SEASON RESULTS

Race	Track	Fin	Qlfy	Pts	Winnings
Daytona 500	Daytona	22	1	97	$43,515
Goodwrench 500	Rockingham	40	42	43	6,900
Purolator 500	Atlanta	22	1	97	18,240
Winston Select 500	Talladega	40	2	43	8,720
Coca-Cola 600	Charlotte	11	37	130	22,700
Budweiser 500	Dover Downs	15	39	118	9,665
UAW-GM Teamwork 500	Pocono	31	31	70	7,750
Miller Genuine Draft 400	Michigan	24	1	96	14,055
Pepsi 400	Daytona	40	2	48	8,705
Miller Genuine Draft 500	Pocono	18	8	109	9,260
DieHard 500	Talladega	37	3	57	9,781
GM Goodwrench Dealer 400	Michigan	22	14	97	9,365
Mountain Dew Southern 500	Darlington	21	42	100	7,200
Miller Genuine Draft 400	Richmond	31	35	70	6,805
Splitfire Spark Plug 500	Dover Downs	22	40	97	9,115
Mello Yello 500	Charlotte	27	34	82	5,150
AC-Delco 500	Rockingham	42	17	37	6,900
Slick 50 500	Phoenix	41	42	40	5,825
Hooters 500	Atlanta	42	17	37	6,100

Ernie Irvan

Sponsor: **Texaco Havoline**
Team: **Robert Yates Racing**
Driver: **Ernie Irvan**
Owner: **Robert Yates**
Crew Chief: **Larry McReynolds**
Car Type: **Ford**

28

1994 SEASON RESULTS

Race	Track	Fin	Qlfy	Pts	Winnings
Daytona 500	Daytona	2	3	180	$190,750
Goodwrench 500	Rockingham	5	6	155	26,410
Pontiac Excitement 400	Richmond	1	7	185	71,175
Purolator 500	Atlanta	1	7	185	86,100
TranSouth Financial 400	Darlington	6	11	155	22,875
Food City 500	Bristol	33	7	64	18,225
First Union 400	North Wilkesboro	3	1	175	41,565
Hanes 500	Martinsville	2	5	175	41,750
Winston Select 500	Talladega	2	1	180	67,990
Save Mart 300	Sears Point	1	1	185	78,810
Coca-Cola 600	Charlotte	5	14	160	47,800
Budweiser 500	Dover Downs	2	1	180	54,830
UAW-GM Teamwork 500	Pocono	7	7	151	23,705
Miller Genuine Draft 400	Michigan	18	23	114	22,640
Pepsi 400	Daytona	2	5	180	50,275
Slick 50 300	New Hampshire	30	1	83	31,600
Miller Genuine Draft 500	Pocono	37	5	57	19,310
DieHard 500	Talladega	3	5	175	47,130
Brickyard 400	Indianapolis	17	17	117	52,000
The Bud at the Glen	Watkins Glen	2	4	170	42,015

DRIVER INFO

Hometown: **Salinas, California**
Birthdate: **January 13, 1959**
Height: **5' 9"**   *Weight:* **180**

Ernie Irvan continues his miraculous recovery after injuries suffered from a practice session crash at Michigan in August of 1994. He hopes to return to racing in the future. His first Winston Cup race was in 1987 at Richmond, and he was runner-up to Ken Bouchard for 1988 Rookie of the Year honors. In 196 Winston Cup starts, he has 12 wins, 16 poles, and $5,599,121 in winnings. At the time of his crash he trailed Dale Earnhardt by only 27 points. Despite missing the last third of the season, he won the True Value Hard Charger Award for leading the most miles of the season. His career-best in the standings was a fifth in 1991, the same year he won the Daytona 500.

In high school Ernie raced as a hobby. His father helped him build his first race car, and they won the Stockton Track championship together in 1977.

A man of many talents and interests, Ernie will do television work during the race telecasts. In his spare time he enjoys movies, music, and basketball.

Career Starts	Wins	Top Five	Top Ten
196	12	51	77
100%	6.12%	26.02%	39.29%

(1992-1994) Starts	Wins	Top Five	Top Ten
79	9	34	40
100%	11.39%	43.04%	50.63%

1994 Starts	Wins	Top Five	Top Ten
20	3	13	15
100%	15.00%	65.00%	75.00%

Dale Jarrett

DRIVER INFO

Hometown: **Conover, North Carolina**
Birthdate: **November 26, 1956**
Height: **6' 2"**   Weight: **215**

Dale Jarrett made his Winston Cup debut in 1984. After 228 career starts, he has three wins and $3,704,244 in earnings. His first win came in the 1991 Champion 400 at Michigan International Speedway. His career-best in the standings was a fourth in 1993, the year he won the Daytona 500. In 1994 Dale finished 16th and won $881,754; his sole victory came in the Mello Yello 500 at Charlotte. He did, however, have four top-fives and nine top-tens.

The son of Ned Jarrett, two-time Winston Cup champion, Dale was born into racing. His early experience was at Hickory Motor Speedway where his father was track promoter. Dale has had success in the Busch Grand National circuit, having eight victories to his credit.

A man with diverse talents, Dale is a very good golfer. In his leisure time he enjoys being with his children and participates in a variety of outdoor sports.

Career Starts	Wins	Top Five	Top Ten
228	3	25	58
100%	1.32%	10.96%	25.44%
(1992-1994) Starts	Wins	Top Five	Top Ten
89	2	19	35
100%	2.25%	21.35%	39.33%
1994 Starts	Wins	Top Five	Top Ten
30	1	4	9
100%	3.33%	13.33%	30.00%

Sponsor: **Texaco Havoline**
Team: **Robert Yates Racing**
Driver: **Dale Jarrett**
Owner: **Robert Yates**
Crew Chief: **Larry McReynolds**
Car Type: **Ford**

28

1994 SEASON RESULTS

Race	Track	Fin	Qlfy	Pts	Winnings
Daytona 500	Daytona	35	41	63	$38,325
Goodwrench 500	Rockingham	18	41	109	20,635
Pontiac Excitement 400	Richmond	10	22	134	21,825
Purolator 500	Atlanta	35	36	63	19,820
TranSouth Financial 400	Darlington	4	14	165	27,550
Food City 500	Bristol	36	36	55	12,025
First Union 400	North Wilkesboro	25	31	88	16,275
Hanes 500	Martinsville	21	20	100	16,475
Winston Select 500	Talladega	21	9	100	20,860
Save Mart 300	Sears Point	12	20	127	20,755
Coca-Cola 600	Charlotte	4	16	165	54,600
Budweiser 500	Dover Downs	29	13	76	19,665
UAW-GM Teamwork 500	Pocono	20	22	108	20,680
Miller Genuine Draft 400	Michigan	14	35	121	22,675
Pepsi 400	Daytona	11	11	130	24,265
Slick 50 300	New Hampshire	14	31	121	23,775
Miller Genuine Draft 500	Pocono	10	17	134	24,510
DieHard 500	Talladega	39	13	46	20,690
Brickyard 400	Indianapolis	40	14	43	33,225
The Bud at the Glen	Watkins Glen	11	14	130	20,250
GM Goodwrench Dealer 400	Michigan	30	31	73	19,965
Goody's 500	Bristol	26	29	90	19,285
Mountain Dew Southern 500	Darlington	9	35	138	23,370
Miller Genuine Draft 400	Richmond	16	25	115	18,830
Splitfire Spark Plug 500	Dover Downs	34	19	61	19,405
Goody's 500	Martinsville	5	8	155	26,775
Mello Yello 500	Charlotte	1	22	180	106,800
AC-Delco 500	Rockingham	12	27	127	21,850
Slick 50 500	Phoenix	9	5	143	21,920
Hooters 500	Atlanta	9	23	138	23,325

Steve Grissom

Sponsor: *Meineke Discount Mufflers*

Team: **Diamond Ridge Motorsports**
Driver: **Steve Grissom**
Owner: **Gary &
Carolyn Bechtel**
Crew Chief: **Bryant Frazier**
Car Type: **Chevrolet**

29

1994 SEASON RESULTS

Race	Track	Fin	Qlfy	Pts	Winnings
Goodwrench 500	Rockingham	30	12	73	$ 7,650
Pontiac Excitement 400	Richmond	23	15	94	7,550
Purolator 500	Atlanta	20	31	103	10,310
TranSouth Financial 400	Darlington	14	28	121	9,280
Food City 500	Bristol	12	30	127	10,230
Hanes 500	Martinsville	14	23	121	7,525
Winston Select 500	Talladega	10	11	134	18,600
Save Mart 300	Sears Point	35	40	58	7,205
Coca-Cola 600	Charlotte	39	28	46	6,300
Budweiser 500	Dover Downs	27	15	82	10,565
UAW-GM Teamwork 500	Pocono	26	37	85	10,600
Miller Genuine Draft 400	Michigan	26	27	85	11,185
Pepsi 400	Daytona	33	21	64	8,885
Slick 50 300	New Hampshire	33	25	64	12,300
Miller Genuine Draft 500	Pocono	29	39	76	10,360
DieHard 500	Talladega	18	24	109	14,480
The Bud at the Glen	Watkins Glen	23	32	94	9,740
GM Goodwrench Dealer 400	Michigan	19	20	106	11,815
Goody's 500	Bristol	34	30	61	7,735
Mountain Dew Southern 500	Darlington	23	32	94	9,560
Miller Genuine Draft 400	Richmond	7	8	146	19,380
Splitfire Spark Plug 500	Dover Downs	8	34	147	16,815
Goody's 500	Martinsville	12	30	127	13,025
Tyson Holly Farms 400	North Wilkesboro	20	33	103	7,725
Mello Yello 500	Charlotte	26	42	85	7,265
AC-Delco 500	Rockingham	30	16	73	9,600
Slick 50 500	Phoenix	22	33	97	9,760
Hooters 500	Atlanta	26	29	85	9,370

DRIVER INFO

Hometown: **Gadsden, Alabama**
Birthdate: **June 26, 1963**
Height: **6' 3"**   Weight: **220**

Steve is new to Winston Cup racing. He made his debut at Atlanta in 1990 and in his first full season, 1994, finished second to Jeff Burton for Rookie of the Year. He finished 28th in the point standings and posted three top-ten finishes. In 30 Winston Cup starts, he has earned $313,975.

Steve began racing on Alabama short-tracks in the area of his home town. After racing in the Winston All-Pro Series where he was 1985 All-Pro Champion, he joined the Busch Grand National circuit in 1988. There he drove cars owned by his father, Wayne. In 182 BGN starts he has eight wins, and he claimed the NASCAR Busch Grand National Series Championship in 1993. He was nominated for Alabama Pro Athlete of the Year in 1986 and 1994.

Racing was important in Steve's family. His father sponsored local Alabama drivers, and Steve began working on cars at an early age. He was also a talented athlete, captain of the football team and on the basketball team. While away from cars and racing, Steve enjoys golf, action movies, and music.

Career Starts	Wins	Top Five	Top Ten
29	0	0	3
100%	0.00%	0.00%	10.34%

(1992-1994)* Starts	Wins	Top Five	Top Ten
29	0	0	3
100%	0.00%	0.00%	10.34%

1994 Starts	Wins	Top Five	Top Ten
28	0	0	3
100%	0.00%	0.00%	10.71%

*2 years (1993 & 1994)

Michael Waltrip

DRIVER INFO

Hometown: *Owensboro, Kentucky*
Birthdate: *April 30, 1963*
Height: *6' 5"*   **Weight:** *220*

Michael Waltrip made his Winston Cup debut in 1985 in the World 600 at Charlotte. His best career finish is a second in 1988 in the Miller 500 at Pocono, and his career-best in the standings is a 12th in 1994. In 268 starts he has two poles and $3,296,523 in winnings.

Michael's racing career started in the early eighties in Kentucky. In the Mini-modified Division he was the Kentucky Motor Speedway track champion. From there he went on to the Dash Series where he was a champion and Most Popular Driver in 1983 and in 1984. He has seven Busch Grand National victories and won the Winston Open in 1991 and 1992.

Because of his brother Darrell, Michael was drawn to racing. He also has other associations in the sport, as he lived with Richard and Lynda Petty when he moved to North Carolina.

Michael enjoys some non-racing activities such as golf and basketball, but he also likes anything that has an engine, such as motorcycles and boats.

Career Starts	Wins	Top Five	Top Ten
268	0	13	48
100%	0.00%	4.85%	17.91%

1992-1994 Starts	Wins	Top Five	Top Ten
90	0	3	17
100%	0.00%	3.33%	18.89%

1994 Starts	Wins	Top Five	Top Ten
31	0	2	10
100%	0.00%	6.45%	32.26%

Sponsor: **Pennzoil**
Team: **Bahari' Racing**
Driver: **Michael Waltrip**
Owner: **Chuck Rider &**
          Lowrance Harry
Crew Chief: **Doug Hewitt**
Car Type: **Pontiac**

30

1994 SEASON RESULTS

Race	Track	Fin	Qlfy	Pts	Winnings
Daytona 500	Daytona	31	14	70	$36,545
Goodwrench 500	Rockingham	10	31	134	19,140
Pontiac Excitement 400	Richmond	31	14	70	12,825
Purolator 500	Atlanta	23	32	94	16,030
TranSouth Financial 400	Darlington	15	30	118	15,025
Food City 500	Bristol	5	23	155	20,135
First Union 400	North Wilkesboro	11	18	130	13,525
Hanes 500	Martinsville	17	7	112	13,225
Winston Select 500	Talladega	3	8	165	50,995
Save Mart 300	Sears Point	16	9	115	15,005
Coca-Cola 600	Charlotte	10	30	134	26,800
Budweiser 500	Dover Downs	7	34	151	20,515
UAW-GM Teamwork 500	Pocono	11	10	130	17,355
Miller Genuine Draft 400	Michigan	8	11	142	22,350
Pepsi 400	Daytona	13	23	124	19,180
Slick 50 300	New Hampshire	37	12	57	13,800
Miller Genuine Draft 500	Pocono	14	41	121	16,860
DieHard 500	Talladega	11	9	130	19,830
Brickyard 400	Indianapolis	8	15	142	72,300
The Bud at the Glen	Watkins Glen	20	19	103	14,630
GM Goodwrench Dealer 400	Michigan	14	10	121	18,190
Goody's 500	Bristol	7	28	151	18,365
Mountain Dew Southern 500	Darlington	31	26	75	12,040
Miller Genuine Draft 400	Richmond	26	20	85	13,180
Splitfire Spark Plug 500	Dover Downs	33	28	64	12,055
Goody's 500	Martinsville	19	31	111	11,975
Tyson Holly Farms 400	North Wilkesboro	21	13	100	11,500
Mello Yello 500	Charlotte	10	2	134	31,450
AC-Delco 500	Rockingham	26	33	85	14,300
Slick 50 500	Phoenix	36	25	55	10,535
Hooters 500	Atlanta	10	27	134	21,200

Ward Burton

Sponsor: **Hardee's**
Team: **A.G. Dillard Motorsports**
Driver: **Ward Burton**
Owner: **Alan Dillard**
Crew Chief: **Philippe Lopez**
Car Type: **Chevrolet**

31

1994 SEASON RESULTS

Race	Track	Fin	Qlfy	Pts	Winnings
Pontiac Excitement 400	Richmond	35	29	58	$6,775
Purolator 500	Atlanta	40	8	43	8,285
TranSouth Financial 400	Darlington	21	38	100	6,670
Food City 500	Bristol	25	21	88	8,585
Hanes 500	Martinsville	16	33	115	6,825
Save Mart 300	Sears Point	36	27	55	7,195
Coca-Cola 600	Charlotte	37	8	52	6,850
Budweiser 500	Dover Downs	37	11	52	7,780
UAW-GM Teamwork 500	Pocono	42	25	37	7,150
Miller Genuine Draft 400	Michigan	29	15	76	8,555
Pepsi 400	Daytona	31	40	55	8,795
Slick 50 300	New Hampshire	42	33	37	9,500
Miller Genuine Draft 500	Pocono	2	2	175	39,720
Brickyard 400	Indianapolis	31	33	70	23,500
The Bud at the Glen	Watkins Glen	24	30	91	6,880
GM Goodwrench Dealer 400	Michigan	29	26	76	8,615
Goody's 500	Bristol	36	7	55	7,735
Mountain Dew Southern 500	Darlington	34	3	61	5,750
Miller Genuine Draft 400	Richmond	25	15	88	7,005
Splitfire Spark Plug 500	Dover Downs	27	3	82	8,465
Goody's 500	Martinsville	35	18	58	4,375
Tyson Holly Farms 400	North Wilkesboro	18	21	114	7,550
Mello Yello 500	Charlotte	41	1	45	29,655
AC-Delco 500	Rockingham	9	7	143	12,450
Slick 50 500	Phoenix	21	27	100	7,685
Hooters 500	Atlanta	41	26	45	8,900

DRIVER INFO

Hometown: **South Boston, Virginia**
Birthdate: **October 25, 1961**
Height: **5' 6"**   Weight: **145**

In 1994 Ward Burton began his Winston Cup driving career, finishing just behind his brother Jeff for NASCAR Rookie of the Year. His first pole was at Charlotte, where he set a new track record, and at Pocono he had a runner-up finish, the best for a '94 rookie. He drove in 26 races, finished 35th in the standings, and won $302,950.

At the age of eight Ward began racing go-karts. He moved on to Street Stock and Late Model Stocks on the Virginia short tracks around South Boston. In 1989 he was honored with the Most Popular Driver title at the South Boston Speedway. He went on to the Busch Grand National Division the next year and got off to a fine start. That year he finished second behind Joe Nemechek for BGN Rookie of the Year. In 111 BGN starts he has four wins.

Many interests other than racing fill Ward's spare time. He is a marksman, winning first place on the Rifle Team at Hargrove Military Academy. He loves all sorts of outdoor activities, including hunting, skeet shooting, and water sports.

Career Starts	Wins	Top Five	Top Ten
26	0	1	2
100%	0.00%	3.85%	7.69%

1992-1994* Starts	Wins	Top Five	Top Ten
26	0	1	2
100%	0.00%	3.85%	7.69%

1994 Starts	Wins	Top Five	Top Ten
26	0	1	2
100%	0.00%	3.85%	7.69%

*1 year (1994)

Chuck Bown

DRIVER INFO

Hometown: **Portland, Oregon**
Birthdate: **Febuary 22, 1954**
Height: **5' 9"**   Weight: **165**

Chuck Bown's Winston Cup debut came in the 1972 Winston Western 500 at Riverside, when he was only 17 years old. He qualified 27th out of 100. He says he was inspired by his father, Dick, who began racing in 1953. Now, after 60 career Winston Cup starts, Chuck has four top-tens and $328,175 in winnings.

The Winston Cup circuit has not been Chuck's only racing arena. In 1976, he was the Winston West Champion, and in 1977 the Winston West Most Popular Driver. In 1985 he was the NASCAR North Most Popular Driver, and in 1990 he was the Busch Grand National Champion.

In addition to racing, Chuck enjoys golf and coaching Little League. He is also an accomplished carpenter and studied solar home building in Oregon Community College.

Career Starts	Wins	Top Five	Top Ten
60	0	0	4
100%	0.00%	0.00%	6.67%

(1992-1994)* Starts	Wins	Top Five	Top Ten
14	0	0	1
100%	0.00%	0.00%	7.14%

1994 Starts	Wins	Top Five	Top Ten
13	0	0	1
100%	0.00%	0.00%	7.69%

*2 years (1993 & 1994)

Sponsor: *Active Trucking*
Team: **Active Motorsports**
Driver: **Chuck Bown**
Owner: **Dean Myers**
Crew Chief: **To Be Announced**
Car Type: **Chevrolet**

1994 SEASON RESULTS

Race	Track	Fin	Qlfy	Pts	Winnings
Daytona 500	Daytona	23	37	94	$36,860
Goodwrench 500	Rockingham	25	25	88	14,535
Pontiac Excitement 400	Richmond	17	3	112	14,300
Purolator 500	Atlanta	41	9	40	12,285
TranSouth Financial 400	Darlington	12	4	127	15,470
Food City 500	Bristol	23	1	94	19,105
First Union 400	North Wilkesboro	35	21	58	8,200
Hanes 500	Martinsville	7	36	146	24,575
Winston Select 500	Talladega	27	14	82	15,110
Save Mart 300	Sears Point	21	41	100	14,230
Coca-Cola 600	Charlotte	13	20	124	22,600
Budweiser 500	Dover Downs	21	35	100	15,165
UAW-GM Teamwork 500	Pocono	39	41	46	11,225

Sponsor: **Skoal Bandit Racing**
Team: **Leo Jackson Motorsports, Inc.**
Driver: **Robert Pressley**
Owner: **Leo E. Jackson, Jr.**
Crew Chief: **Charley Pressley**
Car Type: **Chevrolet**

33

1994 SEASON RESULTS

Race	Track	Fin	Qlfy	Pts	Winnings
Daytona 500	Daytona	40	19	43	$28,490
Mello Yello 500	Charlotte	31	40	70	4,720
Hooters 500	Atlanta	35	35	58	6,275

DRIVER INFO

Hometown: **Asheville, NC**
Birthdate: **April 8, 1959**
Height: **6' 0"**   Weight: **198**

Robert Pressley began the 1995 season competing for Rookie of the Year honors. Up to then he had started three Winston Cup races and won $39,485.

Robert won track championships at New Asheville Speedway and Greenville-Pickens Speedway. In 1988 he helped form a Busch Grand National team and won one race in 1989 as a rookie.

As Robert's father, Bob, raced stock cars in the Asheville, North Carolina, area, Robert came to the sport naturally. As a matter of fact, the elder Pressley still races. Robert's brother Charley, the crew chief for the Skoal Bandit racing team, was also involved in short-track racing. All the Pressley sons spent time involved in their father's racing and learned the sport from the ground up.

Career Starts	Wins	Top Five	Top Ten
3	0	0	0
100%	0.00%	0.00%	0.00%

(1992-1994)* Starts	Wins	Top Five	Top Ten
3	0	0	0
100%	0.00%	0.00%	0.00%

1994 Starts	Wins	Top Five	Top Ten
3	0	0	0
100%	0.00%	0.00%	0.00%

*1 year (1994)

John Andretti

Hometown: **Indianapolis, Indiana**
Birthdate: **March 12, 1963**
Height: **5'5"**   Weight: **140**

John Andretti is new to the Winston Cup scene. He made his debut at North Wilkesboro in the fall of 1993, when he finished 24th. In 33 career Winston Cup starts, he has $416,835 in winnings. His best finish of the 1994 season was 11th in the fall race at Richmond. He became the first driver in history to compete in the Indy 500 (finishing 10th) at Indianapolis and the Coca-Cola 600 at Charlotte (finishing 36th with engine failure), both on the same day.

When he was nine years old, John began racing go-carts, and by 1979 he had begun open wheel road racing. He attended driving schools in Belgium and Pocono, subsequently racing on the Sprint and Midget circuits. In 1988 he had his first LeMans 24-hour start and also drove in the Indy 500. John claimed his first Indy victory in 1991 in Australia, at the Gold Coast Gran Prix. That same year he was fifth in the Indy 500.

John's interest are diverse. He graduated from college with a degree in business management and is a part owner in a couple of auto parts stores.

Career Starts	Wins	Top Five	Top Ten
33	0	0	0
100%	0.00%	0.00%	0.00%

(1992-1994)* Starts	Wins	Top Five	Top Ten
33	0	0	0
100%	0.00%	0.00%	0.00%

1994 Starts	Wins	Top Five	Top Ten
29	0	0	0
100%	0.00%	0.00%	0.00%

*2 years (1993 & 1994)

Sponsor: **K-Mart**
Team: **Kranefuss-Hass Racing**
Driver: **John Andretti**
Owner: **Michael Kranefuss
         & Carl Hass**
Crew Chief: **Tim Brewer**
Car Type: **Ford**

1994 SEASON RESULTS

Race	Track	Fin	Qlfy	Pts	Winnings
Daytona 500	Daytona	42	15	37	$32,365
Goodwrench 500	Rockingham	24	35	91	15,285
Pontiac Excitement 400	Richmond	30	24	73	12,945
Purolator 500	Atlanta	42	26	37	12,785
TranSouth Financial 400	Darlington	38	18	49	9,510
First Union 400	North Wilkesboro	31	23	70	10,750
Hanes 500	Martinsville	35	27	58	10,375
Winston Select 500	Talladega	29	36	76	14,800
Save Mart 300	Sears Point	19	38	106	14,955
Coca-Cola 600	Charlotte	36	9	55	11,050
Budweiser 500	Dover Downs	22	33	97	12,615
UAW-GM Teamwork 500	Pocono	35	21	58	11,450
Miller Genuine Draft 400	Michigan	36	33	55	12,025
Pepsi 400	Daytona	35	28	58	12,825
Slick 50 300	New Hampshire	27	24	82	14,800
Miller Genuine Draft 500	Pocono	25	36	93	12,460
DieHard 500	Talladega	40	21	43	14,525
Brickyard 400	Indianapolis	28	28	79	39,000
GM Goodwrench Dealer 400	Michigan	17	2	112	13,690
Goody's 500	Bristol	30	23	73	7,735
Mountain Dew Southern 500	Darlington	16	29	115	11,930
Miller Genuine Draft 400	Richmond	11	19	130	11,680
Splitfire Spark Plug 500	Dover Downs	25	23	93	10,765
Goody's 500	Martinsville	21	4	100	8,075
Tyson Holly Farms 400	North Wilkesboro	17	28	112	9,050
Mello Yello 500	Charlotte	24	3	96	11,125
AC-Delco 500	Rockingham	25	36	88	10,500
Slick 50 500	Phoenix	43	17	34	6,825
Hooters 500	Atlanta	13	9	129	15,025

Sponsor: **Kendall Motor Oil**

Team: *Sabco Racing*
Driver: *To Be Announced*
Owner: *Dick Brooks*
& Felix Sabates
Crew Chief: *Jeff Hammond*
Car Type: *Pontiac*

40

**DRIVER
TO BE
ANNOUNCED**

1994 SEASON RESULTS

**DRIVER
TO BE
ANNOUNCED**

Ricky Craven

DRIVER INFO

Hometown: **Newburgh, Maine**
Birthdate: **May 24, 1966**
Height: **5' 11"**   Weight: **165**

Ricky Craven is new to Winston Cup racing. Before the 1994 season his only start was in the 1991 AC Delco 500 at Rockingham, where he finished 34th and won $3,750. Many considered him to be a Rookie of the Year competitor in 1995.

He is not, of course, new to racing. In 1991 he was a NASCAR Busch North champion and in 1992 was the Busch Grand National Rookie of the Year and came in second in BGN points in 1993 and 1994. He had two BGN victories, eight top-fives, and 16 top-tens in only 28 races. In 1994 BGN competition, only Ricky's third full season, he won $273,000.

Sponsor: **Kodiak**
Team: **Larry Hedrick Motorsports**
Driver: **Ricky Craven**
Owner: **Larry Hedrick**
Crew Chief: **Rick Pen**
Car Type: **Chevrolet**

41

1994 SEASON RESULTS

ROOKIE SEASON 1995

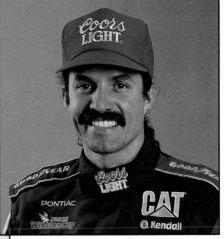

Kyle Petty

Sponsor: **Coors Light**
Team: **Sabco Racing, Inc.**
Driver: **Kyle Petty**
Owner: **Felix Sabates**
Crew Chief: **Barry Dodson**
Car Type: **Pontiac**

42

1994 SEASON RESULTS

Race	Track	Fin	Qlfy	Pts	Winnings
Daytona 500	Daytona	39	26	46	$39,075
Goodwrench 500	Rockingham	8	7	147	22,635
Pontiac Excitement 400	Richmond	5	19	155	26,500
Purolator 500	Atlanta	13	27	124	21,580
TranSouth Financial 400	Darlington	11	33	130	19,400
Food City 500	Bristol	20	14	103	19,511
First Union 400	North Wilkesboro	4	28	160	32,165
Hanes 500	Martinsville	26	9	85	15,675
Winston Select 500	Talladega	13	27	124	23,185
Save Mart 300	Sears Point	11	10	130	16,755
Coca-Cola 600	Charlotte	26	41	85	18,400
Budweiser 500	Dover Downs	11	31	130	21,615
UAW-GM Teamwork 500	Pocono	12	14	127	20,805
Miller Genuine Draft 400	Michigan	17	41	112	21,275
Pepsi 400	Daytona	34	36	61	19,855
Slick 50 300	New Hampshire	8	41	142	25,975
Miller Genuine Draft 500	Pocono	27	37	82	19,360
DieHard 500	Talladega	19	23	106	22,200
Brickyard 400	Indianapolis	25	36	88	39,000
The Bud at the Glen	Watkins Glen	37	20	52	18,000
GM Goodwrench Dealer 400	Michigan	6	40	150	36,690
Goody's 500	Bristol	15	32	118	19,935
Mountain Dew Southern 500	Darlington	12	37	127	19,970
Miller Genuine Draft 400	Richmond	38	24	49	17,755
Splitfire Spark Plug 500	Dover Downs	6	15	150	24,965
Goody's 500	Martinsville	24	16	91	15,875
Tyson Holly Farms 400	North Wilkesboro	26	22	85	15,925
Mello Yello 500	Charlotte	30	41	78	16,015
AC-Delco 500	Rockingham	36	29	55	20,575
Slick 50 500	Phoenix	6	15	150	24,370
Hooters 500	Atlanta	22	41	97	18,730

DRIVER INFO

Hometown: **Trinity, North Carolina**
Birthdate: **June 2, 1960**
Height: **6' 2"**   *Weight:* **195**

The first of Kyle Petty's Winston Cup wins occurred at Richmond in his 170th start. His career statistics for his 411 starts are impressive: seven wins, eight poles, and $6,488,824 in winnings. In 1992, the last year his father Richard was to drive, Kyle was the first in the Petty family to win one million dollars or more in a season. In 1994 he won $806,332 and finished 15th in the standings.

Family history plays a big part in Kyle's story, as he is the first, third-generation driver to win a Winston Cup race. His grandfather, Lee, won in 1949, his father, Richard, in 1960. Kyle started racing young. His first race on a closed course was when he won the ARCA 200 at Daytona in 1979.

Kyle is known to be multi-talented, having dabbled in performance in music and stand-up comedy. He enjoys all sorts of hobbies and activities, including motorcycle riding and golf.

Career Starts	Wins	Top Five	Top Ten
411	7	48	139
100%	1.70%	11.68%	33.82%

(1992-1994) Starts	Wins	Top Five	Top Ten
90	3	20	39
100%	3.33%	22.22%	43.33%

1994 Starts	Wins	Top Five	Top Ten
31	0	2	7
100%	0.00%	6.45%	22.58%

Bobby Hamilton

Hometown: **Nashville, Tennessee**
Birthdate: **May 29, 1957**
Height: **5' 10"**   Weight: **185**

Bobby Hamilton's first Winston Cup race was in 1989, but his first full season did not come until 1991 when he edged out Ted Musgrave for NASCAR's Winston Cup Rookie of the Year honors. His best finish before the 1994 season also came in 1991, with a sixth in the 1991 AC-Delco 500. A year later he had his best start — a second — in that same race.

In 1994 he had one top-ten finish, earned $514,520, and finished 23rd in the standings. He began the 1995 season with $1,299,570 in career winnings in 106 starts.

Bobby is a former Nashville Speedway track champion. One of his career highlights came in 1988, when he beat three superstars — Darrell Waltrip, Sterling Marlin, and Bill Elliott — in a special four-car Showdown at Nashville. He won as a rookie at Richmond during the 1989 Busch Grand National season.

The Hamilton family provided a racing background for Bobby, as his father and grandfather worked with the race cars of the legendary country singer Marty Robbins.

Career Starts	Wins	Top Five	Top Ten
106	0	0	8
100%	0.00%	0.00%	7.55%

(1992-1994) Starts	Wins	Top Five	Top Ten
74	0	0	4
100%	0.00%	0.00%	5.41%

1994 Starts	Wins	Top Five	Top Ten
30	0	0	1
100%	0.00%	0.00%	3.33%

Sponsor: **STP**
Team: **Petty Enterprises**
Driver: **Bobby Hamilton**
Owner: **Richard Petty**
Crew Chief: **Robbie Loomis**
Car Type: **Pontiac**

43

1994 SEASON RESULTS

Race	Track	Fin	Qlfy	Pts	Winnings
Daytona 500	Daytona	12	23	132	$51,265
Goodwrench 500	Rockingham	38	10	49	10,960
Pontiac Excitement 400	Richmond	33	35	64	12,285
Purolator 500	Atlanta	19	33	106	16,630
TranSouth Financial 400	Darlington	25	32	88	12,490
Food City 500	Bristol	9	34	138	19,280
First Union 400	North Wilkesboro	14	24	126	12,875
Hanes 500	Martinsville	13	15	124	13,725
Winston Select 500	Talladega	12	39	132	21,915
Save Mart 300	Sears Point	33	30	64	13,255
Coca-Cola 600	Charlotte	17	23	112	17,900
Budweiser 500	Dover Downs	34	8	61	12,005
UAW-GM Teamwork 500	Pocono	27	32	82	13,950
Miller Genuine Draft 400	Michigan	41	42	40	12,380
Pepsi 400	Daytona	24	42	91	15,945
Slick 50 300	New Hampshire	40	38	43	13,500
Miller Genuine Draft 500	Pocono	23	16	94	15,060
DieHard 500	Talladega	22	41	97	16,950
Brickyard 400	Indianapolis	24	32	91	35,200
The Bud at the Glen	Watkins Glen	34	31	61	12,145
Goody's 500	Bristol	28	17	79	13,810
Mountain Dew Southern 500	Darlington	22	16	97	13,780
Miller Genuine Draft 400	Richmond	34	7	66	11,255
Splitfire Spark Plug 500	Dover Downs	31	11	70	14,165
Goody's 500	Martinsville	13	29	124	13,725
Tyson Holly Farms 400	North Wilkesboro	12	8	127	13,200
Mello Yello 500	Charlotte	19	26	106	13,100
AC-Delco 500	Rockingham	33	42	64	11,200
Slick 50 500	Phoenix	11	29	130	16,820
Hooters 500	Atlanta	24	42	91	13,800

Dave Marcis

Sponsor: **Olive Garden**
Team: **Marcis Auto Racing**
Driver: **Dave Marcis**
Owner: **Helen Marcis**
Crew Chief: **Dale Fischlein**
Car Type: **Chevrolet**

71

1994 SEASON RESULTS

Race	Track	Fin.	Qlfy.	Pts.	Winnings
Daytona 500	Daytona	25	27	88	$31,150
Goodwrench 500	Rockingham	35	40	58	7,100
Purolator 500	Atlanta	36	38	55	10,380
TranSouth Financial 400	Darlington	28	26	84	7,950
Food City 500	Bristol	10	29	134	15,280
First Union 400	North Wilkesboro	29	20	76	6,800
Winston Select 500	Talladega	16	22	120	14,235
Save Mart 300	Sears Point	25	39	88	9,900
Budweiser 500	Dover Downs	18	29	114	11,650
UAW-GM Teamwork 500	Pocono	33	34	64	7,600
Pepsi 400	Daytona	27	32	82	11,310
Slick 50 300	New Hampshire	18	17	114	14,425
Miller Genuine Draft 400	Pocono	26	34	85	10,710
DieHard 500	Talladega	27	34	82	12,040
Brickyard 400	Indianapolis	41	16	40	21,825
The Bud at the Glen	Watkins Glen	21	34	100	9,655
GM Goodwrench Dealer 400	Michigan	36	37	55	8,190
Mountain Dew Southern 500	Darlington	28	38	79	8,595
Miller Genuine Draft 400	Richmond	29	22	76	8,905
Splitfire Spark Plug 500	Dover Downs	35	24	58	7,805
Tyson Holly Farms 400	North Wilkesboro	24	6	91	6,950
AC-Delco 500	Rockingham	34	12	61	7,100
Slick 50 500	Phoenix	19	34	106	10,295

DRIVER INFO

Hometown: **Wausau, Wisconsin**
Birthdate: **March 1, 1941**
Height: **5' 10"**   Weight: **165**

Dave Marcis, who is now an owner/driver, drove in his first Winston Cup race in the Daytona 500 in 1968. In 1975 he was runner-up to Richard Petty for the Winston Cup championship. With 761 starts, he is the most experienced NASCAR Winston Cup driver on the tour. His career encompasses five wins, 14 poles, and $4,277,429 in career winnings. He won three straight pole positions at Talladega in the seventies. In 1994 he finished 35th in the Winston Cup standings and won $261,650.

Dave's Winston Cup accomplishments are not his only racing honors. In 1965 he was a short-track champion in Wisconsin. He also has to his credit two USAC stock car wins, as well as three Late Model Sportsman victories (Late Model Sportsman is now Busch Grand National.)

When he was very young, Dave became interested in cars and how fast they would go. Because of his father's garage and wrecking yard, he had hands-on experience. His involvement with racing extends beyond the competitions, as he has for years been a testing and development driver.

Career Starts	Wins	Top Five	Top Ten
761	5	94	222
100%	0.66%	12.35%	29.17%

(1992-1994) Starts	Wins	Top Five	Top Ten
75	0	0	1
100%	0.00%	0.00%	1.33%

1994 Starts	Wins	Top Five	Top Ten
23	0	0	1
100%	0.00%	0.00%	4.35%

Todd Bodine

DRIVER INFO

Hometown: Chemung, New York
Birthdate: February 27, 1964
Height: 5' 7"   **Weight: 168**

Following in the family footsteps, Todd Bodine made his Winston Cup debut in 1992 at Bud at the Glen. After 41 starts he has $561,046 in career winnings. In 1994 he finished 20th in the point standings and had two top-five finishes, a third at Atlanta in the Hooter's 500 and a fifth in New Hampshire.

Like his older brothers, Todd came naturally to racing. He started in 1983 in Northeast Modifieds, moving on to Late Model Stocks in 1986 and Sportsman Cars in 1989 - 1990. With less than 40 starts, he joined the Busch Grand National circuit in 1991 where he scored seven victories in three full seasons. The 1992 BGN event at Michigan International was important for Todd, as he beat eight Winston Cup regulars.

Other interests of Todd's include country music and comedy movies. In addition he rides his horse and finds time to spend time with his remote controlled cars.

Career Starts	Wins	Top Five	Top Ten
41	0	2	7
100%	0.00%	4.88%	17.07%

(1992-1994) Starts	Wins	Top Five	Top Ten
41	0	2	7
100%	0.00%	4.88%	17.07%

1994 Starts	Wins	Top Five	Top Ten
30	0	2	7
100%	0.00%	6.67%	23.33%

Sponsor: **Factory Stores of America**
Team: **Butch Mock Motorsports**
Driver: **Todd Bodine**
Owner: **Butch Mock**
Crew Chief: **Troy Selberg**
Car Type: **Ford**

75

1994 SEASON RESULTS

Race	Track	Fin	Qlfy	Pts	Winnings
Daytona 500	Daytona	36	11	60	$35,870
Goodwrench 500	Rockingham	34	14	61	8,700
Pontiac Excitement 400	Richmond	25	14	88	9,375
Purolator 500	Atlanta	33	19	64	10,490
TranSouth Financial 400	Darlington	22	41	97	9,050
Food City 500	Bristol	26	8	85	10,355
First Union 400	North Wilkesboro	19	26	106	8,025
Hanes 500	Martinsville	6	12	150	14,775
Winston Select 500	Talladega	28	3	84	11,155
Save Mart 300	Sears Point	38	31	49	7,155
Coca-Cola 600	Charlotte	8	31	142	26,400
Budweiser 500	Dover Downs	16	12	115	12,065
UAW-GM Teamwork 500	Pocono	14	28	121	12,505
Miller Genuine Draft 400	Michigan	31	36	70	10,560
Pepsi 400	Daytona	7	17	146	19,675
Slick 50 300	New Hampshire	5	15	155	21,850
Miller Genuine Draft 500	Pocono	11	31	135	13,710
DieHard 500	Talladega	16	7	115	14,450
Brickyard 400	Indianapolis	9	25	143	63,600
The Bud at the Glen	Watkins Glen	15	24	118	11,340
GM Goodwrench Dealer 400	Michigan	38	8	49	8,140
Goody's 500	Bristol	8	36	142	15,465
Mountain Dew Southern 500	Darlington	26	23	85	9,015
Miller Genuine Draft 400	Richmond	20	16	103	10,380
Splitfire Spark Plug 500	Dover Downs	16	9	115	11,865
Goody's 500	Martinsville	33	33	64	4,875
Mello Yello 500	Charlotte	38	17	49	4,470
AC-Delco 500	Rockingham	21	28	100	11,100
Slick 50 500	Phoenix	32	23	67	8,135
Hooters 500	Atlanta	3	36	170	44,000

Kenny Wallace

Sponsor: **TIC Financial**

Team: **Filmar Racing**
Driver: **Kenny Wallace**
Owner: **Filbert Martocci**
Crew Chief: **Gil Martin**
Car Type: **Ford**

81

DRIVER INFO

Hometown: **St. Louis, Missouri**
Birthdate: **August 23, 1963**
Height: **5' 10"**   *Weight:* **162**

In 1990 Kenny Wallace had his first Winston Cup start at North Wilkesboro, where he was in the top ten before he had an accident. After 48 starts, his best finish is a fourth in the 1994 Martinsville fall race. In the point standings for 1994 he finished 40th, and his career earnings stand at $629,705.

Kenny began his racing career in go-karts in the midwest. Like his brother Rusty, he progressed to ASA and was Rookie of the Year in 1986. He was Busch Grand National Rookie of the Year in 1989 and runner-up for the 1991 BGN Championship.

Kenny is also interested in slot car racing and finds time for racquetball and golf. He was a TNN commentator for several Winston Cup races and is interested in working in that area after his racing career.

1994 SEASON RESULTS

Race	Track	Fin	Qlfy	Pts	Winnings
Miller Genuine Draft 400	Michigan	19	22	106	$ 9,825
DieHard 500	Talladega	9	16	138	13,370
Goody's 500	Bristol	13	15	129	20,490
Mountain Dew Southern 500	Darlington	11	11	130	20,765
Miller Genuine Draft 400	Richmond	32	25	67	18,380
Splitfire Spark Plug 500	Dover Downs	20	7	108	20,965
Goody's 500	Martinsville	4	12	160	30,650
Tyson Holly Farms 400	North Wilkesboro	10	9	134	20,355
Mello Yello 500	Charlotte	14	21	126	22,100
AC-Delco 500	Rockingham	15	23	118	20,225
Slick 50 500	Phoenix	18	11	109	19,195
Hooters 500	Atlanta	25	2	88	18,685

Career Starts	Wins	Top Five	Top Ten
48	0	1	6
100%	0.00%	2.08%	12.50%

1992-1994 Starts	Wins	Top Five	Top Ten
47	0	0	6
100%	0.00%	0.00%	12.77%

1994 Starts	Wins	Top Five	Top Ten
12	0	1	3
100%	0.00%	8.33%	25.00%

Joe Nemechek

DRIVER INFO

Hometown: *Lakeland, Florida*
Birthdate: *September 26, 1963*
Height: *5' 9"*   **Weight:** *180*

Joe Nemechek's Winston Cup debut was in 1993 at Loudon, New Hampshire. He has 34 starts and $442,895 in Winston Cup winnings. In 1994 he finished third, behind Jeff Burton and Steve Grissom, in the Rookie of the Year competition.

Although he is new to Winston Cup racing, Joe has been a racing champion for some time. He began racing at the age of 13 in Motocross and had over 300 wins in six years. He switched to stock cars in 1986 and was the Southeastern Mini-Stock Series Champion in 1987. In 1988 he was United Stockcar Alliance Series Rookie of the Year and Series Champion. Then in 1989 he claimed All Pro Late Model Rookie of the Year honors and was Short Track Driver of the Year. He started his Busch Grand National career in 1990 and again won Rookie of the Year honors. With his own team, he won the Busch Grand National Championship in 1992 and was Most Popular Driver that year and the next.

Joe majored in mechanical engineering at Florida Institute of Technology. He finds time for leisure activities including movies, skiing, and fishing.

Career Starts	Wins	Top Five	Top Ten
34	0	1	3
100%	0.00%	2.94%	8.82%

(1992-1994)* Starts	Wins	Top Five	Top Ten
34	0	1	3
100%	0.00%	2.94%	8.82%

1994 Starts	Wins	Top Five	Top Ten
29	0	1	3
100%	0.00%	3.45%	10.34%

Sponsor: **Burger King**
Team: **NEMCO Motorsports**
Driver: **Joe Nemechek, III**
Owner: **Joe Nemechek, III**
Car Type: **Chevrolet**

87

1994 SEASON RESULTS

Race	Track	Fin	Qlfy	Pts	Winnings
Goodwrench 500	Rockingham	36	23	55	$ 7,025
Pontiac Excitement 400	Richmond	21	11	100	9,850
Purolator 500	Atlanta	18	5	109	13,440
TranSouth Financial 400	Darlington	19	29	106	9,670
Food City 500	Bristol	16	6	115	11,480
Hanes 500	Martinsville	22	29	97	7,575
Winston Select 500	Talladega	42	37	37	8,720
Save Mart 300	Sears Point	22	32	97	10,105
Coca-Cola 600	Charlotte	33	2	64	13,050
Budweiser 500	Dover Downs	14	3	121	13,115
UAW-GM Teamwork 500	Pocono	32	11	67	9,200
Miller Genuine Draft 400	Michigan	7	17	146	20,450
Pepsi 400	Daytona	39	38	46	8,745
Slick 50 300	New Hampshire	19	35	106	15,225
Miller Genuine Draft 500	Pocono	3	11	165	29,790
DieHard 500	Talladega	35	42	58	9,430
Brickyard 400	Indianapolis	20	30	103	36,650
The Bud at the Glen	Watkins Glen	8	23	142	16,980
GM Goodwrench Dealer 400	Michigan	21	6	100	11,665
Goody's 500	Bristol	29	5	81	9,285
Mountain Dew Southern 500	Darlington	42	4	37	5,330
Miller Genuine Draft 400	Richmond	28	33	79	8,930
Splitfire Spark Plug 500	Dover Downs	36	21	60	8,280
Goody's 500	Martinsville	22	26	97	7,375
Tyson Holly Farms 400	North Wilkesboro	34	32	61	4,250
Mello Yello 500	Charlotte	11	4	130	19,300
AC-Delco 500	Rockingham	17	13	112	12,450
Slick 50 500	Phoenix	25	16	88	9,335
Hooters 500	Atlanta	23	7	94	10,115

Mike Wallace

Sponsor: *Heilig-Meyers Furniture*

Team: **Donlavey Racing**
Driver: **Mike Wallace**
Owner: **Junie Donlavey**
Car Type: **Ford**

90

1994 SEASON RESULTS

Race	Track	Fin	Qlfy	Pts	Winnings
Purolator 500	Atlanta	27	42	82	$11,425
TranSouth Financial 400	Darlington	18	23	109	10,415
Food City 500	Bristol	28	25	79	10,080
Winston Select 500	Talladega	15	19	118	15,325
Save Mart 300	Sears Point	23	28	94	9,980
Coca-Cola 600	Charlotte	23	35	94	10,525
Budweiser 500	Dover Downs	13	41	124	14,015
UAW-GM Teamwork 500	Pocono	36	38	55	7,375
Pepsi 400	Daytona	12	18	127	16,570
Slick 50 300	New Hampshire	28	36	79	13,100
Miller Genuine Draft 400	Pocono	30	25	73	10,210
DieHard 500	Talladega	13	14	124	16,130
GM Goodwrench Dealer 400	Michigan	16	27	115	14,240
Goody's 500	Bristol	24	27	91	10,060
Mountain Dew Southern 500	Darlington	17	39	112	11,160
Miller Genuine Draft 400	Richmond	23	26	94	9,480
Splitfire Spark Plug 500	Dover Downs	29	25	76	10,265
Goody's 500	Martinsville	28	36	79	6,525
Mello Yello 500	Charlotte	17	13	112	10,600
AC-Delco 500	Rockingham	16	31	115	12,750
Slick 50 500	Phoenix	28	26	79	8,985
Hooters 500	Atlanta	5	34	160	23,800

DRIVER INFO

Hometown: **St. Louis, Missouri**
Birthdate: **March 10, 1959**
Height: **6' 0"**   Weight: **220**

Mike Wallace made his Winston Cup debut at the Pyroil 500 at Phoenix in 1991. This was the first time three brothers (Mike, Rusty, and Kenny) had competed in Winston Cup racing during the modern era. Mike's best finish is a fifth at Atlanta in 1994, his first full season. He was the highest-finishing rookie five times in that year and won $265,115, to bring his Winston Cup career total to $322,455.

As Mike started racing at the age of 16, he has chalked up many short track wins and championships. During the 70's and 80's he won over 300 short track races in the Midwest. In his 66th Busch Series start, he won his first race at Dover in 1994.

Mike does find time for other interests, among them boating and water sports. Though he loves driving in races, he does not spend a lot of time as a spectator at the tracks. He does, however, have vivid memories of the 1976 Daytona 500 when David Pearson and Richard Petty crashed while battling for the lead on the last lap of the race.

Career Starts	Wins	Top Five	Top Ten
31	0	1	1
100%	0.00%	3.23%	3.23%

1992-1994 Starts	Wins	Top Five	Top Ten
29	0	1	1
100%	0.00%	3.45%	3.45%

1994 Starts	Wins	Top Five	Top Ten
22	0	1	1
100%	0.00%	4.55%	4.55%

Bill Elliott

DRIVER INFO

Hometown: *Dawsonville, Georgia*
Birthdate: *October 8, 1955*
Height: *6' 1"*   **Weight:** *180*

Bill Elliott made his Winston Cup debut in 1976, but his first full season was in 1983. His first win came in his 116th start in the 1983 Winston Western 500 at Riverside. After 407 starts, he has 40 wins and is tied for 12th on the all-time list. He has forty-five poles (making him eighth on the all-time list) and has accumulated $14,543,633 in career winnings. In 1988 he was the Winston Cup champion and was runner-up in 1985, 1987, and 1992. He claimed American Driver of the Year honors in 1985 and 1988, and has been Most Popular Driver for nine different years, including 1994. He tied the modern-era record for consecutive races won by winning four consecutive times in 1992. He also owns the fastest recorded time in a stock car, going 212.809 in the 1987 Talladega qualifying.

Bill finds time to spend with his family and to enjoy his avocations. He loves snow skiing and flying. He has a pilot's license, so he is able to fly the three planes he owns.

Career Starts	Wins	Top Five	Top Ten
438	40	142	240
100%	9.13%	32.42%	54.79%

(1992-1994) Starts	Wins	Top Five	Top Ten
90	6	26	44
100%	6.67%	28.89%	48.89%

1994 Starts	Wins	Top Five	Top Ten
31	1	6	12
100%	3.23%	19.35%	38.71%

Sponsor: **McDonald's**
Team: *Elliott-Hardy Racing*
Driver: *Bill Elliott*
Owner: *Bill Elliott & Charles Hardy*
Crew Chief: *Tony Gibson*
Car Type: *Ford*

94

1994 SEASON RESULTS

Race	Track	Fin	Qlfy	Pts	Winnings
Daytona 500	Daytona	9	8	138	$65,615
Goodwrench 500	Rockingham	39	8	46	11,925
Pontiac Excitement 400	Richmond	12	26	127	15,025
Purolator 500	Atlanta	32	21	67	14,585
TranSouth Financial 400	Darlington	3	1	170	35,285
Food City 500	Bristol	30	15	73	13,625
First Union 400	North Wilkesboro	18	4	109	12,175
Hanes 500	Martinsville	9	10	138	16,175
Winston Select 500	Talladega	19	30	106	16,790
Save Mart 300	Sears Point	30	11	73	13,540
Coca-Cola 600	Charlotte	22	43	97	14,950
Budweiser 500	Dover Downs	31	5	70	14,165
UAW-GM Teamwork 500	Pocono	10	16	134	20,155
Miller Genuine Draft 400	Michigan	11	3	130	20,250
Pepsi 400	Daytona	19	43	106	19,240
Slick 50 300	New Hampshire	16	21	115	19,925
Miller Genuine Draft 500	Pocono	17	19	112	16,160
DieHard 500	Talladega	2	11	175	52,445
Brickyard 400	Indianapolis	3	6	170	164,850
The Bud at the Glen	Watkins Glen	12	8	127	15,810
GM Goodwrench Dealer 400	Michigan	7	4	151	23,015
Goody's 500	Bristol	5	11	155	22,275
Mountain Dew Southern 500	Darlington	1	9	180	68,330
Miller Genuine Draft 400	Richmond	15	38	118	14,855
Splitfire Spark Plug 500	Dover Downs	28	13	79	14,415
Goody's 500	Martinsville	3	10	165	29,525
Tyson Holly Farms 400	North Wilkesboro	6	2	155	15,940
Mello Yello 500	Charlotte	33	28	64	8,565
AC-Delco 500	Rockingham	6	18	155	20,650
Slick 50 500	Phoenix	35	3	63	11,860
Hooters 500	Atlanta	38	43	49	10,140

Jeremy Mayfield

Sponsor: **RCA**
Team: **Cale Yarborough Motorsports**
Driver: **Jeremy Mayfield**
Owner: **Cale Yarborough**
Crew Chief: **Tony Furr**
Car Type: **Ford**

98

DRIVER INFO

Hometown: **Owensboro, Kentucky**
Birthdate: **May 27, 1969**
Height: **6' 0"**   Weight: **165**

Jeremy Mayfield began his racing career in 1982. He had competed in go-karts, street stocks, Sportsman, Late-model Stocks and ARCA cars. He drove one Winston Cup race in 1993, and in the same year won ARCA Rookie of the Year, with eight top-fives and ten top-tens.

In 1994 Jeremy ran 20 races and earned $226,265. He is still after his first top-ten finish in Winston Cup competition.

Jeremy's home town is Owensboro, Kentucky, which is also the home of racing brothers Michael and Darrell Waltrip and David and Jeff Green.

One of Jeremy's favorite activities — other than automobile racing — is golf.

1994 SEASON RESULTS

Race	Track	Fin	Qlfy	Pts	Winnings
Daytona 500	Daytona	30	40	73	$27,645
Pontiac Excitement 400	Richmond	27	18	82	6,925
First Union 400	North Wilkesboro	30	11	73	5,325
Winston Select 500	Talladega	37	24	52	8,360
Coca-Cola 600	Charlotte	21	19	100	9,300
Miller Genuine Draft 400	Michigan	25	18	88	8,945
Pepsi 400	Daytona	30	30	73	9,500
Slick 50 300	New Hampshire	26	37	85	11,400
Miller Genuine Draft 500	Pocono	21	23	100	11,960
DieHard 500	Talladega	32	25	67	9,590
Brickyard 400	Indianapolis	26	31	85	29,100
GM Goodwrench Dealer 400	Michigan	23	39	94	11,365
Goody's 500	Bristol	21	25	100	10,935
Mountain Dew Southern 500	Darlington	33	25	64	7,785
Miller Genuine Draft 400	Richmond	37	37	52	6,755
Splitfire Spark Plug 500	Dover Downs	24	33	91	10,915
Tyson Holly Farms 400	North Wilkesboro	27	34	82	6,800
Mello Yello 500	Charlotte	20	32	103	9,350
AC-Delco 500	Rockingham	19	39	106	11,750
Slick 50 500	Phoenix	20	41	103	11,560

Career Starts	Wins	Top Five	Top Ten
21	0	0	0
100%	0.00%	0.00%	0.00%

(1992-1994)* Starts	Wins	Top Five	Top Ten
21	0	0	0
100%	0.00%	0.00%	0.00%

1994 Starts	Wins	Top Five	Top Ten
20	0	0	0
100%	0.00%	0.00%	0.00%

*2 years (1993 & 1994)

REFERENCE

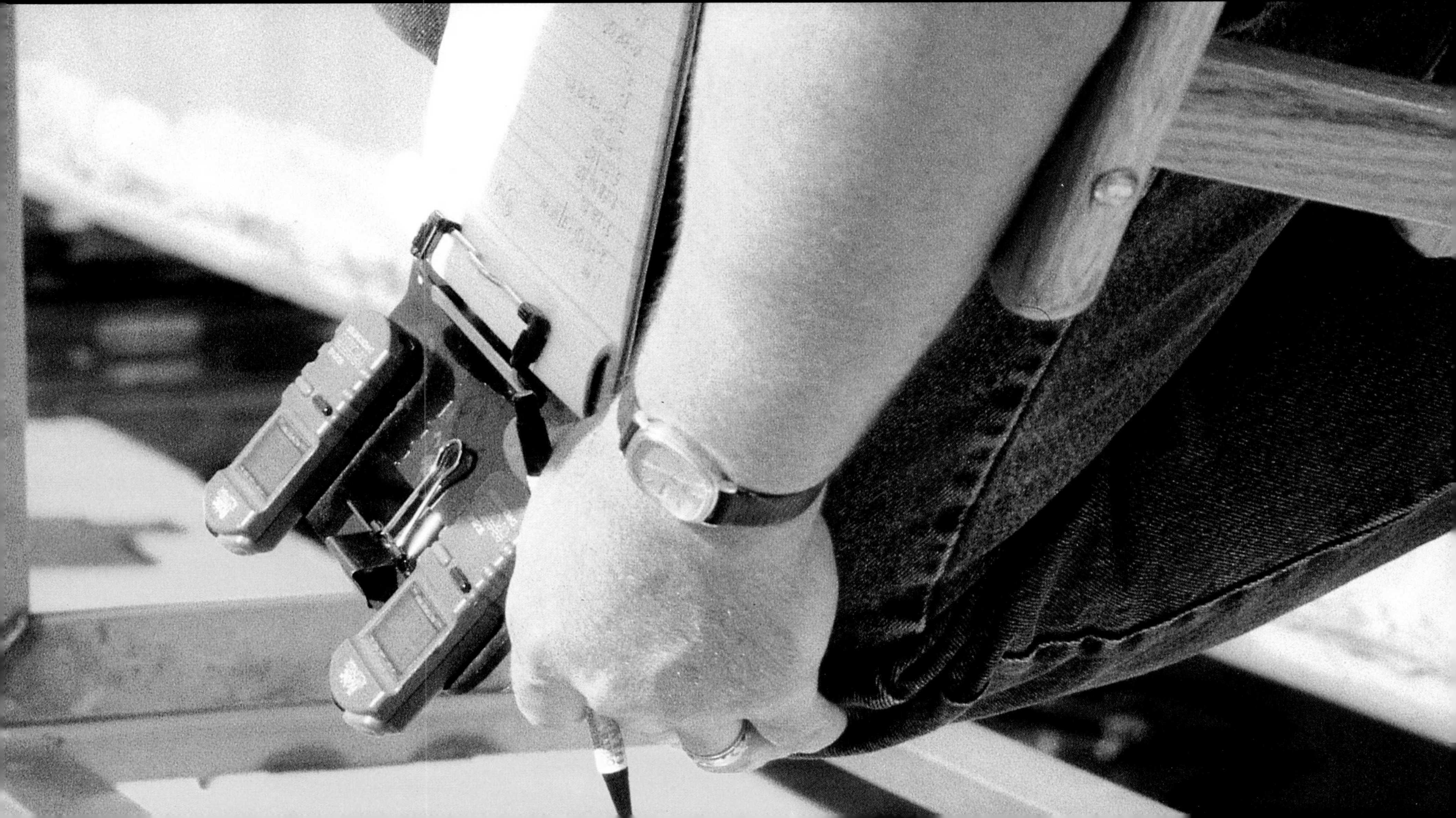

ALL- TIME DRIVER RECORDS   1949-1993

ALL RACES

Most Wins, Career - 200, Richard Petty, 1958-92.
Most Wins, Season - 27, Richard Petty, 1967.
Most Consecutive Wins - 10, Richard Petty, 1967.
Most Wins From Pole, Career - 61, Richard Petty, 1958-1992.
Most Wins From Pole, Season - 15, Richard Petty, 1967.
Oldest Driver to Win a Race - Harry Gant, 52 years, 219 days (Aug. 16, 1992).
Youngest Driver to Win a Race - Donald Thomas, 20 years, 129 days (Nov. 16, 1952).
Most Consecutive Races Won from Pole, Individual - 4, Richard Petty, 1967; Darrell Waltrip, 1981.
Most Consecutive Races Won from Pole - 6, D. Pearson, J. Paschal 2, R. Petty 3, 1966.
Most Years Won at Least 1 Race from Pole - 16, Richard Petty, 1958-92.
Most Consecutive Years Won at Least 1 Race from Pole - 13, Richard Petty, 1960 - 72.
Most Wins at 1 Track - 15, Richard Petty, at Martinsville Speedway and North Wilkesboro Speedway.
Most Consecutive Wins at 1 Track - 7, Richard Petty, Richmond Fairgrounds Raceway, 1970 -73;
        Darrell Waltrip, Bristol International Raceway, 1981-84.

SUPERSPEEDWAYS

Most Wins, Career - 55, Richard Petty, 1958 - 92.
Most Wins, Season - 11, Bill Elliott, 1985
Most Consecutive Wins - 4, Bobby Allison (twice), 1971; Richard Petty, 1971 -72; David Pearson, 1973; Bill Elliott, 1985.
Oldest Driver to Win a Race - Harry Gant, 52 years, 219 days (Aug. 16, 1992).
Most Wins from Pole, career - 20, David Pearson, 1960 - 86.
Most Wins from Pole, season - 6, David Pearson, 1976; Bill Elliott, 1985.
Most Consecutive Races Won from Pole - 2, held by many; last was Bill Elliott, who did it twice in 1985.
Most Years Won at Least 1 Race from Pole - 7, Cale Yarborough, David Pearson.
Most Consecutive Years Won at Least 1 Race from Pole - 5, David Pearson, 1972 -76.
Most Wins at 1 Track - 11, Richard Petty, at North Carolina Motor Speedway.
Most Consecutive Wins at 1 Track - 4, Bill Elliott, Michigan International Speedway,1985 - 86

SHORT TRACKS

Most Wins, Career - 145, Richard Petty , 1958 - 92.
Most Wins, Season - 24, Richard Petty, 1967.
Most Consecutive Wins - 10, Richard Petty, 1967.
Most Wins from Pole, Career - 54, Richard petty, 1958 - 1992.
Most Wins from Pole, Season - 14, Richard Petty, 1967.
Most years Won at least 1 Race from Pole - 14, Richard Petty, 1958 -1992.
Most Consecutive Years Won at least 1 Race from Pole - 12, Richard Petty, 1960 - 71.
Most Wins at 1 Track - 15, Richard Petty, at Martinsville Speedway and North Wilkesboro Speedway.
Most Consecutive Wins at 1 Track - 7, Richard Petty, Richmond Fairgrounds Raceway, 1970 -73;
        Darrell Waltrip, Bristol International Raceway, 1981-84.

WINNING STREAKS ON THE NASCAR WINSTON CUP SERIES

Most Consecutive Wins - Modern Era * (1972 -1993): Four
Cale Yarborough - 1976 (Richmond, Dover, Martinsville and N. Wilkesboro in fall).
Darrell Waltrip - 1981 (Martinsville, N. Wilkesboro, Charlotte and Rockingham in fall).
Dale Earnhardt - 1987 (Darlington, N. Wilkesboro, Bristol and Martinsville in spring).
Harry Gant - 1991 (Darlington, Richmond, Dover and Martinsville in summer/fall).
Bill Elliott - 1992 (Rockingham, Richmond, Atlanta and Darlington in spring).
Mark Martin - 1993 (Watkins Glen, Michigan, Bristol and Darlington).

* In 1971, both Bobby Allison and Richard Petty won five straight races in 46 race season.

STATISTICS

ALL - TIME WINSTON CUP RACE WINNERS

#	Driver	Wins		#	Driver	Wins
1	Richard Petty	200			Danny Letner	2
2	David Pearson	105			Elmo Langley	2
3	Darrell Waltrip	84			Tom Pistone	2
	Bobby Allison	84			Marvin Porter	2
5	Cale Yarborough	83			Bobby Johns	2
6	Dale Earnhardt	59			Gober Sosebee	2
7	Lee Petty	54			Ray Elder	2
8	Ned Jarrett	50			Emanuel Zervakis	2
	Junior Johnson	50			Johnny Beauchamp	2
10	Herb Thomas	48			Al Keller	2
11	Buck Baker	46			Red Byron	2
12	Tim Flock	40			Gwyn Staley	2
13	Bill Elliott	39			Jim Pardue	2
14	Bobby Isaac	37			Billy Myers	2
15	Fireball Roberts	34		87	Bobby Hillin, Jr.	1
16	Rusty Wallace	31			Lake Speed	1
17	Rex White	28			Phil Parsons	1
18	Fred Lorenzen	26			Ron Bouchard	1
19	Jim Paschal	25			Dick Brooks	1
20	Joe Weatherly	24			Jody Ridley	1
21	Benny Parsons	21			Greg Sacks	1
	Jack Smith	21			Lennie Pond	1
23	Speedy Thompson	20			John Kieper	1
24	Buddy Baker	19			Harold Kite	1
	Fonty Flock	19			Donald Thomas	1
	Davey Allison	19			Johnny Allen	1
27	Harry Gant	18			Richard Brickhouse	1
	Neil Bonnett	18			Bob Burdick	1
	Curtis Turner	18			Marvin Burke	1
30	Marvin Panch	17			June Cleveland	1
31	Geoff Bodine	14			Neil Cole	1
	Ricky Rudd	14			Jim Cook	1
	Dick Hutcherson	14			Bobby Courtright	1
	Lee Roy Yarbrough	14			Mark Donohue	1
35	Dick Rathmann	13			Joe Eubanks	1
	Tim Richmond	13			Lou Figaro	1
37	Mark Martin	12			Jim Florian	1
38	Terry Labonte	10			Larry Frank	1
	Donnie Allison	10			Danny Graves	1
40	Ernie Irvan	9			Jim Hurtubise	1
	Cotton Owens	9			Royce Hagerty	1
	Paul Goldsmith	9			Joe Lee Johnson	1
43	Jim Reed	8			Paul Lewis	1
44	Kyle Petty	7			Danny Weinberg	1
	Bob Welborn	7			Jack White	1
	A. J. Foyt	7			Art Watts	1
	Darel Dieringer	7			Johnny Mantz	1
49	Marshall Teague	7			Sam McQuagg	1
	Alan Kulwicki	5			Lloyd Moore	1
	Dave Marcis	5			Norm Nelson	1
	Ralph Moody	5			Bill Norton	1
53	Dan Gurney	5			Dick Passwater	1
	Ken Schrader	4			Bill Rexford	1
	Morgan Shepherd	4			Shorty Rollins	1
	Hershel McGriff	4			Jim Roper	1
	Glen Wood	4			Earl Ross	1
	Charlie Glotzbach	4			John Rostek	1
	Bob Flock	4			Johnny Rutherford	1
	Lloyd Dane	4			Leon Sales	1
	Eddie Gray	4			Frankie Schneider	1
	Pete Hamilton	4			Wendell Scott	1
	Parnelli Jones	4			Buddy Shuman	1
	Eddie Pagan	4			John Soares	1
	Nelson Stacy	4			Chuck Stevenson	1
	Billy Wade	4			Tommy Thompson	1
66	Dick Linder	3			Whitey Norman	1
	Tiny Lund	3			Bill Amick	1
	Bill Blair	3			Mario Andretti	1
70	Frank Mundy	3			Earl Balmer	1
	Dale Jarrett	2			Brett Bodine	1
	Derrike Cope	2				
	James Hylton	2				

MODERN ERA WINSTON CUP RACE WINNERS 1971 -1993

#	Driver	Wins		#	Driver	Wins
1	Darrell Waltrip	84			Bobby Isaac	5
2	Richard Petty	81		25	Ken Schrader	4
3	Cale Yarborough	69			Morgan Shepherd	4
4	Bobby Allison	65			A. J. Foyt	4
5	Dale Earnhardt	59		28	Dale Jarrett	2
6	David Pearson	47			Derrike Cope	2
7	Bill Elliott	39			Ray Elder	2
8	Rusty Wallace	31		31	Bobby Hillin, Jr.	1
9	Benny Parsons	21			Greg Sacks	1
10	Davey Allison	19			Lake Speed	1
11	Harry Gant	18			Ron Bouchard	1
12	Neil Bonnett	18			Dick Brooks	1
13	Buddy Baker	16			James Hylton	1
14	Ricky Rudd	14			Phil Parsons	1
15	Geoff Bodine	14			Charlie Glotzbach	1
16	Tim Richmond	13			Earl Ross	1
17	Mark Martin	12			Mark Donohue	1
18	Terry Labonte	10			Lennie Pond	1
19	Ernie Irvan	9			Jody Ridley	1
20	Kyle Petty	7			Brett Bodine	1
21	Dave Marcis	5			Pete Hamilton	1
	Alan Kulwicki	5				
	Donnie Allison	5				

NASCAR WINSTON CUP CHAMPIONS 1949-1994

YEAR	CAR #	DRIVER	CAR OWNER	CAR	WINS	POLES	MONEY
1994	3	Dale Earnhart	Richard Childress	Chevy	4	2	$3,300,733
1993	3	Dale Earnhardt	Richard Childress	Chevy	6	2	3,353,789
1992	7	Alan Kulwicki	Alan Kulwicki	Ford	2	6	2,322,561
1991	3	Dale Earnhardt	Richard Childress	Chevy	4	0	2,396,685
1990	3	Dale Earnhardt	Richard Childress	Chevy	9	4	3,083,056
1989	27	Rusty Wallace	Baymond Beadle	Pontiac	6	4	2,247,950
1988	9	Bill Elliott	Harry Melling	Ford	6	6	1,574,639
1987	3	Dale Earnhardt	Richard Childress	Chevy	11	1	2,099,243
1986	3	Dale Earnhardt	Richard Childress	Chevy	5	1	1,783,880
1985	11	Darrell Waltrip	Junior Johnson	Chevy	3	4	1,318,735
1984	44	Terry Labonte	Billy Hagan	Chevy	2	2	713,010
1983	22	Bobby Allison	Bill Gardner	Buick	6	0	828,355
1982	11	Darrell Waltrip	Junior Johnson	Buick	12	7	873,118
1981	11	Darrell Waltrip	Junior Johnson	Buick	12	11	693,342
1980	2	Dale Earnhardt	Ros Osterlund	Chevy	5	0	588,926
1979	43	Richard Petty	Petty Ent.	Chevy	5	1	531,292
1978	11	Cale Yarborough	Junior Johnson	Olds	10	8	530,751
1977	11	Cale Yarborough	Junior Johnson	Chevy	9	3	477,499
1976	11	Cale Yarborough	Junior Johnson	Chevy	9	2	387,173
1975	43	Richard Petty	Petty Ent.	Dodge	13	3	378,865
1974	43	Richard Petty	Petty Ent.	Dodge	10	7	299,175
1973	72	Benny Parsons	L.G. DeWitt	Chevy	1	0	114,345
1972	43	Richard Petty	Petty Ent.	Plym	8	3	227,015
1971	43	Richard Petty	Petty Ent.	Plym	21	9	309,225
1970	71	Bobby Isaac	Nord Krauskopf	Dodge	11	13	121,470
1969	17	David Pearson	Holman-Moody	Ford	11	14	183,700
1968	17	David Pearson	Holman-Moody	Ford	16	12	118,842
1967	43	Richard Petty	Petty Ent.	Plym	27	18	130,275
1966	6	David Pearson	Cotton Owens	Dodge	14	7	59,205
1965	11	Ned Jarrett	Bondy Long	Ford	13	9	77,966
1964	43	Richard Petty	Petty Ent.	Plym	9	8	98,810
1963	21	————	Wood Brothers	Ford	3	5	77,636
1963	8	Joe Weatherly	————	Merc	3	6	58,110
1962	8	Joe Weatherly	Bud Moore	Pontiac	9	6	56,110
1961	11	Ned Jarrett	W.G. Holloway,Jr.	Chevy	1	4	27,285
1960	4	Rex White	White-Clements	Chevy	6	3	45,260
1959	42	Lee Petty	Petty Ent.	Plym	10	2	45,570
1958	42	Lee Petty	Petty Ent.	Olds	7	4	20,600
1957	87	Buck Baker	Buck Baker	Chevy	10	5	24,712
1956	300	Buck Baker	Carl Kiekhaefer	Chry	14	12	29,790
1955	300	Tim Flock	Carl Kiekhaefer	Chry	18	19	33,750
1954	92	————	Herb Thomas	Hudson	12	8	27,540
1954	42	Lee Petty	————	Chry	7	3	26,706
1953	92	Herb Thomas	Herb Thomas	Hudson	11	10	27,300
1952	91	Tim Flock	Ted Chester	Hudson	8	4	20,210
1951	92	Herb Thomas	Herb Thomas	Hudson	7	4	18,200
1950	60	Bill Rexford	Julian Buesink	Olds	1	0	6,175
1949	22	Red Byron	Raymond Parks	Olds	2	1	5,800

MULTIPLE WINSTON CUP CHAMPIONS

DRIVER	YEARS
Dale Earnhardt	1994-93-91-90-87-86-80
Richard Petty	1979-75-74-72-71-67-64
Darrell Waltrip	1985-82-81
Cale Yarborough	1978-77-76
David Pearson	1969-68-66
Lee Petty	1959-58-54
Ned Jarrett	1965-61
Joe Weatherly	1963-62
Buck Baker	1957-56
Tim Flock	1955-52
Herb Thomas	1953-51

TOP 10 CLOSEST WINSTON CUP CHAMPIONSHIPS

YEAR	CHAMPION	RUNNER-UP	POINT MARGIN
1992	Alan Kulwicki	Bill Elliott	10
1979	Richard Petty	Darrell Waltrip	11
1989	Rusty Wallace	Dale Earnhardt	12
1980	Dale Earnhardt	Cale Yarborough	19
1988	Bill Elliott	Rusty Wallace	24
1990	Dale Earnhardt	Mark Martin	26
1983	Bobby Allison	Darrell Waltrip	47
1981	Darrell Waltrip	Bobby Allison	53
1984	Terry Labonte	Harry Gant	65
1982	Darrell Waltrip	Bobby Allison	72

WINSTON CUP ROOKIE OF THE YEAR
1958-1994

	DRIVER	YEAR	RACES	WINS	POLES	TOP 5	TOP 10	WINNINGS
1	Jeff Gordon	1993	30	0	1	7	11	$765,168
2	Jeff Burton	1994	30	0	0	2	3	594,700
3	Davey Allison	1987	22	2	5	9	10	361,060
4	Dick Trickle	1989	28	0	0	6	9	343,728
5	Dale Earnhardt (a)	1979	27	1	4	11	17	264,086
6	Bobby Hamilton	1991	28	0	0	0	4	259,105
7	Geoff Bodine	1982	25	0	2	4	10	258,500
8	Jimmy Hensley	1992	22	0	0	0	4	247,660
9	Ken Schrader	1985	28	0	0	0	3	211,523
10	Jody Ridley	1980	31	0	0	2	18	196,617
11	Rusty Wallace (b)	1984	30	0	0	2	4	195,927
12	Rob Moroso	1990	25	0	0	0	1	162,002
13	Ron Bouchard	1981	22	1	1	5	12	152,855
14	Sterling Marlin	1983	30	0	0	0	1	143,564
15	Ken Bouchard	1988	24	0	0	0	1	109,410
16	Alan Kulwicki (c)	1986	23	0	0	1	4	94,450
17	Ronnie Thomas	1978	27	0	0	0	2	73,037
18	Ricky Rudd	1977	25	0	0	1	10	68,448
19	Earl Ross	1974	21	1	0	5	10	64,830
20	Bruce Hill	1975	26	0	0	3	11	58,138
21	Skip Manning	1976	27	0	0	0	4	55,820
22	James Hylton	1966	41	0	1	20	32	29,575
23	Dick Brooks	1969	28	0	0	3	12	27,532
24	Walter Ballard	1971	41	0	0	3	11	25,598
25	Lennie Pond	1973	23	0	0	1	9	25,155
26	Larry Smith	1972	23	0	0	0	7	24,215
27	Donnie Allison	1967	20	0	0	4	7	16,440
28	Bill Dennis	1970	25	0	0	0	5	15,670
29	Sam McQuagg	1965	15	0	0	2	5	10,555
30	Doug Cooper	1964	39	0	0	4	11	10,445
31	Tom Cox	1962	40	0	0	12	20	8,980
32	Billy Wade	1963	22	0	0	4	11	8,710
33	Shorty Rollins	1958	21	1	0	10	17	8,515
34	Pete Hamilton	1968	16	0	0	3	6	8,239
35	Richard Petty (d)	1959	22	0	0	6	9	7,630
36	David Pearson (e)	1960	22	0	1	3	7	5,030
37	Woody Wilson	1961	5	0	0	0	1	2,625

a Won Winston Cup Championships - 1980,1986,1987,1990,1991,1993,1994
b Won Winston Cup Championship - 1989
c Won Winston Cup Championship - 1992
d Won Winston Cup Championships - 1964,1967,1971,1972,1974,1975,1979 championship.
e Won Winston Cup Championships - 1966,1968,1969 championships.

DRIVERS WITH 300 CONSECUTIVE STARTS
(Through Feb. 1, 1994)

	DRIVER	START	END	RACES
1	Richard Petty	Nov. 14, 1971	March 19, 1989	513
2	Terry Labonte	Jan. 14, 1979		444
3	Darrell Waltrip	Jan. 18, 1976		431
4	Dale Earnhardt	Sept. 9, 1979		421
5	Ricky Rudd	Jan. 11, 1981		382
6	Bobby Allison	Nov. 9, 1975	June 19, 1988	374
7	Bill Elliott	Oct. 31, 1982		324
8	Benny Parsons	Nov. 14, 1971	July 4, 1982	321

OTHERS

9	Rusty Wallace	Feb. 19, 1984		291
10	Dave Marcis	Aug. 5, 1979	April 9, 1989	284
11	Harry Gant	June 17, 1979	June 5, 1988	264
12	Ken Schrader	Feb. 17, 1985		261

MOST COMPETITIVE WINSTON CUP RACES
(Since 1976)

	EVENT	SITE	NO. LEAD CHANGES	LAPS
1	1984 Winston 500	Talladega, AL	75	188
2	1984 Talladega 500	Talladega, AL	68	188
3	1978 Talladega 500	Talladega, AL	67	188
4	1981 Champion 400	Brooklyn, MI	65	200
5	1977 Winston 500	Talladega, AL	63	188
6	1983 Daytona 500	Daytona, FL.	59	200
7	1979 Coca-Cola 500	Pocono, PA	58	200
8	1979 World 600	Charlotte, NC	54	400
9	1982 Winston 500	Talladega, AL	51	188
10	1986 Talladega 500	Talladega, AL	49	188
	1989 Die-Hard 500	Talladega, AL	49	188

TOP 40 200-PLUS QUALIFIERS

	DRIVER	SPEED	RACE
1	Bill Elliott	212.809	1987 Winston 500
2	Bill Elliott	212.229	1986 Winston 500
3	Bobby Allison	211.797	1987 Winston 500
4	Davey Allison	210.610	1987 Winston 500
5	Darrell Waltrip	210.471	1987 Winston 500
6	Bill Elliott	210.364	1987 Daytona 500
7	Dale Earnhardt	210.360	1987 Winston 500
8	Kyle Petty	210.346	1987 Winston 500
9	Sterling Marlin	210.194	1987 Winston 500
10	Terry Labonte	210.101	1987 Winston 500
11	Phil Parsons (tie)	209.963	1987 Winston 500
	Lake Speed (tie)	209.963	1987 Winston 500
13	Geoff Bodine	209.710	1987 Winston 500
14	Buddy Baker	209.701	1987 Winston 500
15	Bill Elliott	209.398	1985 Winston 500
16	Bobby Allison	209.274	1986 Winston 500
17	Davey Allison	209.084	1987 Daytona 500
18	Bill Elliott	209.005	1986 Talladega 500
19	Ron Bouchard	208.910	1987 Winston 500
20	Rusty Wallace	208.251	1987 Winston 500
21	Ken Schrader	208.227	1987 Daytona 500
22	Geoff Bodine	208.169	1986 Winston 500
23	Ken Schrader	208.160	1987 Winston 500
24	Bobby Hillin Jr.	208.142	1987 Winston 500
25	Ricky Rudd	208.138	1987 Winston 500
26	Cale Yarborough (tie)	208.092	1986 Winston 500
	Cale Yarborough (tie)	208.092	1987 Winston 500
28	Dale Earnhardt	208.052	1986 Talladega 500
29	Morgan Shepherd	207.831	1987 Winston 500
30	Bobby Allison	207.795	1987 Daytona 500
31	Sterling Marlin	207.776	1986 Winston 500
32	Benny Parsons	207.659	1987 Winston 500
33	Bill Elliott	207.578	1985 Talladega 500
34	Tim Richmond	207.538	1986 Talladega 500
35	Benny Parsons (tie)	207.403	1886 Talladega 500
	Neil Bonnett (tie)	207.403	1987 Winston 500
37	Morgan Shepherd	207.389	1986 Winston 500
38	Greg Sacks	207.246	1987 Winston 500
39	Sterling Marlin	207.192	1986 Talladega 500
40	Buddy Baker	207.151	1986 Winston 500

58 drivers have run 200 or better during their Winston Cup careers.
Cale Yarborough has topped 200 15 times to lead this list.

WINSTON CUP CAR OWNER ALL-TIME STANDINGS
1949-1993

ALL RACES

	CAR OWNER	YEARS	RACES	ENTRIES	WINS	POLES	WINNINGS
1	Junior Johnson	29	777	952	136	126	$19,235,402
2	Richard Childress	20	550	553	52	17	18,693,212
3	Rick Hendrick	10	291	688	33	54	17,170,122
4	Harry Melling	12	314	314	34	40	11,039,319
5	Petty Enterprises	45	1,562	1,921	268	146	8,977,556
6	Bud Moore	30	832	846	62	42	8,955,442
7	Wood Brothers	41	782	806	96	116	7,402,769
8	Jack Roush	6	175	234	12	21	6,938,647
9	Raymond Beadle	8	233	234	20	13	6,745,189
10	Billy Hagan	20	526	531	6	15	6,744,843

SUPERSPEEDWAYS

	CAR OWNER	YEARS	RACES	ENTRIES	WINS	POLES	WINNINGS
1	Junior Johnson	29	497	622	67	67	$10,752,024
2	Rick Hendrick	10	209	503	24	38	10,487,137
3	Richard Childress	20	378	381	33	11	7,687,273
4	Petty Enterprises	44	576	757	61	29	6,039,360
5	Bud Moore	30	501	515	27	13	5,982,813
6	Harry Melling	12	232	232	33	35	5,937,873
7	Wood Brothers	34	544	558	80	87	5,907,470
8	Billy Hagan	20	371	375	5	14	4,158,268
9	Jack Roush	6	127	170	8	15	3,964,148
10	Stavola Brothers	11	211	295	4	1	3,586,818

"Crown Jewel" Winners 1969-1994

Year	Daytona 500	Winston Select 500	Coca-Cola 600	Southern 500
1994	S. Marlin	D. Earnhardt	J. Gordon	B. Elliott
1993	D. Jarrett	E. Irvan	D. Earnhardt	M. Martin
1992	Da. Allison	Da. Allison	D. Earnhardt	D. Waltrip
1991	Ernie Irvan	Harry Gant	Davey Allison	Harry Gant
1990	Cope	Earnhardt	Wallace	Earnhardt
1989	D. Waltrip	Da. Allison	D. Waltrip	Earnhardt
1988	B. Allison	Parsons	D. Waltrip	Elliott
1987	Elliott	Da. Allison	K. Petty	Earnhardt
1986	G. Bodine	B. Allison	Earnhardt	Richmond
1985	Elliott (c)	Elliott	D. Waltrip	Elliott
1984	C. Yarborough	C. Yarborough	B. Allison	Gant
1983	C. Yarborough	R. Petty	Bonnett	B. Allison
1982	B. Allison	D. Waltrip	Bonnett	C. Yarborough
1981	R. Petty	B. Allison	B. Allison	Bonnett
1980	Bdy. Baker	Bdy. Baker	Parsons	T. Labonte
1979	R. Petty	B. Allison	Waltrip	Pearson
1978	B. Allison	C. Yarborough	Waltrip	C. Yarborough
1977	C. Yarborough	D. Waltrip	R. Petty	Pearson
1976	Pearson (a)	Bdy. Baker	Pearson	Pearson
1975	Parsons	Bdy. Baker	R. Petty	B. Allison
1974	R. Petty	Pearson	Pearson	C. Yarborough
1973	R. Petty	Pearson	Bdy. Baker	C. Yarborough
1972	A.J. Foyt	Pearson	Bdy. Baker	B. Allison
1971	R. Petty	D. Allison	B. Allison	B. Allison
1970	Hamilton	Hamilton	D. Allison	Bdy. Baker
1969	L. Yarbrough (b)	N/A	L. Yarbrough	L. Yarbrough

(a) - David Pearson won three or the Big Four races.
(b) - LeeRoy Yarbrough won the NASCAR Triple Crown.
(c) - Bill Elliott became the first driver to win the Winston Million.
The $1 million from Winston cigarettes goes to any driver who wins three of the four Crown Jewels.
The award was initiated in 1985

**RaceFans
Reference**